A SON TO ME

An Exposition of 1 & 2 Samuel

PETER J. LEITHART

canonpress
Moscow, Idaho

Published by Canon Press
P.O. Box 8729, Moscow, ID 83843
800.488.2034 | www.canonpress.com

Library of Congress Cataloging-in-Publication Data

Leithart, Peter J.
    A son to me : an exposition of 1 & 2 Samuel / by Peter J. Leithart.
        p. cm.
Includes index.
    ISBN-13: 978-1-885767-99-8
    ISBN-10: 1-885767-99-4
    1. Bible. O.T. Samuel—Commentaries. 2. Typology (Theology) I.Title.
BS1325.53 .L46 2002
222'.407—dc21
                                                2002000982

09 10 11 12 13 14 15 16   9 8 7 6 5 4 3

To Christian David
May you live up to your name

Against Christianity

Ascent to Love
A Guide to Dante's Divine Comedy

The Baptized Body

Blessed Are the Hungry
Meditations on the Lord's Supper

Brightest Heaven of Invention
A Christian Guide to Six Shakespeare Plays

Deep Comedy
Trinity, Tragedy, and Hope in Western Culture

From Silence to Song
The Davidic Liturgical Revolution

A Great Mystery
Fourteen Wedding Sermons

Heroes of the City of Man
A Christian Guide to Select Ancient Literature

A House For My Name
A Survey of the Old Testament

Miniatures and Morals
The Christian Novels of Jane Austen

The Promise of His Appearing
An Exposition of 2 Peter

Wise Words
Family Stories that Bring the Proverbs to Life

CONTENTS

ACKNOWLEDGMENTS

The book of Samuel has been well-plowed ground over the past two decades, the subject of a number of popular and scholarly commentaries, as well as a host of monographs. This book hovers somewhere between the scholarly and the popular; I have not included a full academic apparatus, but there are probably far too many footnotes for some readers. In any case, the commentaries that I found most helpful were those of Robert Bergen, Ronald Youngblood, Robert Gordon, Joyce Baldwin, and Robert Alter. I have worked through portions of commentaries by Walter Brueggemann and Kyle McCarter and S. R. Driver's classic notes on Samuel; found useful insights in Robert Polzin's *Samuel and the Deuteronomist*, Peter Miscall's *1 Samuel: A Literary Reading*, and J. P. Fokkelman's awesome literary work on Samuel; and drawn heavily on Moshe Garsiel's stimulating study of narrative analogies in 1 Samuel, wishing all the while that I could read modern Hebrew in order to make use of Garsiel's work on 2 Samuel. Everett Fox's inventive translation of Samuel, *Give Us A King!*, offered fresh readings and proved useful as I worked on the Hebrew text. Given the nature of this book, my debt to these scholars is not fully represented in the citations, and I hope this acknowledgment compensates in a small way for that inadequacy.

Over the past several years, I have had taught on all or part of the book of Samuel in several different settings, and I am grateful for all of these opportunities. The elders of Christ Church, Moscow, Idaho, allowed me to teach Samuel in the adult Sunday School class for the past two years, and I am particularly grateful to those who regularly attended the class and whose provocative questions and comments have helped to shape this book. During the summer of 2000, I was invited to present a week-long series on 1 Samuel at a Family Camp sponsored by Reformation Covenant Church of Oregon City, Oregon. Thanks to Pastor Dennis Turri and the elders of that congregation for the invitation, and for insisting that I strive to make the talks practical. I trust that the pastoral thrust of that series of lectures has not been lost in the book. Finally, I taught Samuel at the Reformed Seminary of St. Petersburg, Russia, in March 2001, and I am grateful to Rev. Blake Purcell and the boisterous student body for their vigorous disagreements, laughter, and lunchtime borsch.

I have had help with research from a number of people. My oldest son, Woelke, turned some of my lecture notes and outlines into prose, but the bulk of that work was done by Gene Liechty, whose labors were an immeasurable help in getting the book done in a timely way. Nate Smith found and copied many articles to which I had no access at home, and I am grateful for his faithfulness and timeliness.

James B. Jordan read through the entire manuscript, and took considerable time from his own research to produce two audio tapes of criticisms, comments, and suggestions, and his corrections and additional insights continued to come my way after I thought I had finished the book. Jim's thoughts helped me to discern some the large thematic structures of Samuel and gave unity to a book that threatened to become a collection of random notes.

Finally, thanks to Doug Jones and his staff at Canon Press, for their generosity and labor.

This book is dedicated to Christian David, my fourth son, who shares a name with the poet-warrior of the book of Samuel. At this point in his life, Christian is more the poet than the warrior, and he will enjoy the play of type and antitype, the recurring narrative rhythms, and the arresting turns of phrase that I have highlighted. Beyond that, my hope is that this book might inspire Christian to use his poetic gifts as a Christian warrior, and that he might see giants fall at his feet.

Peniel Hall
Trinity Season, 2001

INTRODUCTION

Stephen Fowl has noted that, with the modern decline of typological interpretation, "there is little, if any, professional space for those who wish to read the Old Testament through lenses ground by the New Testament and Christian theology or by the Talmud and the midrashim."[1] Professionally suicidal as it may be, this book is precisely such an exercise in Christian interpretation, an effort to read the Old Testament as a figure of the New, and to read both together as what the sociologists like to call a "symbolic universe" for making sense of and acting faithfully in today's church and world. That is, this commentary has both a theological and a practical orientation, and both rest on a typological reading of an Old Testament book.

To show in more detail what that orientation involves, it will be useful to consider the main features of typological reading of Scripture. According to Hans Frei's account, precritical interpretation (or what I am calling typological interpretation) had three main features. First, "a biblical story was to be read literally" and therefore "it followed automatically that it referred to and described actual historical occurrences."[2] In typological interpretation, historical, literary, and theological considerations are inseparable. The Bible reports historical events, but, like any historical writing, it reports from a perspective and in a particular form of words, and the perspective embodied in the literary form exhibits the theological significance of the events.[3] Though for various reasons the focus of this commentary is literary and theological, the conviction

---

[1]Stephen E. Fowl, *Engaging Scripture: A Model for Theological Interpretation*, Challenges in Contemporary Theology (London: Blackwell, 1998), 27.

[2]Hans W. Frei, *The Eclipse of Biblical Narrative: A Study in Eighteenth and Nineteenth Century Hermeneutics* (New Haven: Yale, 1974), 1–3.

[3]Though he does not defend typological interpretation, N. T. Wright provides a sophisticated discussion of the necessary interrelations of history, literature, and theology in *The New Testament and the People of God*, Christian Origins and the Question of God, #1 (London: SPCK, 1992), part II.

that these cannot be separated from history is a basic assumption behind my work.

Second, Frei continues, since the world described by the Bible is "a single world of one temporal sequence," it followed that there is "one cumulative story to depict it." Interpreters showed the coherence of the single story of Scripture by pointing to resemblances between earlier and later events; earlier events were "figures or types" of later ones, and most crucially, the events of the Old Testament prefigured the later work of Jesus. The text describing those events brought out correspondences between the events in various ways (see below), and thus following the text's guidance in finding analogies between one biblical account and another was a central concern of the interpreter. Importantly, Frei notes that

> Far from being in conflict with the literal sense of biblical stories, figuration or typology was a natural extension of literal interpretation. It was literalism at the level of the whole biblical story and thus of the depiction of the whole of historical reality. Figuration was at once a literary and a historical procedure, an interpretation of stories and their meanings by weaving them together into a common narrative referring to a single history and its patterns of meaning.

Finally, the world described by the one story of Scripture was "the one and only real world," and therefore it must "embrace the experience of any present age and reader." It was the reader's "duty" to discover how his own experience and world were figures of the biblical world.[4]

CHRISTOLOGICAL INTERPRETATION

I wish to discuss two related elements of this account at more length. First, typological interpretation is Christological interpretation. Having said that, I am immediately faced with the objection that Christological readings of the Old Testament are strained,

---

[4] Frei, *Eclipse*, 1–3.

artificial, and eisegetical, an objection that comes from formidable commentators like Robert Gordon. In the introduction to his commentary on Samuel, Gordon admits that, given the New Testament's emphasis on Jesus' Davidic ancestry, "the tendency to see David as a 'type' foreshadowing in his life's circumstances the experiences of Christ the promised scion easily developed." Yet, "the New Testament does not indulge in wholesale typological comparisons between David and Christ." Instead, it employs a "contrastive method of approach as against the comparative emphasis of typology," and Gordon goes on briefly to develop three intriguing examples of the New Testament's "contrastive" use of the story of David.[5] In general, he makes no effort "to 'Christianize' 1 and 2 Samuel at every conceivable point."[6]

No doubt Gordon would disagree, I have made no effort to "Christianize" the book of Samuel either. To suggest that the text needs to be "Christianized" is to start off on the wrong foot, for it implies that the text is not Christian to begin with; something from the outside—namely, "Christianity"—overlays what is essentially *not* a Christian book. I make no effort to "Christianize" because I reject the assumption that Samuel is a "non-Christian" text.

Though meant seriously, the previous paragraph is a semi-playful response to the sort of objection that Gordon brings forward. More seriously, it must be admitted that efforts to read the Old Testament as a Christian book have not always been successful or plausible. And so it is necessary to present at least a few points to explain in what sense the present commentary offers a Christological interpretation of Samuel, and how I arrived at that intepretation.[7]

[5] Robert Gordon, *I & II Samuel: A Commentary,* Library of Biblical Interpretation (Grand Rapids: Zondervan, 1986), 49–53.
[6] Ibid., 9.
[7] The following pages overlap with my discussion in *A House for My Name: A Survey of the Old Testament* (Moscow: Canon Press, 2000), 27–40, but attack on a different front.

First, as noted above, the book of Samuel presents historical events, but does not provide a transparent window to those events. That is to say, the text interprets as well as records. It is a truism that historical writing is always an interpretation: A writer's choice to use *these* words rather than *those* words, to emphasize *these* features of the event rather than *those* features, to tell the story in *this* order rather than *that* order—all these choices interpret the events in question. Writing things down always means limitation, and limitation, for any rational writer, has a rationale. Thus, while it is important to determine "what really happened," this is not the only matter that demands attention. Something happened, but that something may be subject to a number of more or less conflicting, more or less valid, interpretations. With respect to the current book, I am operating on the belief that *to read Scripture typologically is to accept that the Bible's interpretation of events provides a true and the most essential interpretation of the events it records.* Other ways of presenting those events were available, and might also be true; but even an interpretation consistent with the Bible's interpretation would not have the same weight as the Bible.

Sometimes, rarely, the Bible's interpretation is sometimes stated explicitly. Hophni and Phinehas, the sons of the high priest Eli, were historical characters, and they were, as Scripture says, "sons of Belial" who "did not know Yahweh" and who committed "very great" sins (1 Sam. 2:12, 17). If independent historical evidence were found that explained the practices of Hophni and Phinehas as innocent liturgical innovations, no effort could be made to "reconcile" the biblical record with the new evidence. The two interpretations would simply be at war.[8] Similarly, it is not only true that David's adultery with Bathsheba "really happened," but it is also true that "the thing that David had done was evil in the sight of the Lord" (2 Sam. 11:27).

---

[8] Certain kinds of evidence might force a new interpretation, of course: A newly discovered and highly reliable text might give a different spin to things, philological research might prove that the text had simply been misunderstood, and so on.

In most instances, however, the Bible uses more subtle means to present its interpretation of events. A number of devices are used. In a superb review of Robert Alter's *The David Story*, Hillel Halkin argues that certain of these devices are inherent in the structure of the Hebrew language. "All languages," he writes, "have words with multiple meanings," but languages with a restricted vocabulary, like Hebrew, exploit these multiple meanings more often and more readily than languages, like English, that have a much larger and more finely grained vocabulary.[9] Since they were writing in Hebrew, therefore, it is not surprising that Old Testament writers had to rely on punning and similar devices to bring out meanings. Further, "In general, a language with a relative paucity of rhetorical means must resort to its own literary stratagems. And so, as Alter observes, 'the Bible turns everywhere not on variation,' as is generally the case with English, but on 'significant repetition.'"[10] Thus, to offer an obvious example, the repetition of the word "take" in Samuel's speech in 1 Samuel 8:10–18 highlights the oppressiveness of the "king like the kings of the nations" that Israel asked for. Throughout this commentary, I shall attend to these kinds of "key word" repetitions as a way of explaining how the Bible is portraying Israel's history.

Another very common device is the use of analogy, and here we begin to arrive at typology per se. As Frei points out, typology means that earlier characters and events are understood as figures of later characters and events, and the text is written in a way that brings out the connection. Through analogy, the writer guides his reader's responses and judgments about characters and events. A character, for example, described in terms reminiscent of Esau (abundant hair, a hunter, very hungry) is almost bound to be a villain, and if he is not, we will conclude that he is deliberately being contrasted with Esau. A writer who describes a character in a way that reminds readers of Joseph (handsome, successful, resistant to

---

[9] "Sacred Implications," in *The New Republic* (February 21, 2000), 39.
[10] Ibid., 39–40.

sexual temptation) wants to comment this "new Joseph" to his readers. The analogies between different characters can be brought out by names, quotations, allusions, physical details, actions, and so forth. The analogies between different events can be brought out by location, similar sequences of events, repetition of key words or phrases, and so on. Whatever the specific means used, biblical writers resort to internal typology to guide the reader.

Moshe Garsiel has explored the use of such "comparative structures" in 1 Samuel.[11] He points out, for example, that 1 Samuel draws out a number of striking analogies between the judges on the one hand, and Samuel and Saul on the other.[12] Samuel functioned as a judge (1 Sam. 7:15–17) and explicitly placed himself among the judges of Israel (1 Sam. 12:11). Alongside these explicit statements are numerous analogies that are left to the discernment of the Scripturally-aware reader. Like Deborah, Samuel held court, judging Israel (1 Sam. 7:15–17; Judg. 4:4–5). Just as Deborah commanded Barak to fight Sisera, so Samuel ordered Saul to fight Amalek, and in both stories the phrase "ten thousand men" appears (1 Sam. 15:1–4; Judg. 4:6), and Kenites are mentioned (1 Sam. 15:6; Judg. 4:17–22). These analogies between two judges and two battles serves to highlight a crucial discontinuity: "Barak follows [Deborah's] instructions and steadily pursues Sisera . . . , while Saul takes pity on Agag, King of Amalek."[13] And of course, any comparison of Saul with the timid Barak implies some degree of criticism.

It was not always so. Early in the account of Saul's life, analogies to the judges were used to commend Saul. As Garsiel points out, Samuel's speech informing the people that Saul had been chosen king recalls the prophet's speech announcing the coming of Gideon (1 Sam. 10:17–19; Judg. 6:8–10), and Saul's initial battle with the Ammonites is described in a way that makes comparisons with Gideon's battle with the Midianites virtually unavoidable:

[11] Moshe Garsiel, *The First Book of Samuel: A Literary Study of Comparative Structures, Analogies and Parallels* (Jerusalem: Rubin Mass, 1990).
[12] Ibid., 54–56, 78–81, 87–93.
[13] Ibid., 55.

Gideon (Judges)	Saul (1 Samuel)
father a mighty man, 6:12	father a mighty man, 9:1–2
humility, 6:15	humility, 9:21
the Spirit clothes, 6:34	the Spirit comes upon, 11:6
messengers through the land, 6:35	messengers through the land, 11:7
division into three companies, 7:16	division into three companies, 11:11
attacks Midianite camp, 7:19	attacks Ammonite camp, 11:11
attacks during the middle watch, 7:19	attacks at the morning watch, 11:11

At the battle of Michmash (1 Sam. 14), however, the writer compares Saul to Jephthah, with more ambiguous effects. Like Jephthah, Saul made a vow before a battle (1 Sam. 14:24–26; Judg. 11:29–31), and in both cases, the vow terminated on a beloved child (Jephthah's unnamed daughter; Jonathan). Jephthah's vow, however, followed hard upon the coming of the Spirit of Yahweh (Judg. 11:29–30), and this suggests that his vow, troubling as it turned out, was righteous.[14] 1 Samuel 14 says nothing to suggest that Saul's vow was similarly inspired by the Spirit, and therefore the comparison with Jephthah's vow puts Saul in an unfavorable light. Meanwhile, the text shifts attention to Jonathan, and by describing Jonathan in a way reminiscent of Gideon, shows that the initiative in leading Israel had moved away from the king to the prince.

Analogies thus provide clues and signposts to show the attentive reader the point of the story and to help him form the judgments that the writer intended. Readers who fail to catch the significance of these analogies will be misled about who's the villain and who's the hero, about what's a sin and what's not. The fact that Saul's first battle so closely resembled Gideon's war, for example, exposes the error of those commentators who believe that Saul was wicked or incompetent from the beginning,[15] and that interpretive

[14] I do not believe that Jephthah slaughtered his daughter and burned her on the altar. Instead, I believe she went to serve the priests at the tabernacle as a dedicated virgin.
[15] E.g., Robert Bergen, *1, 2 Samuel: An Exegetical and Theological Exposition of Holy Scripture,* The New American Commentary (Nashville: Broadman & Holman, 1996), 121: Saul's failure to find his father's donkeys points to his "unfitness to serve as a shepherd of the Lord's flock."

error leads commentators to misconstrue the entire shape of Saul's life. Saul's is a story of rise and fall, a movement from Gideon to Abimelech. It is not the story of a Cain or an Esau who was wicked from the moment he appeared in the text.

Such analogies are foundational for the theological conclusions that can be drawn from an Old Testament book, and thus fundamental to any Christian reading of the Old Testament. It is commonly said that typology should not be used to formulate doctrine. This claim, popular as it is, is not only wrong; it is preposterous. The whole of New Testament Christology is built on analogies (i.e., typologies) between Jesus and Aaron, Jesus and Moses, Jesus and Melchizedek, Jesus and David, Jesus and Jeremiah, and so on. Even apparently more "literal" Christological titles and descriptions are fundamentally typological: To say Jesus is Son of Man is to say He is Last Adam; to say He is Son of God is to say (among other things) that He is the Heir to the Davidic throne (2 Sam. 7:14); to say that he is Prince of Peace is to say that He is a new Solomon. No one with a knowledge of the Old Testament can read the gospels and fail to realize that virtually every line assumes the Old Testament background. Even the most "systematic" of New Testament writers, Paul, draws not only theological but ethical conclusions from an avowedly "allegorical" reading of the story of Ishmael and Isaac (Gal. 4:21–31) and from a typological summary of Israel's wilderness experience (1 Cor. 10:1–10). Far from being illegitimate grounds for theology, typology, I submit, is the only ground for understanding the theological contribution of the Old Testament.

Here especially Gordon's objections come into play. To Gordon, reading the life of David and searching for analogies to the life of Christ distorts the life of David. I cannot answer this objection fully here, but at least I can explain what it means to find Christ revealed in the life of David. To be sure, a Christological reading of the Old Testament is not only an effort to discover "snapshots" of Jesus in the history of Israel. I believe that there are many such snapshots, and many will be pointed to in this commentary.

David foreshadowed Jesus by his patience in the face of persecution, his sufferings on the way to receiving his kingdom, his kindness to Saul's house, his victories over Israel's enemies, his intention to build a house for the Lord, his exile from Jerusalem during the rebellion of Absalom, and in many other more specific ways. On two occasions in 2 Samuel, the death of a son of David preserves David and his kingdom (the first son of Bathsheba; Absalom), and this, I submit, points to the cross.

Illuminating and exciting as these things can be, a Christological reading of David's life must also operate at another level. It is not merely that David foreshadows Christ in isolated events, but that a Davidic royal theology is developed by the literary-historical presentation of David's life, and this provides a crucial element of the framework for understanding the ministry of Jesus (that is, it provides a fundamental Christology in the systematic theological sense). One of the main themes of my treatment of David's life is that David is presented in Samuel as the new and true Israel. This is true in two senses: First, David's life followed the pattern of the life of Jacob, the eponym of Israel, and, second, David is the head of the corporate Israel, the representative Israelite, and this is evident in the way his life story both recapitulated the earlier history of Israel and foreshadowed her future.

But this David-Jacob-Israel connection is understood fully only when it is seen as essential groundwork for the gospels and Paul, where Jesus is seen as the true Israel, recapitulating and redeeming Israel's history in his own history. As N. T. Wright especially has shown, the notion that Israel was embodied in the one person of Jesus is crucial to Paul's Christology and soteriology,[16] and this notion was introduced by the book of Samuel. (To be sure, the Aaronic priest was a representative Israelite, but Jesus is more often contrasted with Aaron than compared with him.) Jesus as son of David functions as representative, and this was made possible by

---

[16] N.T. Wright, *The Climax of the Covenant, Christ and the Law in Pauline Theology* (Minneapolis: Fortress, 1993), e.g., 29.

the arrangements of the Davidic covenant. Typology thus grounds not only Christology (who Jesus is—"son of David") but soteriology (what He accomplished, the "mechanism" of His atonement, and the effects of His work).

PRACTICAL

Like systematic theologians, biblical scholars have often attempted to do their work from "midair," positioned above the conflicts and debates of the contemporary world. The perfect commentary is the "timeless" commentary, as the perfect systematics is the one that presents the "enduring system of doctrine found in Scripture." I am not at war with systematics as such, but the pretense that a theologian can escape from his own time is false, and the *desire* to escape into a timeless systematic Nirvana is a rebellious affront to the theologian's calling. Theology is a pastoral vocation, a ministry to the church, and not to the church of the future or to the church of all times and places, but to the church as the theologian finds her. Biblical interpretation should thus have a practical and pastoral thrust, and, if the proper approach to interpretation is typological, then I must show that typology is practical. My argument will be that typology not only can be made practical, but that, rightly done, it is the only possible basis for practical use of the Old Testament. Proving that assertion will take some doing.

During the 1930s and 1940s, Dutch Reformed theologians were engaged in a debate concerning the question of how to preach the historical books of the Old Testament. On one side were theologians who insisted on a "redemptive-historical" method, emphasizing the unfolding work of God in history, which comes to its climax in Christ. On the other side were those theologians who practiced and defended what was called an "exemplarist" approach, an effort to "get on the inside" of the characters of Scripture by highlighting their struggles, their strengths and weakness, and their psychological state and piety and by holding up the characters of the Bible as examples to imitate or to spurn. As Sidney Greidanus has pointed out, the exemplarists were deeply concerned with making preaching relevant to contemporary congregations, something they believed an exclusive redemptive-historical approach failed to provide.[17]

Though the Dutch debate was not centrally about typology, the exemplarists raised an objection that is often brought against typological interpretation: However exhilarating it may be to discover Christ in every nook and cranny of Scripture, typological commentary and preaching fails to address the concrete practical lives of the congregation and the specific challenges they face. "Jesus in the wilderness reverses the sin of Adam in the garden—lovely, but the baby has chicken pox and I've got to get the twins to the baseball game and help organize the reception for the new assistant youth pastor's wife's mother and finish dinner by six. . . . It is certainly wonderful to know that Jesus is a new Solomon, building up His temple, but I have to close out a big contract on Tuesday, and the boss is breathing down my neck. . . . I'm glad to know Jesus is a greater David who can fight giants, but I got a D on my final and don't know how to tell my parents." Pastorally, it is not a sufficient answer to say, "Give it to Jesus; cast your cares on him." True as that counsel is, Christians demand and deserve specific direction in specific circumstances.

Do we abandon typology to provide this kind of specific counsel? Or should we try out "typology plus"—that is, we read typologically for aesthetic purposes, but when things get ethical, we abandon it and look for proof texts? These questions, and the objection that typology is impractical, arise from a misconception of what typology is and does, a misconception that has, admittedly, been fed by the malpractice of some practitioners of typological interpretation. Perhaps more fundamentally, it arises from a misconception about how we make ethical decisions. The question "What has typology to do with the practical details of the Christian life?" is similar to the question "What have story and metaphor

[17] Sidney Greidanus, *Sola Scriptura: Problems and Principles in Preaching Historical Texts* (Toronto: Wedge Publishing Foundation, 1970), 39–49.

to do with ethics?" And the answer in both cases is, "Much every way."[18]

It is clear from the quotations from Frei earlier that premodern typological interpretation was not merely mental play, performed for the sheer ecstasy of seeing the pattern in the carpet. Rather, the pattern of life found in the type shaped the pattern of life found in the antitype, and both type and antitype were to impress their pattern of life on the reader. George Lindbeck has explained more concretely how the process worked in Western history (read it carefully, because it's crammed!):

> Typology was used to incorporate the Hebrew Scriptures into a canon that focused on Christ, and then, by extension, to embrace extrabiblical reality. King David, for example, was in some respects a typological foreshadowing of Jesus, but he was also, in Carolingian times, a type for Charlemagne and, in Reformation days, as even Protestants said, for Charles V in his wars against the Turks. Thus an Old Testament type, filtered through the New Testament antitype, became a model for later kings, and, in the case of Charlemagne, provided a documentable stimulus to the organization of the educational and parish systems that stand at the institutional origins of Western civilization.[19]

As Lindbeck points out, one of the key features of premodern interpretation of Scripture was "the direction of interpretation":

> Typology does not make scriptural contents into metaphors for extrascriptural realities, but the other way around. It does not suggest, as is often said in our day, that believers find their

---

[18] Though this introduction focuses on the first question, I hope it also contributes to consideration of the second.

[19] George Lindbeck, *The Nature of Doctrine: Religion and Theology in a Postliberal Age* (Philadelphia: Westminster Press, 1984), 117. As I have pointed out elsewhere, the Gelasian theory of church-state relations (a "two-powers" theory), which was a fundamental axiom of medieval political, was formulated in a discussion of the typology of Melchizedek and Christ. For a brief excerpt from Gelasius' "Bond of Anathema," see Oliver O'Donovan and Joan Lockwood O'Donovan, eds., *From Irenaeus to Grotius: A Sourcebook in Christian Political Thought* (Grand Rapids: Eerdmans, 1999), 177–179.

stories in the Bible, but rather that they make the story of the Bible their own story. The cross is not to be viewed as a figurative representation of suffering nor the messianic kingdom as a symbol for hope in the future; rather, suffering should be cruciform, and hopes for the future messianic. . . . Intratextual theology redescribes reality within the scriptural framework rather than translating Scripture into extrascriptural categories. It is the text, so to speak, which absorbs the world, rather than the world the text.[20]

Instead of seeing the text through the lenses of some extrabiblical system, the extrabiblical world was seen through the lenses of Scripture. And not only the world, but the individual person sought to read his life in terms of Scriptural types.[21]

Since the eighteenth century, as Frei's book demonstrates at length, this style of interpretation has fallen into disrepute, and the most fundamental shift can be characterized in the terms that Lindbeck provides: For modern interpretation, "reality" is the world as experienced and as described by science and social science. At best, Scripture provides a set of symbols and metaphors for this "real" world. In short, the world absorbs the text. The similarity between modern methods of interpretation and ancient allegorical interpretation should be noted. In both, reality is named by some extrabiblical system, whether Neoplatonic or Stoic philosophy, or evolutionary science and "scientific" historical research. Both methods seek the meaning of the text in some reality "behind" or "underneath" the text, and thus both read the text in the context of the world rather than the world in the context of the text.

An example pertaining to 1–2 Samuel might help to illustrate how modern critical study resembles allegory, and to demonstrate how typological interpretation stands in opposition to both. In a much-cited article published in 1969, Christian E. Hauer examined

---

[20] Ibid., 118.

[21] See, for example, the stimulating discussion of the idea of Dante's "Scriptural self" in Peter S. Hawkins, *Dante's Testaments: Essays in Scriptural Imagination* (Stanford: Stanford University Press, 1999), chapter 1. Hawkins borrows the phrase "Scriptural self" from John A. Alford.

the "shape of Saulide strategy."[22] While admitting that Saul suffered a measure of "psychological instability," Hauer argues that
the information in 1 Samuel gives evidence of reasonable military
and political strategy, developed in three stages: "(1) the securing
of the Israelite center as the aftermath of the battle of Michmash
[1 Sam. 14], (2) the securing of the (Judean) south, and (3) an abor-
tive attempt to secure the far north," which ended in failure with
Saul's death at the battle of Mount Gilboa (1 Sam. 31).[23]

To fill out the details: After Jonathan had led Israel to victory
over the Philistines, Saul had control of the center of Israelite territory and began to pursue a dual policy of securing those gains on
the one hand and forging stronger bonds between Judah and the
northern tribes on the other. In this context, Hauer suggests that
Saul's pursuit of David was strategically rational; David, after all,
was a rival for the loyalty of Judah, and to unify the nation, Saul
had to neutralize his influence. Once David escaped to Philistia,
however, Saul determined that the south was securely behind him,
and this freed him to turn toward the Philistines in the north,
where they had a long-established foothold in Israelite territory.
Unfortunately, he badly miscalculated Philistine power. As Hauer
summarizes this last phase of Saul's military career,

> [Saul] fell in a grand adventure fraught with momentous pos-
> sibilities. When he moved north, Saul left two thirds of the
> traditional Israelite land claim reasonably secure in his rear.
> His only serious rival for power [David] was a fugitive in en-
> emy service. Those inclined to historical speculation may muse
> at will upon the consequences which would have flowed from
> success in the third strategic place envisioned here. Certainly
> they would have been great.[24]

All this "leads to a heightened respect for Saul," and "helps to
explain David's own high regard for his predecessor."[25]

[22] *Catholic Biblical Quarterly* 31 (1969), 153–176.
[23] Ibid., 153.
[24] Ibid., 166.
[25] Ibid., 167.

In some respects, Hauer's article is illuminating, since it provides some insight into what Saul might have convinced himself he was doing as he chased David through the wilderness. In the end, though, there is no way to reconcile Hauer's account with the portrayal of Saul in Samuel. According to the book of Samuel, after Saul's failure to destroy the Amalekites (1 Sam. 15), the Spirit of Yahweh departed and he was thereafter inspired by an "evil spirit from Yahweh" (16:14) that prompted his hostility towards David (18:10–11). Attacking David was not a defensible point of grand strategy, but an assault on the Lord's man, the new anointed one. Throughout this period, moreover, Saul received no guidance from the Lord; Samuel stopped speaking to him, and he was incapable of consulting with the priests. Hauer may have discerned a logic in Saul's actions, but the Bible presents this as an infernal logic.

Behind Hauer's specific interpretation of Saul is the methodological assumption that motivations of strategy and power-politics are somehow more basic, more real, than the motivations recounted in the biblical story. Explaining Saul's behavior by appeals to strategy makes rational sense of the events; explaining Saul's behavior as the product of demonic inspiration does not. As in allegorical interpretation, the claims and namings of the text become pointers to something more fundamental, in this case, strategies of power.

An even more fundamental presupposition is that the world is quite within its rights to absorb the text. Hauer's approach permits us to absorb the story of Saul into the modern prejudice that out of politics and geostrategy flow the issues of life. The text as read by Hauer does not challenge this assumption but perpetuates it. A typological method would assume that the world has to find its place in the text, and that means that the text's own description of events must be understood as the most basic description. If we follow the text's own leading, the story of Saul becomes a profoundly disturbing portrait of how politics and military strategy can become enthralled to Satanic influence. This becomes especially pointed if Hauer is right that "there is no clear evidence [that Saul's insanity] prevented resolute prosecution of security affairs," since it raises the question of whether "resolute prosecution of security affairs" might be a euphemism for demonic prosecution of murderous policy. It is no accident that the modern church has both rejected typology and has become a mirror image of the world; there is a chicken and egg problem here, but surely the two developments are related. A church that refuses typology cannot hear the word of Yahweh, because it has allowed the Word to be situated by the world. A church that refuses typology will therefore be enslaved to the words, words, words that circulate through the culture.

Let me attempt to bring this back to the congregation in the pews: The answer to the charge of irrelevance is that typology is the only basis for making the Bible practically relevant. Only if there are correspondences between events—that is, only if one event may be a "type" of a future event—can the Bible be relevant, since the Bible obviously does not speak about our circumstances directly. This does not mean that *we* are the antitype in some direct way; rather, it means that the types of Scripture provide us with a set of names and symbols by which we may evaluate our world and which provide a motivation for action. A preacher can urge the members of his congregation to "dare to be a Daniel" only if there is some correlation between Daniel's situation and that of his congregation. Once the connection is made, the analogy with Daniel becomes a source of motivation, zeal, and confidence, and a guide for behavior: "If I'm like Daniel, I had better act like a Daniel." All application of Scripture is presumptively, even when not explicitly, typological.

In short: If the world absorbs the text, as in allegorical or historical-critical interpretation, we can discover nothing in the text that we did not know before; the text can only illustrate truths we learned from other sources, and it will not challenge or rebuke us. If the text absorbs the world, as typological interpretation demands, it is useful for correction, reproof, and training in righteousness. Interpreted typologically, Scripture is unleashed to function as revelation.

And that, after all, is what it is.

STRUCTURAL AND HISTORICAL OVERVIEW

As I pointed out in the introduction, this commentary on 1–2 Samuel is mainly concerned with literary and theological issues. Historical questions are discussed when such discussion is necessary to make sense of the story or when an historical perspective illuminates a theological point. Only rarely have I attempted to deal with historical, textual, or compositional difficulties; this limitation is due to lack of competence, lack of space, and (especially on the issue of compositional history) to settled lack of interest and an even more settled incredulity about the usefulness of scholarly speculations.[1] Yet, some historical orientation will be useful at the outset, and that is one goal of this opening chapter.

My other goal in this chapter is to offer a structural overview of the whole book. Throughout the commentary, I have included outlines, many of them chiastic and many of them confined to footnotes, of smaller sections of 1–2 Samuel. Yet, whole books of the Bible, and not merely individual passages, have a discernible literary architecture, and in this chapter I offer what I believe is a plausible blueprint. Further, biblical books, notoriously various in incident as they are, tell a single story; they have a *plot*. In this opening chapter, I discuss the overall narrative shape of the book. Literary questions will be discussed first, and then I turn to issues of history and chronology.

---

[1] Readers interested in such questions should consult Joyce G. Baldwin, *1 & 2 Samuel: An Introduction and Commentary*, Tyndale Old Testament Series (Downers Grove: InterVarsity Press, 1988), 15–47; Gordon, *I & II Samuel*, 19–68; Bergen, *1, 2 Samuel*, 17–56; Ronald F. Youngblood, *1, 2 Samuel*, The Expositor's Bible Dictionary, 10 vols. (Grand Rapids: Zondervan, 1992), 553–562.

STRUCTURAL AND NARRATIVE OVERVIEW

The subtitle of this volume refers to 1–2 Samuel as a "book" and considers the two volumes of our English Bibles as a single story crucial to understanding the sweep of narrative.[2] The unity of the story is apparent when we look at its beginning and end.[3] It begins with a world falling apart: The lamp was still burning, but only dimly, and the woman was barren. Early in 1 Samuel, the Philistines captured the ark and took it to Philistia. At the same time, Eli and his sons died, and the Mosaic tabernacle at Shiloh was destroyed (1 Sam. 4–6). To be sure, the ark was returned to Israel and David later set it in Jerusalem, but throughout 1–2 Samuel, the worship system described in Exodus and Leviticus was simply not operating. The early chapters of 1–2 Samuel report the death of the Mosaic order. Meanwhile, with the dark age descending, Yahweh intervened to open the womb, to trim the wick, and to create, as He always does, a future. The first major character, Samuel, was called as a prophet to speak the words that would initiate the construction of a new Israel. Samuel guided Israel through a period of liturgical and political chaos, and in the process laid foundations for a new order.

2 Samuel ends with David's census, which led to a plague that devastated Israel (2 Sam. 24). To stop the plague, David purchased the threshing floor of Araunah and offered sacrifice on it. At first glance, this seems an odd place to end the story of David. It provides a fitting climax, however, because it brings the story of the house of God to a conclusion (at least, to a penultimate conclusion). The threshing floor of Araunah becomes the location for the temple (2 Chr. 3:1). And so the story that began with the desolation of the Mosaic tent ends with David purchasing the place for

---

[2] In addition to the narrative and structural considerations discussed here, the textual history indicates that 1–2 Samuel was originally a single book. On the textual unity and textual history, see Gordon, *I & II Samuel*, 19–22, 57–66. To avoid confusion, I have used the conventional citations that assume two books of Samuel.

[3] See also the discussion in my book *A House for My Name*, chapter 4.

the Solomonic house. The big story in the book of Samuel is the transition from tabernacle to temple.[4]

Political transitions accompanied this change in liturgy and worship. First, there was a shift from rule by Gentiles to rule by Israelites. At the beginning of 1 Samuel, the Philistines were dominating Israel, but by the end of 2 Samuel David had eliminated the Philistine threat and established a settled dynasty that would endure for several centuries. Second, 1–2 Samuel records a movement from rule by judges to rule by kings. Eli was a judge, and Samuel was the last of that breed. Though anointed king, Saul was something of a transitional figure, who remained at home plowing when he was not fighting Ammonites (1 Sam. 11). With David, however, Israel came fully into the monarchical period.

Within these larger transitions, the main story has to do with the "crossing fates" of Saul and David.[5] Saul's rise and fall is like an expanded retelling of the story of Adam, and if Saul was like the first Adam, David was a type of the Last Adam, called to replace the fallen king as the head of God's people, persecuted without cause by his rival, waiting patiently until the Lord gave him the kingdom. This is not to say that David is perfect by any means, but David is a man after the Lord's own heart, and foreshadows the work of his greater Son, Jesus.

Viewing the book of Samuel from this perspective helps us to identify its particular relevance for our times. As I complained in the introduction, many biblical commentators, like systematic theologians, attempt to do their work from "midair," floating above the conflicts of the contemporary world and attempting to provide a "timeless" and "definitive" explanation of the biblical text. Being middle-aged and possessed of a growing midriff, I have no allusions about being able to float in midair, and my study of 1–2 Samuel

---

[4] According to Chronicles, David was preoccupied with preparations for the building of the temple and with organizing the Levites for the worship of the temple.

[5] The phrase "crossing fates" comes from the title to the second volume of J. P. Fokkelman's monumental *Narrative Art and Poetry in the Books of Samuel* (Assen: Van Gorcum, 1986).

has explored how it might provide guidance for the church in the twenty-first century. Since it tells a story in which one world gives birth to another, it offers wisdom for Christians as we grope our way through (and, hopefully, out of) our present ecclesiastical crises toward the light.[6] It points to the things we must do if we want to see the lamp burning again, if we hope to see the barren give birth.

Perhaps most importantly, what 1–2 Samuel highlights is the decisive importance of leadership, and specifically of leadership over generations. Americans like to pretend that the world works democratically, that reformations come from the masses. Surely, there is a symbiotic relation between leaders and the led; a leader with no following is no leader. But all societies are led, and all social transitions are the product of the vision, labor, and perseverance of leaders. As Oliver O'Donovan has pointed out, the modern obsession with the social sciences has obscured the fact that "the societies we inhabit are *politically formed*," that is, "they depend upon the art of government."[7] Political and cultural leadership, or lack of it, determines the health of a civilization, and, likewise, the health of the church. It is not simply that good leaders *do* things that restore health to a civilization; the mere *fact* of righteous and godly leadership marks a rebirth.

At the outset of 1 Samuel, Israel was sick because she was ruled by Philistines and, worse, Eli, Hophni, and Phinehas. At the birth of Samuel, Hannah celebrated because she discerned that Yahweh had begun a revolution of the elites, casting down oppressive Philistines and wicked priests and raising up new nobles and, ultimately, a king (1 Sam. 2:1–10). And Hannah's hope was vindicated over the subsequent decades. Yahweh eliminated Eli and his sons and began to raise up a faithful priest, and through the efforts

---

[6] Though my focus is on the relevance of 1–2 Samuel for the church, I believe that a rebirth of the church would be a profoundly important political and cultural event.

[7] *The Desire of the Nations: Rediscovering the Roots of Political Theology* (Cambridge: University of Cambridge Press, 1996), 16.

of Samuel, Saul, and David, the Philistines were driven from the land. 2 Samuel ends with an Israelite king sitting on the throne, receiving tribute from nations that had once oppressed the people of God. Israel's condition at the end of 2 Samuel is by no means ideal, and much of the wisdom that the book offers is given through negative examples. Saul turned from the Lord early in his reign, and he threw the nation into confusion by his obsession with David. David too fell into sin with Bathsheba and never recovered his earlier vigor. David's weakness opened the door for opportunists and rebels, Joabs and Absaloms. Yet, Israel's condition at the end of David's reign was an undeniable and vast improvement.

1–2 Samuel pay particular attention to the failure of Israel's leaders to raise up leaders from a new generation. Eli, apparently a well-meaning priest who had no clue about how to control his sons, set the pattern at the outset, and was followed by Samuel and, to a large extent, David. Surprisingly, the only leader to produce utterly faithful sons was Saul. In 1–2 Samuel, the pattern of a faithless son replaced by a faithful adopted son is typological, but this pattern also highlights a key failure of Israel's leaders during the early monarchy.

The promise of faithful leadership that Hannah looked to was finally fulfilled in Jesus. He is the True King, who rises like a sun and causes the vegetation of the land to flourish. Yet Jesus does not govern alone. Throughout the prophetic books of the Old Testament, the promise of a new covenant included the promise that Israel's corrupt and ungodly leaders would be replaced with true shepherds (Jer. 3:11–18; 23:1–4; Ezek. 34:1–31), a promise fulfilled when Jesus ascended on high and gave gifts to men (Eph. 4:8–13). Jesus' gathering of apostles was not just a pragmatic necessity, a way of ensuring that His "movement" would spread. His installation of new "bishops" over Israel was part of the good news for which Israel had been waiting, part of the gospel. And it is a gospel that we crave to see fulfilled in our time. How we get from where we are to where we hope to be is one of the main practical messages of

1–2 Samuel. We will know that reformation of the new Israel has occurred, and is occurring when Davids replace the Elis and the Philistines that rule the church today. The church will simply not be revived until that is fulfilled which was spoken by the Psalmist: "His office let another man take."

FORMAL STRUCTURE

So much for the "plot" of 1–2 Samuel. With respect to formal structure, many portions of 1–2 Samuel are chiastically arranged, and I have provided many detailed outlines in the following chapters. The entire book, however, may also be seen as a large chiasm. David Dorsey has suggested the following outline:[8]

A   Samuel succeeds elderly Eli and rules over all Israel, 1 Sam. 1–7
  B   Saul's failure, 1 Sam. 8–15
    C   David's initial rise, 1 Sam. 16–20
      D   Turning point: Yahweh reverses fortunes of Saul and David, 1 Sam. 21–31
    C'   David's initial rise to power over all Israel, 2 Sam. 1–8
  B'   David's failure, 2 Sam. 9–20
A'   Solomon succeeds David, 2 Sam. 21–1 Kgs. 2

Though plausible, this outline has a number of weaknesses. First, a number of Dorsey's sections would be better divided into smaller units. To subsume the ark narrative of 1 Samuel 4–6, for example, under the heading of "Samuel succeeds elderly Eli" obscures crucial aspects of the opening chapters of the book. Eli's death is recorded in 1 Samuel 4 and he is never mentioned again in these chapters, and Samuel does not even make an appearance in chapters 4–6. Making 1 Samuel 21–31 a single section, moreover, blurs the distinction between David's "wanderings in the wilderness" and his "exile in Philistia," a distinction that is important narratively and theologically. Finally, though 2 Samuel 9–20 do hang together as a record of "David's failure," the chapters describe

---

[8] *The Literary Structure of the Old Testament: A Commentary on Genesis-Malachi* (Grand Rapids: Baker, 1999), 135.

not only David's sin with Bathsheba, but also the struggle between
Absalom and Amnon, Absalom's rebellion, and the secession led by
Sheba. To include all this in one section again seems clumsy.[9]

Second, at least one of the strongest parallels between A and
A' makes sense only if 1 Kings 1–2 is included with 1–2 Samuel.
Solomon is not even mentioned in the closing chapters of 2 Samuel,
and so it is odd, to say the least, to title A' "Solomon succeeds
elderly David." I am certainly open to the possibility that Samuel
and Kings form one large book and that the whole has a chiastic
arrangement. But 1–2 Samuel has its own structural integrity, and
that is obscured by Dorsey's outline. Finally, Dorsey has set up his
outline in a way that obscures some of the important connections
between the beginning and end of the book.

For these reasons, I propose the following as an alternative outline:

A			Birth of Samuel, 1 Sam. 1:1–2:11 (Hannah's song, 2:1–10)
	B		The corruption of Eli's house, 2:12–3:21
		C	Exile and return of the ark, 4:1–7:17
		D	Saul's rise, 8:1–12:25
		E	Saul's fall, 13:1–15:33
		F	David in Saul's house, 15:34–20:42
		G	Saul versus David, 21:1–27:12
		H	Saul's death, 28:1–2 Sam. 1:27 (lament)
		G'	House of Saul v. House of David, 2:1–4:12
		F'	David as King, 5:1–9:13
		E'	David's fall, 10:1–12:31
		D'	Absalom's rise, 13:1–15:12
		C'	Exile and return of David, 15:13–19:43
	B'		Rebellion of Sheba, 20:1–26
A'			The True King, 21:1–24:25 (poems, 22:1–23:7)

[9] Dorsey does acknowledge that 2 Samuel 9–20 "comprises two long sections" and
seeks to show their unity by pointing to "echoes between the two parts" (ibid., 133), but
the distinction between these sections is lost in his larger outline. Though he does not
mention it, Dorsey may be influenced by speculation that 2 Samuel 9–20 forms, along
with 1 Kings 1–2, an originally distinct document known to scholars as the "Succession
Narrative." In responding to this, I can only remind the reader of my settled incredulity
about conjectures concerning the compositional history of 1–2 Samuel.

Though a few of these correspondences appear stretched (even to me!), overall the scheme works well and was arrived at by applying the most rigorous and scientific methods known to man. In any case, one of the features of chiastic structures is that corresponding sections illuminate each other and together form a mini-narrative of their own. Let me attempt to explain how this works with this particular chiasm:

A and A': Both sections contain poetry, and David's psalms in 2 Samuel 22:1–23:7 celebrated the fulfillment of Hannah's hope for an "anointed one" (1 Sam. 2:10). Further verbal parallels between these two poems are explored in chapter 11 of this book. Through the instrumentality of David, who was anointed by the son of Hannah, the doomed "temple" at Shiloh (1 Sam. 1:9) is replaced by the new permanent temple location at the threshing floor of Araunah (2 Sam. 24).

B and B': The division between Samuel and the sons of Eli (1 Sam. 2:12–3:21) foreshadowed the division between Israel and Judah that manifested itself in Sheba's rebellion (2 Sam. 20). Moreover, the structure brings out correspondences between Eli's house and David's: Eli's house was dominated by his wicked sons, while David's house was dominated by the wicked Joab (see the list of David's royal house in 2 Sam. 20:23–26, and chapter 10 of this book). Eli's sons ignored his rebuke, as Joab ignored David's orders.

C and C': In both sections, we have an "exodus and return" story, and the parallel suggestively highlights a correspondence between David and the ark, both bearers of the Lord's presence and Spirit.

D and D': The matching sections bring out important analogies between Saul and Absalom: Both were distinguished by their "head" (Saul's head towered above Israel's and Absalom was known for his hair), both were closely related to David (Saul was father-in-law and Absalom was son), both eventually persecuted David and drove him from the city into the wilderness. Within the two D sections particularly, there is a contrast between Saul's early humility and faithfulness and Absalom's arrogance and violence. Saul received the crown without seeking it; Absalom plotted to overthrow David. Saul sought for donkeys and hid among the baggage, while Absalom gathered horses and a chariot and stationed himself at the gate.

E and E': Both sections record the sins of a king and the prophetic judgment against him. Because of these sins, both kings lost their kingdoms, though David regained his. As we shall see in the commentary, Saul's sins and David's sins shared certain features (impatience, an assault on a "brother," ungodliness in relation to Gentiles).

F and F': In both sections, David is the focus of attention, in F as warrior and servant to Saul, and in F' as warrior-king and head over Israel. In both sections, David acts wisely and prospers wherever he goes. In both sections, David defeats Philistines and other enemies of Israel.

G and G': In both sections, there was struggle between Saul and David; in G, the struggle was between Saul and David personally, while in G' the struggle was between their houses. David's behavior was similar in both sections, as he showed restraint in the face of opposition and treated Saul and Saul's house with respect. But there is also a contrast between David's treatment of Saul in G and Joab's treatment of Abner in G'; Joab's relation to Abner was analogous to David's relation to Saul, but Joab's violent actions exacerbated rather than pacified tensions between the two houses, between "Israel and Judah."

H: The death of Saul is the hinge on which the whole action of the book turns. Described in sacrificial terms in the text, Saul's death cleansed the land and cleared the way for a new king to assume the throne. Further, poetry is found at the center of the book, as at the beginning and end.

More detailed structural analyses will be offered throughout the commentary, and in particular the commentary will defend the sectioning of the text that is assumed in the above outline.

HISTORICAL AND CHRONOLOGICAL OVERVIEW

The history of 1–2 Samuel covers about a century and a half of Israel's history: forty years of Philistine oppression, plus some thirty years as Samuel grows old, and then forty years each for the reigns of Saul and David. The story opens during the forty-year Philistine oppression referred to in Judges 13:1. Joyce Baldwin has offered a concise summary of the larger political situation at the time of the Philistine invasions:

> At this period no great world power was seeking to dominate the New East. Israel's battles were waged against near neighbours, whose territory bordered the land occupied by the twelve tribes, and in particular against the Philistines, a military aristocracy from Crete, small numbers of whom had settled in Canaan in patriarchal times. Soon after Israel's arrival in Canaan, however, they had arrived in force and had occupied the coastal plain of the south-west. There they set up five city-states, organized under . . . 'lords', and demonstrated their mastery of iron technology and their military professionalism in their attacks against Israel. . . . Throughout the reign of Saul, and initially during the reign of David also, they continued to be a thorn in Israel's side; both Saul and Jonathan died at their hands, and the Philistines penetrated to Bethshan, so dominating the Jordan valley.[10]

The early chapters of 1 Samuel report the events of the period of Philistine dominance that overlap with the events in Judges 13–16. 1 Samuel 4 describes the battle of Aphek against the Philistines, and in chapter 7 another battle with the Philistines is chronicled, the battle of Ebenezer. Ebenezer brought an end to the Philistine domination of Israel (1 Sam. 7:13), and was fought twenty years after the death of Eli and the capture of the ark (1 Sam. 7:1-2). Thus, the forty-year oppression by the Philistines was bisected by the capture of the ark at the battle of Aphek. This basic chronology of the early chapters of 1 Samuel may be diagramed as follows:

[10] Baldwin, *1 & 2 Samuel*, 19.

Year of Philistine Oppression	Event	Leaders of Israel
1		Eli as judge and priest
20	Battle of Aphek	Eli died
40	Battle of Ebenezer	Samuel as leader

To get a fuller picture, it is necessary to harmonize this chronology with the information in Judges. Judges 15:20 tells us that Samson was judging Israel for twenty years during the Philistine oppression. Did he judge Israel during twenty years before Aphek, during the twenty years between Aphek and Ebenezer, or during some twenty-year period that straddles Aphek? Several considerations help to answer that question. When Samson was born, the Philistines were already ruling (Judg. 13:1; 14:4), and Samson did not live to see the Philistines defeated. He died when he brought down the temple of Dagon upon the Philistine lords (Judg. 16:23–31), but there is nothing in the text about the Philistine oppression ending at that point (though it must have been a severe blow to their political system, to say the least). Assuming that he began judging Israel around the age of twenty (or even a year or two earlier) and noting that his judgeship lasted for twenty years, his life must have almost exactly corresponded to the period of Philistine dominance. He was thus born early in the forty-year period and grew up during the last twenty years of Eli's priesthood, prior to the battle of Aphek. His twenty years of judging Israel must have begun shortly before the battle of Aphek and must have ended shortly before the battle of Ebenezer. Intriguingly, this was also the time when Samuel is born and is growing up (1 Sam. 1–2).

Once we see the chronological overlap of Samson and Samuel, other connections between them become plausible, though not certain. Samson began his work shortly before the battle of Aphek, and his antics provoked the Philistines to organize an attack on Shiloh. Samson labored as a judge for most of the twenty years between Aphek and Ebenezer, dying in the temple of Dagon shortly before the battle of Ebenezer. Samson's assault on Dagon and the Philistine nobility may well have been the incident that prodded

Samuel to assemble the people at Mizpah to renew the covenant
(1 Sam. 7:3–11). One hint that this was the sequence of events is the
sequence of judges. Eli judged Israel for forty years (1 Sam. 4:18),
and this ended at his death at the battle of Aphek. Samuel did not
begin to judge Israel for another twenty years (7:6). It seems reasonable to assume that Samson judges Israel during the intervening
twenty years.[11] This chronology is summarized in the chart below.

Event	Year of Eli's Priesthood (Age)	Year of Philistine Oppression
Samson's birth	Year 20 (78)	Near Year 1
Samuel's birth	Year 20+ (78+)	Year 1+
Samson begins	Year 39 (97)	Year 19
Aphek	Year 40 (98)	Year 20
Ark captured	Year 40 (98)	Year 20
Eli's death	Year 40 (98)	Year 20
Ark returned		Year 21
Samson destroys temple		Year 39
Ebenezer		Year 40
Samuel begins judging		End of oppression

Samuel remained as judge over Israel until old age (1 Sam.
8:1), which probably means some thirty years after the battle of
Ebenezer. At this point, Israel requested a king and Samuel anointed Saul to be king. Sometime while Saul was pursuing David in the
wilderness, Samuel died. Saul reigned for forty years (Acts 13:21)
and died at the battle of Gilboa. David, who had been anointed
a number of years earlier, became king in Hebron for seven years
and six months, and then moved to Jerusalem, where he reigned
for thirty-three years. The further chronology of 1–2 Samuel is
summarized in the chart below, though a number of the ages are
admittedly somewhat speculative.

---

[11] Several judges were often at work in different parts of the land, so it is reasonable
to conclude that Samson and Eli were judging simultaneously, at least for a time. Indeed,
the chronology demands some overlap.

Event	Samuel's Age	Saul's Age	David's Age
Ebenezer	40?	10?	
Request for a king	70	40	
Saul becomes king	70+	40+	
David born	80	50+	1
David anointed	97	67	17
David and Goliath	97	67	17
Samuel dies	105	72	22
Saul pursues David		72–80	22–30
Saul dies at Gilboa		80	30
David reigns in Hebron			30–37
David reigns in Jerusalem			37–70

Some details of this chronology will be further discussed in the commentary (e.g., Samuel's age at the time of Aphek and Ebenezer, Saul's age at the time of his becoming king), and a more detailed chronology of David's reign is offered in chapter 10.

THE BARREN GIVES BIRTH

First and Second Samuel record a history of political struggle and intrigue, of major shifts in the religious and political life of ancient Israel, of world-historical, epoch-making events. Its major events take place at the sanctuaries of Shiloh and Zion, on the battlefields of Aphek and Gilboa, in the royal homes of Saul and David, in the cities of Ramah and Jerusalem. Yet, at the beginning the writer calls our attention to a humble woman—a humble *woman*[2]—living in the backwaters of the hill country of Ephraim, weeping over her dead womb. Why did the writer choose to begin the story here? What has Hannah to do with high politics? What has Ramathaim-zophim to do with Jerusalem?

"Hannah" means "favored one," and Hannah was the favored wife of Elkanah (v. 5), but her condition contradicted her name: How could the favored one be barren?[3] In her barrenness, Hannah

---

[1] Structurally, this section of 1 Samuel is divided into three main sections: 1:1–2:11; 2:12–4:1a; 4:1b–7:17. Though these form distinct units of the book, it is reasonable to treat chapters 1–7 together here (though see my reservations in chapter 1). In chapters 1–2, the text focuses on the high priest and his unfaithful sons, and the Lord's plan to raise up a new priest; this story starts over in a different "register" in chapter 8, where we are told that Samuel's own sons were unfaithful. Further, the fact that chapter 8 turns our attention to the rise of the monarchy indicates that a new phase of the story is being told. Finally, "Ramah" or "Ramathaim-zophim" is mentioned both at the beginning and end of the passage (1:1, 19; 2:11; 7:17), but nowhere in between, and thus these geographic references frame the whole section.

[2] Of course, Hannah was married, and we know her husband's name and genealogy (1:1), but without doubt the focus is on his wife.

[3] The story is patterned as follows:

A   Hannah's barrenness and rivalry with Peninnah (Ramathaim-zophim), 1:1-8
   B   Hannah's prayer (Shiloh), 1:9-11
     C   Eli and Hannah (Shiloh), 1:12-18
       D   Birth of Samuel (Ramah), 1:19-23
     C'   Eli and Hannah (Shiloh), 1:24-28
   B'   Hannah's song (celebrating answer to prayer), 2:1-10
A'   Hannah's child grows (Ramah), 2:11

takes her place with the wives of the patriarchs. Sarah was barren, Rebekah was barren, Rachel was barren. In Genesis, the woman's barrenness was not only an emotional or family problem but threatened the fulfillment of God's promise of an abundant seed to inherit the land. Barrenness is significant ultimately because of God's promise to raise up a "seed of the woman" to crush the serpent's head (Gen. 3:15). That was the seed promised to Abraham, but so long as Sarah was barren, the promise was not being fulfilled. Without a son, there was no future for Israel. Further, Israel was God's bride, and so a barren woman is a symbol of fruitless Israel (Is. 49:14-21; 54:1-3). Israel was the Hannah, the favored one, of Yahweh. How indeed can the favored one be barren?

A moment's reflection on the historical context of 1 Samuel will answer that question: Israel was barren because Israel was unfaithful (see Deut. 28:15–19), and particularly because her leaders were unfaithful. 1 Samuel opens in the period of the judges, a period marked by repeated apostasy. Apparently, prayer at the Shiloh sanctuary was so rare that Eli could not recognize it when he saw it (1 Sam. 1:12–13). Eli's inability to identify what Hannah was doing, however, points to the apostasy of the priests and Levites during this period. The book of Judges comes to a climax with stories about corrupt Levites (chapters 17–21), and 1 Samuel fills out that portrait. So long as Israel was "husbanded" by the likes of Eli, Hophni, and Phinehas, she would remain a waste land. A priest incapable of distinguishing prayer from drunkenness was hardly a suitable gatekeeper at Yahweh's "house of prayer" (see Acts 2:13).

But we can be more precise: Hannah's was a story of rivalry as well as barrenness. In addition to Hannah, Elkanah was married to Peninnah, a mother of many sons and daughters (1:4) who persecuted Hannah intensely (1:6). As the story unfolds, it becomes clear that Hannah was part of a faithful remnant, one of those who continued to pour out her heart in all its bitterness before the Lord. There were others. The men who objected to the practices of Hophni and Phinehas (2:16) stood in the company of Hannah, the favored one. But the faithful remnant was exactly that, a remnant, weak and beggarly by comparison with the strong and well-fed priests, and the even stronger and better-fed Philistines. Elkanah's family was a microcosm of Israel, divided between the rich and apparently fruitful nobles and the poor and needy who made their home in the dust and ashes. In Hannah's transition from bitterness to joy, we see on a small scale the effect that Samuel would have on the whole of God's barren bride, Israel. Samuel would make the barren, unfruitful remnant rejoice in children, because he would replace the wicked priests.

Neither Hannah nor Samuel was capable of renewing Israel. Only Yahweh, as Hannah knew, "kills and makes alive" (2:6). If Hannah hoped to rejoice as a mother of children, she knew she had to appeal to the only one who could bring life from the dead. If Israel hoped to be revived, her only option was to "pour out her soul before Yahweh" (1:15). Hannah's prayer was an admission of impotence, an acknowledgment that she could do nothing to open the closed door of her womb. Her prayer was an acknowledgment that only Yahweh can open such doors. Every prayer is like the prayer of Hannah: powerless creatures confessing their powerlessness by turning to the Lord and Giver of all life and all good. Israel's renewal began with prayer because it began with Yahweh.

Many believers and churches today find themselves in the situation of Hannah. The favored ones, the remnant earnest to remain faithful to the Lord and His word, suffer because of indifference or active persecution from corrupt leaders. Eli and his sons preside at the sanctuary, and all the big churches, the big budgets, and the big libraries are at Shiloh. Peninnah seems to be the fruitful one, while Hannah remains barren. Seminaries, pastoral internships, leadership seminars—all these have their place in overturning this situation. Since we are a barren people, however, our hope for new "husbands" is in the One who raises the dead, and in Him alone. And our first task is to plead with Him to open the womb.

A couple of side details about Hannah's prayer are interesting. Eli was sitting at the door-post of the "temple" as he watched her pray. The description is odd, since there was in fact no temple in Shiloh. Because the tabernacle had been there throughout the period of the judges (Josh. 18:1), however, it had become virtually a permanent building. Eli's location at the door-post seems an incidental detail, but is not. Sarah stood in a doorway when the angels told Abraham that he was going to have a son (Gen. 18:10), and in the exodus, Israel passed through blood-stained doorways as they came to a "new birth" from slavery in Egypt. In these passages, the doorway symbolizes birth. God "opens" the doorway of the womb so that a child can enter the world. Hannah's child would eventually stand in the same doorway as the "gatekeeper" of Israel (1 Sam. 3:15).

Hannah vowed she would dedicate her son to the Lord forever, as a permanent Nazirite (1:11). According to Numbers 6, the Nazirite separated himself from wine, from grapes, from cutting his hair, and from the dead. In several details, the Nazirite resembled a priest, especially the high priest. Nazirites were to avoid contact with the dead, as high priests were (Lev. 21:1-3, 10-11). Priests were not to drink wine or strong drink in the sanctuary (Lev. 10:9–11), while the Nazirite was not supposed to drink wine or eat grapes at all. Nazirites thus lived as if the whole world was a holy place. Their holy service, which often took the form of holy war, outside the sanctuary was comparable to the holy service of the priests in the sanctuary.

Hannah's prayer emphasized the Nazirite prohibition against cutting the hair. Hair is a natural crown and a sign of glory. As the Proverb says, "the glory of old men is their gray hair" (Prov. 20:29) and Psalm 68:21 speaks of a man's "hairy crown." During the time of his vow, the Nazirite wore his growing crown (analogous to the "crown" on the high priest), and when the vow was finished, he dedicated it to God by putting it on the altar fire with a peace offering, throwing down his crown before the Lord. Literally, Hannah vowed that "a razor shall never come on his *head*" (1:11), and this is consistent with the language of Numbers 6, which speaks about the Nazirite's "dedicated head" rather than his dedicated hair (vv. 9, 11, 18). Hannah's prayer thus initiates the theme of the "head" that runs through 1–2 Samuel. Saul was a head taller than other Israelites (10:23), and later Absalom's hair was a heavy, "glorious" crown.

There are three permanent Nazirites in the Bible: Samson, Samuel, and John the Baptist, and each of them was born to a barren woman. Samuel typifies the ministry of John: As Samuel prepared the people for the reign of David, so John turned the hearts of the fathers to the children and prepared a people for the coming of the Davidic King.

Hannah's etymology of the name "Samuel" introduces another key theme of the book. Verse 20 says he was called Samuel because he had been "asked of Yahweh." The word "asked" is used a number of times in chapter 1 (vv. 17, 20, 27–28),[4] but the name Samuel does not mean precisely this. *Shem* means "name" and *"el"* means "God," so Samuel could be interpreted as "His name is God." The word for "asked" is from the verb *sha'al,* close enough to make a punning etymological connection, but distant enough to make us suspect that something more is afoot.

This etymology becomes more significant as the story of 1 Samuel progresses. In chapter 9, a character is introduced whose name actually means "asked": Saul (Heb., *Sha'ul*). Saul was "asked" for by the people (1 Sam. 8:10), but chapter 1 is already preparing the thematic background for this request, and preparing for the contrast between Samuel and Saul. This contrast helps to explain why the people were wrong to ask for a king. They received *sha'ul* after asking for a king, but they already had a *sha'ul*, one "asked for," namely, Samuel. Israel should have been content with their "asked" judge, and waited for God to introduce the king.

---

[4] The verb *sha'al* is used four times in verses 27-28 alone; the word translated as "dedicated" (NASB) is a form of the same verb.

Samuel's parents brought him to Shiloh after he was weaned (vv. 21–28). Weaning was sometimes elaborately celebrated in the ancient world, since it marked his transfer from his mother's care to his father's (Gen. 21:8). More than Samuel's weaning, however, 1 Samuel focuses attention on Samuel's transfer from his father's house to the house of Eli. Eli was going to raise Samuel and act as a substitute father, and this passage describes Eli's "adoption" of Samuel. Eli's paternal relation to Samuel forms the background for the contrast between Samuel and Eli's natural sons that is developed in chapter 2. Father-son relations are, moreover, prominent throughout 1–2 Samuel. Samuel's troublesome sons provided a pretext for the people to ask for a king, and Saul was "adopted" as Samuel's son. Later, David became a son-in-law to Saul, and much of the account of David's reign in 2 Samuel is taken up with recording David's difficulties with his sons.

In each of these cases, biological sons were replaced by an adopted son. Just as Eli and his sons lost the priesthood and were supplanted by Samuel, so Samuel's sons were supplanted by Saul and Saul's son by David. In contrast to Genesis, the true son in 1–2 Samuel is not a younger biological son but an adopted son who comes from outside the genealogy. This ultimately points to Jesus, the miracle-born son of Adam who displaced His fallen father. 1–2 Samuel thus makes the typology of Genesis more precise by showing that the "seed" would not come through the normal channels of fleshly descent but would be preeminently the one "born according to the Spirit" (cf. Lk. 1:35; Gal. 4:21–31).

According to 3:3, Samuel slept in the "tent of the Lord" (3:3). This adds an important dimension to the ceremony in 1:21–28, because it shows that Samuel was not only being transferred to Eli's house but to Yahweh's. Yahweh was Samuel's Father, Samuel His true priest-son. Here again the later history of 1–2 Samuel is being foreshadowed. Saul was called to look to Yahweh as his Father but failed to listen to his Father's voice, while the Davidic kings were explicitly described as "sons of God" (2 Sam. 7:14).

The opening story of 1 Samuel concludes with the "song of Hannah." In contrast to her earlier prayer, this is a hymn of joy, a prayer not of desperation but of exultation. Clearly, Hannah understood the birth of Samuel as something more than her personal vindication and blessing. She knew that when the Lord started opening barren wombs, He was beginning to act for His people. Yahweh's preeminence, the "prevenience" of His work in Israel, is emphatic in the song. If Samuel's birth marked the beginning of Israel's renewal, it was not because Hannah had been able to psych herself up to pregnancy. Only Yahweh could open her womb, and the favored one celebrated His favor by using Yahweh's seven times in this brief song (a sabbatical theme) and by singing of over a dozen different works that He had done.

Hannah's song begins and ends with references to "horns." Hannah's horn had been raised up, and she looked expectantly for the Lord to raise the horn of His anointed, His Christ (2:1,10). In the first instance, this refers to the horns of a powerful animal that raises its horn in victory and triumph (see Ps. 75). In verse 10, however, there is a pun on "horn." David and other kings were anointed out of a "horn of oil," and Hannah was saying that the king anointed from a horn would also be a mighty animal who exalted his horn in victory over Israel's enemies. Horns were also associated with the altar because ancient altars had projections at each corner called horns. To say that the king's "horn" would be exalted may also carry the connotation that he would be exalted by prayer and worship of Yahweh, just as Hannah had been.[5]

At the heart of Hannah's song is a subversive message about a social revolution (vv. 4–8). Such passages have frequently been spiritualized, so that the upheaval is understood as an overthrow of spiritual forces, wickedness, or immorality. Hannah, however, did not express herself so abstractly. She definitely expected and longed for Israel to be turned upside down. It is a general truth that

[5] This was suggested by James B. Jordan in personal correspondence.

God's faithful people are poor and feeble because elites are hostile to God. In our day, America's political and cultural elites are hostile to Christ and to faithful Christians, and the structures of power encourage wickedness: The more one has to lie and cheat and ruin his family to become a President or U.S. Senator, the less Christians will want to pursue that life. The same dynamics are apparent in the church: The more a preacher has to compromise his message to build a megachurch, the less attractive megachurches will be to serious Christians. Given that the system seems to be set up to encourage compromise and unfaithfulness, we should be joining Hannah in pleading that the Lord would shatter the bows of the mighty and cast down nobles. We should be praying for ecclesiastical (and social) revolution.

In Hannah's time, Israel was being harassed by the Philistines; they were the nobles whom Hannah hoped would soon totter and fall. As noted at the outset of this chapter, moreover, Peninnah's hostility to Hannah represented the hostility of Israel's leaders to the faithful remnant, and Hannah was also celebrating because the Lord was beginning to throw down the "Peninnahs" within Israel. More specifically, Hannah discerned that the birth of her son meant the doom of the priestly house of Eli. When Hannah first sang this song, Eli and his sons were among those who "were full" (see 2:12–17), but soon they would "hire themselves out for bread" (see 2:36). Eli was one of the nobles to be cast down, in favor of a priest who would share the Lord's bread rather than make himself fat with it. Hannah herself had moved from fasting to feasting; she saw that the opposite was going to happen to Eli. Seeing this, she rejoiced.

Of course, none of this social upheaval had even begun to happen yet, but Hannah was confident that it would come. Among the reversals that Hannah celebrated was that the barren would become a mother of seven (she became a mother of six, 2:21), while the fruitful mother would languish. From her experience of barrenness, Hannah knew that the Lord "kills and makes alive." Resurrection hope is also implied in verse 8: Hannah expected the Lord to raise up new life from the dust and the needy from the ashes. Indeed, the whole reversal would be a kind of resurrection, as God brought new life from the barren land and people of Israel. So far, all that had happened was the miraculous birth of Samuel from Hannah's barren womb. All that had happened was life from the dead. But Hannah knew that this resurrection was a pledge of more of the same.

The other source of her confidence was her confidence in God as Creator (v. 8). She sang that "the pillars of the earth are Yahweh's, and He set the world on them," which pictures Yahweh's work in creation as a construction project (Job 38:1-7).[6] In context, the "pillars" are the nobles themselves, the powerful and strong leaders who serve to support the social house (see Ps. 144:12; Is. 19:10; Rev. 3:12). Just as God created the universe at the beginning, so He can create a new "social universe" in Israel. He can break the pillars of Philistia and replace them with the faithful poor.

Hannah's song was a Magnificat, very similar to the song of Mary (Lk. 1:46–55). Both the barren woman and the virgin rejoiced that the Lord was throwing down the high and lifting up the low. Both women celebrated the rebirth of God's people that would take place when arrogant priests and scribes were thrown down, and the house of Israel was set on new pillars.

THE PILLARS OF ISRAEL, 1 SAMUEL 2:11B-3:21

Hannah was the focus of attention in the first section of the book, and Samuel becomes the focus of attention in the following chapters. This passage is held together by repeated notices about Samuel (2:11b, 18, 21, 26; 3:1, 19), which function like a recurring musical theme that makes this passage a unified composition. The surrounding narrative records the "custom of the priests" at Shiloh and the prophetic judgment announced against them. In this context, Samuel, clothed in the linen ephod (2:18), is presented as the alternative to Hophni and Phinehas, and Samuel, the "servant of

[6] See also my book, *A House for My Name*, 47.

Yahweh," is presented as the prophetic alternative to the nearly blind Eli.[7] The first section of this passage (2:11–26) contrasts Samuel and Eli's sons.[8] Samuel was "adopted" into the house of Eli (see 3:6, 16) and served at the house of his heavenly Father. Samuel "became great," while the only "great" thing about the sons of Eli was their sin (2:17). Eli's sons are introduced as "sons of Belial."[9] Translated woodenly, the Hebrew says, "Now the sons of Eli, the sons of Belial, they did not know the Lord," which shockingly draws out a parallel between Eli and Belial.[10] Finally, Samuel "ministered" to

[7] See the outline to this section in ibid., 128, fn. 12. Alternatively, this section can be seen as a double chiasm, the first of which focuses on the priestly aspects of Samuel's ministry, the second highlighting Samuel the prophet. 2:11–26 may be outlined as follows:

A		Samuel ministers to the Lord, 2:11
B		Sins of Eli's sons (sacrifices), 2:12–17
	C	Hannah brings Samuel a robe, 2:18–21
B'		Sins of Eli's sons (women), 2:22–25
A'		Samuel grows, 2:26

Notice that this section centers on the "robe" that Hannah brought Samuel every year, and on the fact that Samuel wore a "linen ephod" (v. 18), both priestly emphases. The following section, 2:27–4:1a, may be outlined in this way:

A		Man of God prophesies against Eli's house, 2:27–36
B		Samuel ministers before the Lord, 3:1
	C	Eli and Samuel, 3:2–9
	D	Yahweh reveals His word to Samuel, 3:10–14
	C'	Eli and Samuel, 3:15–18
B'		Samuel grows, 3:19
A'		Samuel confirmed as prophet, 3:20–4:1a

Not only are there statements about the "word" at the beginning and end of the passage, but Samuel's call to be the "servant" (v. 10) of Yahweh is at the center of the structure. The idea that these chapters focus on Samuel's prophetic and priestly ministries was suggested by John T. Willis, "Cultic elements in the story of Samuel's birth and dedication," *Studia Theologica* 26 (1972), 40–54 and René Péter-Contesse, "La Structure de 1 Samuel 1–3," *The Bible Translator* 27:3 (1976), 313–314.

[8] The following pages overlap with and repeat some material from *A House for My Name*, 123–126.

[9] The etymology and precise meaning of the word *beli'al* is uncertain, but within 1 Samuel there is a connection with Hannah (1:16), where she protested to Eli that she was no "daughter of Belial." This episode throws Eli's lack of discernment into high relief: He had raised "sons of Belial," but he treats a devout woman who is seeking a blessing from the Lord as a daughter of Belial.

[10] The contrast is also reinforced by the use of "lad" (*na'ar*) for Eli's sons and for Samuel, translated "boy" in 2:11 and "young men" in 2:17 (NASB). The word does not necessarily connote "boy" in our sense of preadolescent. After all, the sons of Eli must have

the Lord before Eli (2:11b), while Eli's sons despised the offering of the Lord (2:17). The verb for "minister" is often used to describe the ministry of priests, and in Joel 1:9, 13, the noun form "minister" is synonymous with "priest." Samuel was not a descendant of Aaron, but he was a Levite (1 Chr. 6:22–30). Samuel's "ministry," therefore, was limited to that of a Levite, but the language suggests that his work was at least semi-priestly. He wore a "linen ephod," the garb of priests (see 1 Sam. 22:18). The "ephod" was also associated with oracles in 1–2 Samuel, and Samuel was seer and prophet.[11] The word for the "robe" that Hannah brought to Samuel is used elsewhere to describe the robes of a high priest (Exod. 28:4) and other dignitaries (1 Sam. 15:27). Samuel was the first to wear a robe in 1–2 Samuel, but the robe motif continues throughout the book.

Eli's sons were guilty of two types of sins. First, they committed various sins in connection with the sacrifices. The first offense had to do with the priestly share of the sacrificial meat. The phrase "custom of the priest" (2:13) is from Deuteronomy 18:3, which details the specific portions that the priests received from offerings (cf. Lev. 7:28–34). Eli's sons, however, were not satisfied with the designated portions and instead took whatever they could get, robbing the Israelites in the process (v. 14). The second sin was a direct insult to Yahweh. Instead of waiting for the fat to burn before taking their portions, Hophni and Phinehas seized raw meat from the people. The fat of the animal was the Lord's portion (e.g., Lev. 3:4, 9–10, 14–15, 4:8), called the Lord's "bread" and His "food offering" (Lev. 21:17, 21–22). By seizing meat before the fat was removed,

---

been at least thirty if they were serving as priests, and, given Eli's advanced age (4:15), it is likely that they were probably closer to fifty at the battle of Aphek. Samuel was probably not a "boy" in our sense when he received this revelation. A *na'ar* is often simply an "underling," someone who serves another, regardless of age, and may even connote a religious office of some sort ("deacon"). Ziba was the "boy" of Mephibosheth, though he had fifteen children (2 Sam. 9:9–10), and the "boys" killed by bears in 2 Kings 2:23–25 were most likely functionaries at the idolatrous shrine of Bethel.

[11] Though the ephod used for inquiring of the Lord was not a "linen ephod," the fact that both objects are called "ephods" establishes a conceptual connection between them.

Eli's sons were taking their portion before serving Yahweh His portion, a blatant insult to the Lord and a "very great" sin.

Hophni and Phinehas were also sleeping with the women who served the tabernacle (2:22).[12] In this, we see a contrast between Eli's son Phinehas and his namesake. The earlier Phinehas pierced through a man and woman who were fornicating in the camp (Num. 25:1-9), but at Shiloh an anti-Phinehas fornicated in the tabernacle precincts. This fornication also had symbolic significance. In Leviticus 18, sexual sins are described as an illicit "uncovering nakedness," and the language parallels the language used of approaches to the sanctuary. There is thus a conceptual parallel between the inviolability of the tabernacle and the inviolability of a woman, and the inviolability of the tabernacle is symbolized by the virgin women who served there. Hophni and Phinehas, however, violated these women, a sign that the tabernacle itself was being violated.[13] Uncovering the nakedness of the women was as much as ripping down the curtains of the tabernacle. Instead of guarding the dedicated virgins, the sons of Eli treated them as sacred prostitutes.

One of the key themes of this passage is "hearing."[14] Eli heard reports about his sons (vv. 22-23), but they did not hear his rebuke (v. 25). By contrast, Samuel "heard" the Lord speak, even when Eli did not (3:10), and he "listened" (3:10) when Hophni and Phinehas closed their ears. Eli's sons did not hear because the Lord had determined to eliminate them (2:25). Just as the Lord hardened Pharaoh's heart so that he would not repent, so the Lord was hardening the hearts of the priests in order to destroy them, in preparation for a new "exodus." There might be a connection between the name of Samuel and the Hebrew verb "hear," which is used in the great Israelite "confession of faith," the "Shema" ("Hear, O Israel,"

---

[12] These women are mentioned in Exodus 38:8, and Jephthah's daughter was also dedicated to serve as a perpetual virgin at the tabernacle (Judg. 11:34-40).

[13] The women at the tabernacle are also symbolic of the land. A violated virgin symbolizes a violated land.

[14] I owe this suggestion to Dr. Louis Schuler.

Deut. 6:4–6). "Samuel" might be a play on "God hears," a sign that it was through Samuel that the Lord was raising up a renewed Israel to "hear" the word of the Lord.

Judged by psychological or sociological factors, Shiloh would be the last place we would expect to find a faithful young priest or a prophet-in-training. The fact that Samuel was able to hear the word of Yahweh at Shiloh is further proof that Yahweh Himself was raising up new leadership in Israel. It is also significant that Samuel faithfully served before Eli despite the evils he had to encounter there. Samuel did not become the leader of Israel by seizing power, but by faithfully serving even at an ungodly and doomed sanctuary. In this he foreshadowed David, and also set a pattern for Christians who seek godly leadership. We must always remember that throwing down and setting up pillars is Yahweh's work, not ours.

Eli's sons committed an "abomination of desolation," and in the next section the Lord sent an unnamed "man of God" to announce the sanctuary's destruction. The man of God began with an historical recital of the Lord's favor to Eli. The Lord revealed Himself to the house of Aaron (v. 27) and gave them great privileges: the ministry of incense, the ephod (which refers to consultation with the Lord), and a share of Yahweh's "food offerings." Eli's sons abused these privileges, and the man of God warned that they were about to lose them. Significantly, the indictment was delivered to Eli (v. 29). Though Eli did not abuse the priestly office in the way that his sons did, he sinned by enjoying the fruit of his sons' corruptions. He had become "very heavy" from feasting on sacrificial food. "Heavy," interestingly, is from the same Hebrew word as "glory" or "honor" ("heavy" is *kebed*, and "glory" is *kabod*). Eli is glorifying himself by fattening himself with the Lord's food, instead of glorifying God by offering food to Him.

When the Lord later spoke to Samuel, He said that Eli's great sin was his failure to rebuke his sons (3:13). Eli did rebuke his sons, but did a poor job of it (2:23–25). He heard that his sons were committing fornication, but did not address that point in his rebuke.

Eli's rebuke was too general to cut to the heart. Failure to restrain high-handed sin is judged as high-handed sin, which cannot be atoned by sacrifice or offering (3:14). Fathers' failure to restrain sons will be a persistent theme throughout the books of Samuel. Eli rebuked his sons, but lamely and ineffectually; Saul rebuked both David and Jonathan, but for their righteous works rather than for their wickedness; and David failed to restrain his sons.

The judgment announced by the man of God focused on the "house," a word used eight times in the passage (2:30–36; and note "dwelling" in v. 32). Eli's house would be cut off from the altar so that they would no longer perform altar service or share the sacrifices. Though his house would not be entirely eliminated, none of his descendants would live to an old age. This prophecy was fulfilled progressively during the following century, as the various descendants of Eli were killed (1 Sam. 4:11, 18; 14:3 with 22:9–23) and finally driven from the priesthood by Solomon (1 Kgs. 2:26ff). The punishment fits the crime: Eli's sons had been getting fat from the Lord's bread, and the Lord's judgment was that they would be left begging for bread (cf. 2:5). There is also an interesting foreshadowing of the battle of Aphek: The Lord threatened to "shatter the arms" of Eli's house (2:31), just as He would shatter the arms of Dagon, the Philistine god.

Samuel's ministry as a quasi-priest has been described in chapter 2, and in chapter 3 Samuel was called as a prophet. Samuel was the first named prophet in Israel since Moses, and his call resembled Moses'. The Lord called "Samuel, Samuel," as He called Moses' name twice, and Samuel answered "here I am," which was also Moses' answer (Exod. 3:4). Like Moses, Samuel the prophet was God's instrument to initiate a new era of Israel's history, to speak in faith to form the future.[15] According to 3:1, "the word of the Lord was rare in those days; no vision spread abroad." To be sure, Israel had Scriptures from Moses and Joshua but the Lord was not coming to speak to the people. There was no prophet like

---

[15] For further discussion of the parallels between Moses and Samuel, see *A House for My Name*, 131–132.

Moses, and the priests were not faithful. Therefore, they could not discern the will of God. There was no word or vision, but there was Samuel, wearing an ephod (see Exod. 28:15–30). Samuel was to be the one who delivered the word of the Lord and spread visions abroad. Having heard the word of Yahweh, he would be able to speak it.

Eli's blindness is noted in 3:2, a sign of his lack of spiritual discernment and sound judgment (Ps. 11:4). Eli could not tell the difference between pious Hannah and the real sons of Belial, Hophni and Phinehas, and he could not discern that the Lord was calling Samuel. He was not a "seer," though Samuel would be. Eli was much like Isaac whose blindness was not limited to the pivotal moment when Jacob came to deceive him, but was manifest in years of favorable treatment of his wicked son Esau. Verse 3 mentions that the lamp of God had not gone out. This was the lampstand in the holy place, which was supposed to be lit all the time (Lev. 24:1–4). Verse 3 is phrased to suggest that the lampstand was on the verge of going out. The time was coming when the house would become so desolate that the lamp would go out. But the fact that it was still flickering, however dimly, meant that there was still hope. Because he received the Word that is light, Samuel was himself a flickering wick that kept the knowledge of God alive during a dark period. So long as God was speaking to Samuel, the full darkness of the dark age had not yet arrived.[16]

The text seems to say that Samuel was in the tabernacle when the Lord called him (3:3), and even in the Most Holy Place, and

[16] Further attention to the symbolism of the lampstand enriches this passage. In Exodus 25:31ff, the lampstand is described as a stylized tree. It is a burning bush or tree of gold, and Samuel, like Moses, was called in connection with this "burning bush." Specifically, it had features of an almond tree, and, in this respect, was linked with the priesthood. In Numbers 17, Aaron's rod budded and produced almond blossoms, and in Hebrew, there is a word-play between "watch" and "almond"; the almond tree could be called a watcher tree (see Jer. 1:11–12). Thus, the almond tree, and the lampstand that was almond-like, symbolized the guarding function of the priests. To say that the lamp had not yet gone out (with the implication that it is fading) parallels the statement that Eli's eyes were growing dim. The priest, the guardian who is supposed to judge and discern with his eyes and so be a light to Israel, was not fulfilling that function; he was not a watcher tree, and so the lamp was going out.

some children's books picture Samuel with a sleeping bag on the floor of the tabernacle. This could not be the case. Since Samuel was not a priest, he could not enter the Holy Place, much less the Most Holy Place. Literally, 3:3 must mean that Samuel was sleeping in the tabernacle precincts, not in the tabernacle proper. Yet the hyperbolic phrasing is important. Samuel was a "son" of Eli, but more importantly a son of Yahweh, and so he was pictured as dwelling in his Father's house.

The Lord's word to Samuel was substantially the same as His message through the "man of God," but the repetition provided a testimony of two witnesses against Eli's house. As 2:25 indicates, Hophni and Phinehas had already passed the point of no return. The prophetic word only hardened them further and sealed the doom of Shiloh. The judgment against Shiloh was worse than anything that Israel had experienced since entering the land. As bad as the period of judges has been, this is worse. Shiloh had not been devastated before, the priests had not all died, the lamp had not gone out. Soon, it would be "lights out." The abominations of the sons of Eli were bringing desolation to the house of the Lord and the priesthood.

Samuel's actions in the morning after his prophetic call, however, gave reason for hope. Samuel waited until morning before approaching Eli (v. 15). The announcement of judgment was given at the beginning of a new day because it announced the coming day of the Lord, the day that Hannah hoped for, when the nobles would be cast down and the needy exalted. Samuel also opened the doors of the house of the Lord, a symbolic act with a number of dimensions. Samuel was the replacement for Hophni and Phinehas, who had lain with the women who served at the doorway, and also for Eli, who was introduced into the story standing in the doorway. Neither Eli nor his sons guarded the doorway faithfully, but the fact that Samuel opened the door indicates that he was destined to become the faithful gatekeeper. In addition, the word of the Lord comes from inside the house, since the covenant law was inside the

ark in the Most Holy Place. Samuel heard the word and, opening
the doors, "spread it abroad." Before, "the word of the Lord was
rare in those days; there was no widespread revelation" (3:1), but
now "the word of Samuel came to all Israel" (4:1). Yahweh raised
up Samuel as a faithful priest and faithful prophet. Samuel, whose
birth was prayed for at a doorway, opened the doorway to bring a
new birth for Israel.

THE GLORY DEPARTS, 1 SAMUEL 4:1-7:14[17]

But the transition was not a smooth one. Pillars cannot be cast
down without raising a cloud of dust and creating a pile of rubble.
Before Samuel the son could lead Israel in renewal of the covenant,
the father had to be removed.

And, curiously but importantly, Samuel had no direct part
in the removal. Throughout the first three chapters, the story has
been building up to Samuel's ministry. Samuel has been sharply
contrasted with the priests Hophni and Phinehas—he has received
the prophetic word of the Lord. He has become greater and greater,
in favor with God and man. After 4:1a, however, Samuel drops out
of sight for three chapters. For this reason, some scholars believe
that chapters 4–6 must be from a different source than chapters
1–3, one in which Samuel was not as prominent. But the absence
of Samuel from these chapters is deliberate and makes a theological
and literary point. 1 Samuel 4–6 shows what happened when the
prophet of Israel was not leading the people. At Aphek and after,
Israel got into trouble, but did not "ask" help from the Lord or from

---

[17] This section overlaps with and repeats some material from *A House for My Name*,
129–135. 4:1–7:17 is chiastically arranged:

		Battle of Aphek (Philistine victory), 4:1b–11
A		Battle of Aphek (Philistine victory), 4:1b–11
B		Ark captured and exiled, 4:12–22
C		Ark in Philistia (plagues), 5:1–12
	D	Return of Ark, 6:1–18
C'		Ark in Beth-shemesh (plague), 6:19–21
B'		Ark exiled in Kiriath-jearim, 7:1–2
A'		Battle of Ebenezer (Israelite victory), 7:3–17

the one they should "ask"—the one that Hannah had asked. Only after Eli's house had been removed was Israel ready to ask.

Samuel reappeared in chapter 7, however, and it is important to see the parallel and contrast between the battles of Aphek (chapter 4) and of Ebenezer (chapter 7). Similar words are used to describe the battles: the Israelite shout at Aphek corresponded to the Lord's thunder at Ebenezer (4:5; 7:10), and in both cases the Philistines were filled with fear and panic at the sound (4:7; 7:10). These parallels only serve to heighten the contrast: At Aphek, without Samuel and relying on the corrupt priests, Israel suffered a devastating defeat; led by Samuel at Ebenezer, Yahweh won a great victory.

It is also important to see that Ebenezer came at the end of a sequence of events: Israel was defeated at Aphek, the ark was captured and exiled in Philistia and returned after seven months. These events are crucial for understanding why Israel won the battle of Ebenezer. According to Deuteronomy 28:64ff, the climactic curse of the covenant was the curse of exile. If Israel persisted in idolatry and sin after the Lord brought all the other curses upon her, He would eventually cast her from the land. This was the curse looming in the background in the days of Eli, but this was not what happened. Instead of Israel going into exile, the ark did. Yahweh went into exile, taking on the curse of the covenant for His people, and while in exile He fought for them and defeated the gods of Philistia. Israel suffered humiliating defeat at hands of Philistines, but Yahweh shared in their humiliation, and by taking the most intense weight of that humiliation upon Himself, triumphed over the principalities and powers and rulers of the age.[18]

The exodus from Egypt provides another piece of the theological background to the battle of Aphek. The story line follows the sequence of events in the exodus: The ark of the Lord went into

---

[18] Notice the parallel with the later exile in Babylon. Ezekiel saw the Lord leave His temple and journey east (Ezek. 8–11). Clearly, the Lord's abandonment of His house was a judgment on Israel, but it was also a promise of mercy, because the Lord accompanied His people into exile and even fought for Israel in the days of Daniel.

enemy territory, brought plagues on the enemies of Israel, humbled the gods of the Gentiles, and then returned to the land, full of treasure. The parallels were obvious enough that even the Philistines, who were related to the Egyptians (Gen. 10:13–14; "Mizraim" is the Hebrew name of Egypt), were reminded of Yahweh's treatment of Egypt (4:8; 6:6).[19] As in the exodus from Egypt, Israel moved from oppression and misery to blessedness, from bondage to freedom, from the desert to the garden.

Against this background, we can look at 1 Samuel 4–7 in more detail. "Ebenezer" is mentioned in 4:1, which provides a further link to the battle in chapter 7. Ebenezer is the name Samuel gave to the rock that marked the victory over the Philistines. "Ebenezer" means "Rock of Help," and in 4:1 the name is deeply ironic, for the Israelites got no help from Yahweh at Aphek. Aphek was in the region of Shiloh, and this suggests that the Philistines were heading for the shrine. An attack on Shiloh made military sense for the Philistines. Since the shrine at Shiloh was the center and source

[19] Beyond this similarity in the structure of the story, there are many near-quotations from the Exodus. 1 Samuel 5:6 says that the hand of the Lord was heavy on the Ashdodites and smites them with tumors; similarly, in Exodus 9:3 we read that the hand of the Lord brought severe pestilence on Egypt. When the plagues hit, "the cry of the city went up to heaven," (1 Sam. 5:12); similarly, on the night of Passover, there was a "great cry" throughout the land of Egypt (Exod. 12:30). In 1 Samuel 5:11, the people pleaded with their leaders to get the ark out of Philistia; similarly, in Exodus 10:7, Pharaoh's servants advised Pharaoh to let Israel go before Egypt was completely destroyed. Philistia's priests and diviners advised the rulers how to get the ark out of the land (6:2), just as the Egyptian magicians warned Pharaoh to remove Israel. In 6:6 we learn that the priests and diviners even know part of the Exodus story about Pharaoh hardening his heart, and they warned the Philistines not to do the same. The effect of the whole series of events was that the Philistines come to "know" Yahweh (6:9), and this was also the issue throughout the confrontation between Moses and Pharaoh. There are also many verbal similarities. The word "smite" is used in both Exodus 3:20 and 1 Samuel 5:6, 9; the phrase "strike with plague" occurs in both Exodus 9:14 and 1 Samuel 6:4; and the phrase "destruction of the land" is repeated in Exodus 8:20 and 1 Samuel 6:5. These parallels are drawn from the analysis of Moshe Garsiel, *The First Book of Samuel*, 51–54.

Perhaps we can even speculate that the ark left Philistia about the time of the Passover. The ark was in Philistia seven months, and when the ark got to Beth-shemesh, they were harvesting wheat. The wheat harvest occurred from April to June, depending on altitude. This was in the "valley" (6:13)—the warmer climate would mean an earlier harvest. This wheat harvest could have been as early as April, that is, around the time of Passover. We cannot be sure, but that was fun to think about, wasn't it?

of Israel's national identity, destroying it would demoralize Israel. More theologically, the Philistines no doubt hoped to attack the house of Yahweh to demonstrate the superiority of their gods to the God of Israel, a hope that was dramatically subverted by subsequent events. If, as suggested in the previous chapter, Samson's work provoked this Philistine attack, then the Philistines might be hoping that destroying Shiloh would cut Samson off at the knees. Behind the Philistines' strategic motives, however, was the purpose of Yahweh: He was sending the Philistines to devastate His house, just as He would later send the Babylonians and the Romans for the same purpose.

Israel lost four thousand men in the initial encounter (4:2), a number that symbolizes that the devastation wreaked by the Philistines extended to the "four sides" of the land. Considering their loss, Israel concluded that Yahweh was not among them. There seemed to be an easy solution: Bring the ark of the covenant out to the battlefield; that would guarantee Yahweh's presence. The insistence that this was the "ark of the covenant of Yahweh of hosts" is striking (4:3–5). The text highlights the ark's covenantal significance because Israel hoped that the covenant Lord would defend His covenant people, that Yahweh would deploy His "hosts" against the Philistines.[20] To put it mildly, the plan did not work, and Israel suffered a major defeat.[21] Though the Philistines were frightened by the reminder of the "plagues" (*makkim*) that Yahweh brought to Egypt, they ended up "plaguing" Israel.[22] Yahweh proved Himself the Lord of the covenant and the Lord of hosts; but at Aphek He brought covenant curses on Israel and deployed His (Philistine!) hosts against His rebellious people. Israel's problem, it

---

[20] The word "ark" is used thirty-seven times in 1 Samuel 4:1–7:2, over against a single use in the first three chapters of the book (3:3).

[21] Some commentators suggest that the number "30,000" should be interpreted as "thirty units," and it is possible that a unit did not have a thousand men. But losing thirty units is still a major blow to Israel's military.

[22] The word "plague" in 4:8 is the same word for "slaughter" in verse 6:19.

turned out, was not God's absence. Yahweh was too much among them, but He had bared His arm to become their adversary. The text describes the battle in a way that evokes two earlier battles in Israel's history. At Jericho, the priests carried the ark around the city, and at the end of the week the people shouted to bring the walls of the city down (Josh. 6:1–21). After an initial setback, Aphek began to look like a promising repetition of Jericho: The ark was on the field, carried by priests, and the people were shouting (1 Sam. 4:4–6). Surely Philistine walls would soon crumble. As it turned out, however, the battle of Aphek was more like another battle during the time of Joshua, the battle at Ai. Israel initially lost at Ai because Achan had seized plunder from Jericho; only after removing the "troubler" did Israel conquer that city (Josh. 7:1–26). At Aphek, by contrast, the "Achans," the troublers, were carrying the ark. Engaging the enemy with such men in the midst is not a prescription for victory. A battle that held the promise of Jericho thus ended like Ai.

When Eli heard of the death of his sons and the capture of the ark, he fell from his seat, dethroned (4:18). Hannah knew what she was talking about: Indeed the Lord brings low and raises up; He lifts the needy and makes them sit with nobles in a seat of honor, while toppling the fat from their thrones. It is interesting to note that Eli was sitting at the gate waiting for news of the battle (4:18). According to the custom of ancient cities, judgment was passed at the gate (Ruth 4:1ff.),[23] and here it is passed against the gatekeeper and the "judge" (4:18). Eli was standing in the doorway when Hannah asked for a new birth for Israel, but he died in the gateway before that new birth took effect.

To be sure, Eli had a grandson on the very day of his death, but this birth, unlike Samuel's, was no cause for hope or joy (4:19–22). It simply reinforced the evils that Israel was suffering. Though often

---

[23] In a number of ways, Eli is associated with the Philistines. His question in 4:14, "What does the sound of this tumult mean?" parallels the Philistines' question during the battle (4:6), and his fear and agitation at the news recalls the Philistine reaction to the appearance of the ark.

translated as "the glory has departed," the name "Ichabod" would be better translated as "where is glory?" or "glory has been exiled." Since the Lord was enthroned on the ark, the capture and exile of the ark meant the exile of Yahweh's glory. Further, as noted above, the word for "glory" (*kabod*) and the word that describes Eli's weight (*kebed*) are variants of the same word. The priest should be the glory of Israel, but he had brought shame; his death was mourned as the departure of "glory," but it was, in the final analysis, merely the death of a "gloriously fat" man.

As a result of the battle, Shiloh was devastated by the Philistines (Jer. 7:12, 14; 26:6, 9),[24] and the fall of Shiloh brought an end to an epoch of Israel's history. As James Jordan has emphasized, the Mosaic tabernacle, once destroyed, was never put back together again.[25] During David's reign, the Mosaic tabernacle was set up at Gibeon (1 Chr. 16:37–39), but the ark was never put back inside. As noted above, nothing comparable happened during the period of the judges, and nothing comparable happened again until the Babylonians invaded and destroyed the temple of Solomon. Just as the destruction of the temple of Solomon brought an end to the period of the kingdom and ushered Israel into the "times of the Gentiles," so the destruction of Shiloh marked the end of the Mosaic period and initiated a transition to the period of the kings.

As the story goes on, however, it becomes apparent that, like many of Israel's defeats, Aphek was merely a prelude to victory. Aphek was the site of a defeat in the same way that Golgotha was the place of defeat. At Aphek, God was victorious over the wicked

---

[24] It is interesting that the prophet who announced the division of Israel into Northern and Southern kingdoms was from Shiloh, Ahijah the Shilonite (1 Kgs. 11:29ff; 14:1ff; 15:29). Just as Shiloh was the place where the house of Eli lost its preeminence in the priesthood and had its robe "torn," so a Shilonite announced that the robe of the *kingdom* was going to be torn. Ahijah later announced that the kingdom would be taken from Jeroboam and that the house of Jeroboam would be devastated (1 Kgs. 14:6), which reminds us of the man of God's prophecy against Eli. Ahijah was a good choice to bring this message, for, as a Shilonite, he knew all about the fall of dynastic houses.

[25] James B. Jordan, *Through New Eyes: Developing a Biblical View of the World* (Eugene: Wipf and Stock, 1999), 221–225.

priests Hophni and Phinehas, over Israel's armies, and over Eli himself. He intended to kill Eli's sons, and He accomplished His purpose. The fall of leaders in the church is not always a tragedy; it may well be a sign of God's work to renew His people. The hardening that we see toward the word of God in some mainline churches (e.g., acceptance of sodomy and abortion) may be a cause for rejoicing; God may have closed their ears and hardened them, as a prelude to overthrowing them.

But Eli was not the only one who fell over and broke something in this story. After the Philistines captured the ark, they took it to the house of Dagon, the chief god of the Philistine pantheon. The Philistines considered the ark as a war trophy, and by placing it in the temple of Dagon, they were proclaiming Dagon's victory over Israel (cf. Judg. 16:24). More fundamentally, they were making a theological statement. Dagon, the Philistines believed, was not only superior to Israel, but to Yahweh. The fact that they set the ark "beside" Dagon highlights the intention: Yahweh might prove useful, but henceforth whatever power He possessed would be harnessed to the purposes of Dagon. Like an honored palace servant, Yahweh was allowed to stand "beside" Dagon to serve him.

But Yahweh did not accept this subservient position for long. He humiliated the god of the Philistines, forcing Dagon to bow before His throne (5:3). The priests of Dagon found him fallen before the ark in worship, incapable of getting himself up without help (5:3). Like other idols, Dagon might have had arms and legs, but he could not stand. He had fallen and he could not get up. This discovery occurred "early the next morning," about the time of Israel's morning sacrifice, and Dagon apparently was joining with Israel in prostrating himself before the throne of the God of gods. Early in the morning, the Philistines went to Dagon's temple expecting to find the defeated God, but He was not there. He had risen; Yahweh lives! And the day that the Philistines hoped would be the day of Dagon turned out to be the Day of Yahweh.

The next day, things were even worse. This time, Dagon had fallen over and broken in pieces, with his head and palms cut off. This is the first one of many head wounds in 1–2 Samuel (or the second, if we count Eli). Crushing the head obviously disables the one whose head is crushed, but it also relates to the crushing of the serpent's head in Genesis 3:15. The breaking of the hands was also significant, since hands represent power. While the strong hand of the Lord was against the Philistines (5:7, 9, 11), Dagon's hands were made impotent. Removing hands and head was a ritual execution, a ritual dismemberment, the first of several in the books of Samuel.[26]

The Philistines should have known better. At the battle of Aphek, they realized that the ark was the throne of the God who had devastated Egypt. Soon, they had forgotten, even though they were themselves living through another exodus. In Exodus 12:12, the struggle in Egypt is described as Yahweh's war against the gods of Egypt, and after Aphek Yahweh again humbled the chief god of His enemies. As at the Passover, He carried out His victory at night, so that the morning brought a new day. But the Philistines did not learn the lesson of the exodus and were even less receptive to the lesson of the ark. Some twenty years later, they brought another trophy of Israelite war into the temple of Dagon—Samson—and in that case not only the image of Dagon but the whole temple was destroyed, along with the lords of the Philistines (Judg. 16:18–31). Psalm 78 describes the exile of the ark by bringing out its parallels with the story of Samson. When the Lord left Shiloh, the glory was given into the hands of the adversary; Yahweh delivered Israel to the sword, so that priests fell and the widows mourned (vv. 60–64). Then the Lord awoke as if from sleep, like a warrior overcome with wine (vv. 65–66). Yahweh fought in the house of Dagon—not just a greater Samson but a drunken Samson!

---

[26] When David defeated Goliath, he cut off his head. Goliath was a worshiper of Dagon, and all who worship idols will be like them. When Saul was defeated, intriguingly, his head was also cut off (31:9). In 2 Samuel 4:12, David removed the hands and feet of the men who killed and beheaded Ish-bosheth and hung them up in Hebron.

The Lord was not content to crush and dismember Dagon. He carried His victory throughout the land of Philistia, and His exile turned into a victory procession through enemy territory. Finally, the Egyptian plagues became too much to bear, and the Philistines demanded that the ark be returned. Recalling the exodus (again!), the priests and diviners warned that the ark should be sent away with treasure, like the Israelites as they came from Egypt (6:2–9). So the Philistines filled a box with golden mice and tumors as a "guilt offering" or "trespass offering" (Heb. *'asham*). According to Leviticus 5:1–6:7, the guilt offering was the proper offering for sacrilege, that is, for trespassing on holy things or holy space. Along with an offering, an *'asham* involved restitution for the trespass. The fact that the Philistines sent a "trespass offering" thus indicates that they recognized they had committed sacrilege, misusing Yahweh's consecrated throne. We get a hint of the kind of restitution they offered from the fact that the word for "tumors" also means "fortified city." Apparently, they were offering the cities of Philistia to Yahweh, so that the five tumors represented the five cities (6:17) and the mice represented the villages (6:17–18). This was their way of "giving glory to the God of Israel" rather than "glorifying their hearts" as Pharaoh had (6:5–6; the verb is *kabad*). At Aphek, the Philistines remembered the exodus and fought against Israel more courageously. After being humbled by Yahweh, they remembered the exodus and gave glory to God.

It was just possible, the Philistines believed, that it was all an unfortunate coincidence. Perhaps the ark had nothing to do with the plagues; perhaps the two things just happened to occur simultaneously. Perhaps. To determine whether or not the Yahweh was responsible for the plagues, they set up a test (6:7–9). Two milch cows were chosen, and the ark was placed on a cart behind them. The cows' instinct would be to return to their home to their calves, and if, in spite of this, they turned toward Israel, the Philistines would know that the Lord's hand had been upon them. As it turned out, the cows pulled the cart right back to Beth-shemesh, near

Israel's border with Philistia. Yah returned driving the cart like a hero returning from war.

With the return of the ark the "glory" had returned, but the Israelites who received the ark were no better than Philistines. If the Lord's exile in Philistia was like an exodus-and-return, His reentry into the land was like a new conquest. There is even a reference to a "Joshua" (6:14). Instead of making war against Canaanites, however, Yahweh made war against Israelites who acted like Canaanites. Beth-shemesh was a Levitical city (Josh. 21:13–16), which explains the sudden reference to Levites (6:15). Since there were Levites about, Beth-shemesh was a promising place to receive the ark at its return. Unfortunately, nearly every time Levites appeared in Judges or Samuel, they were wicked men, or at least incompetent. The Levites of Beth-shemesh did not break this mold.

They committed several crucial sins in relation to the ark. First, while offering a burnt offering as thanks for the return of the ark was appropriate, Leviticus 1:3 requires that all burnt offerings be male. These Levites offered the cows (1 Sam. 6:14). But the more important mistakes had to do with the treatment of the ark. The Levites of Beth-shemesh "took down the ark," (v. 15), set it on a large stone (v. 18), and then looked into it (v. 19).[27] Everything they did was wrong. According to Numbers 4:5, the ark should have been covered, and the same chapters tell us that even the Kohathites who carried the ark were never to touch nor even see it (vv. 19–20).

Act like a Philistine and you can expect to be punished like a Philistine. The punishment of the Beth-shemesh—the striking of 50,070—was fitting (6:19), and the parallel with the judgment on Philistia is brought out by the fact that the word "stroke" (*makkah*) is the same as the word for "plague" in 5:6. After committing sacrilege, the people of Beth-shemesh acted like Philistines again by trying to get rid of the ark. Instead of repenting of their sins, they sent the ark out of their country, like the men who urged Jesus

---

[27] The Hebrew might mean that they "looked at it," but this would still be a violation of the law.

to leave them after He killed their swine. "Who is able to stand before Yahweh, this holy God?" they asked (6:20). Certainly not Dagon, certainly not Philistines, and certainly not Israelites who act no better than worshipers of Dagon. The Lord fights Philistines wherever they are; whether they are in Ashdod or Gath, Ekron or Beth-shemesh; whether they are in Beijing or Baghdad, Washington, D.C., or Wheaton.

The ark was sent from Beth-shemesh to Kiriath-jearim to the house of Abinadab, which was on the "high place" (Heb. *gibe'ah*, 7:1), where Abinadab's son Eleazar was consecrated to care for it. Commentators point out that Eleazar was a common priestly name, and perhaps this Eleazar was a priest or Levite. Yet, Kiriath-jearim was one of the cities of the Gibeonites, the people who tricked Joshua into making a covenant with them (Josh. 9:17). When Joshua discovered who they were, they were made servants at the tabernacle, carrying water and hewing wood (Josh. 9:27). Though a city within Israel, Kiriath-jearim was a predominantly Gentile city. Later in 2 Samuel, when the ark was brought to Jerusalem, there was another sojourn in the house of a Gentile, Obed-edom, a Gittite from the Philistine town of Gath (Goliath's home town!). In both of these incidents, the Lord used Gentiles to "provoke Israel to jealousy." Levites mistreated and then rejected the Lord's throne, and so the Lord left Beth-shemesh to dwell in a city of Gentile God-fearers until Israel turned to seek her Lord.

Yahweh's victory over Dagon was the crucial victory over the Philistines, and the victory at the battle of Ebenezer was just the aftermath. By the time Samuel gathered the people at Mizpah to renew the covenant, it had been twenty years since "D-day."[28] As

---

[28] The twenty years which is referred to in chapter 7:2 is the period between the return of the ark and the battle of Ebenezer. After that, Saul reigned for forty years, followed by another seven years or so of the reign of David before the ark was brought into Jerusalem (2 Sam. 6). In addition, there is a period of time briefly summarized at the beginning of chapter 8, the time between the battle of Ebenezer and the request for a king, a period of some thirty years or so. Thus, the ark was at the house of Abinadab for the better part of a century (20 + 30? + 40 + 7 = 97). The notion that the Lord's triumph over Dagon was comparable to "D-Day" is borrowed from Walter Brueggemann, *First and Second Samuel*, Interpretation (Louisville: John Knox, 1990), 39. Brueggemann also points to the analogies between the resurrection and the triumph of the ark, which I have alluded to in the text.

noted in chapter 1, the battle of Aphek bisects the period of the Philistine oppression.[29] Shortly before the battle of Ebenezer, Samson killed the nobles of Philistia who had gathered in the temple of Dagon to mock him, and this incident in all likelihood indicated to Samuel that the moment was right for a covenant-renewal at Mizpah. Thus, after the battle of Ebenezer, there was a complete reversal of the situation at Aphek, when *Israel's* leadership was killed, the sanctuary devastated, and Israel defeated in battle. There had been a resurrection because of the Lord's work in Philistia and the repentance of Israel that followed. Truly, Yahweh was raising the poor from the dust, setting them in the honored seat of the nobles.

The parallels between the battles of Aphek and Ebenezer highlight a number of features of the latter battle. At Aphek, the Philistines heard the shout of Israel and feared the "gods" who brought plagues to Egypt (4:7), while at Ebenezer, Israel was the army to "hear and fear" (7:7). In both battles, the army that was afraid won. By the battle of Ebenezer, Israel had begun to fear her own Lord and won a victory in that fear. In another reversal at Aphek, the cities that had been taken by the Philistines were recovered after the battle of Ebenezer (7:14). The hand of the Lord had been against the Philistines throughout the ark's sojourn in Philistia (5:6, 9, 11), but the effect of Ebenezer was more lasting: "the hand of Yahweh was against the Philistines all the days of Samuel" (7:13).[30]

The outcome at Ebenezer was different because the preparation and leadership were different. Leading up to the battle of Aphek, we had been reading about the wickedness of the sons of Eli, whom the Lord was determined to remove from the priesthood. During the battle, Israel relied on the presence of the ark, which was carried by the very same sons of Eli. Clearly, the root problem had not been solved. Leading up to the battle of Ebenezer,

---

[29] See the chronological information in chapter 1.

[30] It is true that the Philistines made gains again before Samuel died, but apparently this period was not included in the "days of Samuel." Though Samuel was still alive, Saul had taken over leadership of the nation.

Samuel had been the leader of Israel for some twenty years. After twenty years of Samuel's faithful leadership (which corresponded to Samson's more colorful ministry), twenty years of the word of the Lord spreading to Israel, and twenty years of prophetic ministry, Israel knew where to turn for deliverance. Instead of bringing the ark to the field, Israel "asked" for Samuel's help and prayers. Samuel took the place of the ark. Just as the ark contained the tablets of the law, so Samuel delivered the word of Yahweh. As the ark moved from place to place, so Samuel moved around the countryside judging Israel. And just as the ark was a mediator of God's presence to Israel, so Samuel was. With Samuel among them, the people were victorious.[31]

Like Moses, Samuel led Israel to victory by crying out to the Lord in prayer (7:10–11; see Exod. 17:8–16). At the battle of Ebenezer, in fact, there was little military engagement at all. Samuel cried out to the Lord and offered a burnt offering of a suckling (see Lev. 22:27).[32] While Samuel was engaged in worship and covenant renewal, Yahweh thundered against the Philistines and threw them into a panic. Like so much of 1 Samuel 1–7, this was already foreshadowed in the song of Hannah: The Lord thundered against His enemies and the voice/word of the Lord was victorious (2:10).

Things were looking up for Israel. All Israel was asking for the one whom Hannah had asked for. Before long, however, Israel was asking for someone else to lead them.

---

[31] Pouring out water is an unusual rite (v. 6), not found in the law at all. Here, it is connected with fasting and confession of sin. Perhaps it conveys the idea of "pouring out" one's soul in repentance and mourning before the Lord (see 1 Sam. 1:15). Perhaps it is also a picture of Israel receiving the Spirit, a symbol of Israel's prayer that the Spirit would be poured out like water upon the barren ground and that the Spirit would "clothe" them as He clothed the judges for battle.

[32] Samuel here offers a burnt offering. Is this legitimate? It seems that Samuel would not be allowed to do this. First, no burnt offering is supposed to be offered outside the sanctuary precincts, and, second, in order to offer a burnt offering, you needed a priest to sprinkle the blood and put the flesh on the altar. This is not a violation of the law, however. Since Shiloh had been destroyed, and the ark had not been placed back in the tabernacle, the land was not at rest, and the requirements of Deuteronomy 12 concerning the centralization of sacrifice were not operative.

CHAPTER**THREE**
1 SAMUEL 8–15

A KING LIKE THE KINGS OF THE NATIONS

Yahweh made the barren woman from the hill country fruitful, and what fruit! Hannah's son, the miraculous seed springing from dead ground, became the leading figure in Israel for several decades and led Israel from demoralization and defeat to renewed covenant and victory. Under his leadership, Israel turned to the Lord in repentance and successfully resisted the Philistine menace. Though he had been raised in the house of Eli, Samuel proved himself more a son of his heavenly Father. It would be hard to imagine a leader less like Eli than Samuel.

Yet, as the next section of 1 Samuel opens, we read that Samuel was in the same position as his priestly mentor. Whereas Eli's sons abused faithful worshipers and despised the sacrifices of Yahweh, Samuel's sons "turned aside after dishonest gain and took bribes and perverted justice" (8:3). Though Scripture never explicitly blames Samuel for the conduct of his sons, the text makes an implicit comparison with Eli; as with Eli, Samuel must find an adopted son to replace his fallen sons.

That "adopted" son was Saul, who plays a prominent role in the remainder of 1 Samuel. Saul's story was one of "rise and fall," a fact indicated by the organization of chapters 8–15. This section of Samuel is divided into two large passages: 8:1–12:25 and 13:1–15:35.[1] The first section is organized in a roughly concentric pattern:

A	Israel requests a king; Samuel's speech, 8:1–22
B	Saul is privately anointed king, 9:1–10:16
C	Saul publicly acknowledged as king, 10:17–27 (sons of Belial)
D	Saul defeats Nahash, 11:1–11
C'	Saul refuses to take vengeance, 11:12–13 (sons of Belial)
B'	Israel gathered to Gilgal to renew the kingdom, 11:14–15
A'	Samuel's farewell speech, 12:1–25

[1] Chapters 8–15, like chapters 1–7, are framed by references to "Ramah" (8:4; 15:34–35).

Central to the whole section is Saul's battle with the Ammonites. Samuel claimed that the attack of Nahash was one of the reasons the elders of Israel asked for a king (12:12), and by his victory,
Saul proved capable of fulfilling Israel's hopes in a king. He fought in
the power of the Spirit (11:6) and was implicitly compared to Gideon
and other faithful judges.[2] Elsewhere in these chapters, Saul's upright character was evident. He was humble and not ambitious for
the kingship (9:20–21) and meek before opposition (11:12–13), like
Moses, the meekest man on the face of the earth (Num. 12:3).

On the other hand, this positive portrayal of Saul's reign is
surrounded by speeches by Samuel that have a different tone. When
the elders asked for a king, Samuel warned about the "custom" that
the king would follow (8:11–18), and in his "farewell speech" Samuel warned that the king would be swept away if the people turned
from the Lord. These speeches strike an ominous note, pointing
ahead to the fall of Saul and the future activity of the kings of
Israel. Though the king started well, these speeches leave us uneasy
about his future. These hints of a catastrophic future are confirmed
in chapters 13–15, which record two battles of Saul, the first at
Michmash against the Philistines (13–14) and the second a prosecution of "holy war" against the Amalekites (15). Saul won both
battles, yet when the dust had settled he had lost the kingdom.[3]

---

[2] See the discussion in the introduction.

[3] These chapters may be outlined in several different ways. First, there is a kind of
conceptual chiasm:

    A   Rejection, 13:1–15a
      B   Victory at Michmash, 13:15b–14:52
      B' Victory over Amalekites, 15:1–9
    A'   Rejection, 15:10–35

One of the striking aspects of this outline is the fact that Saul was rejected from
being king before ever joining battle with the Philistines. Alternatively, a more textually
grounded chiasm may be offered:

    A   Saul moves against the Philistines, 13:1–7
      B   Saul's sin and confrontation by Samuel, 13:8–15a
        C   Victory at Michmash, 13:15b–14:46
          D Saul's kingdom and household established, 14:47–52
        C'   Victory over Amalekites, 15:1–9
      B'   Saul's sin and confrontation by Samuel, 15:10–31
    A'   Samuel hews Agag before the Lord, 15:32–33

This outline strikingly places the notice about the establishment of Saul's kingdom
at the center of the passage.

ASKING FOR A KING, 1 SAMUEL 8–12[4]

An unspecified period of time passed between the battle of Ebenezer and Israel's request for a king. Samuel was an adult at the battle of Ebenezer, leading the people to victory, but by the time the elders came to him at Ramah, he had full-grown sons and had become "old" (8:1–2). This suggests a passage of some thirty years, yet the writer of 1 Samuel has ignored this time period and has placed chapter 8 right after chapter 7.

Several reasons for this are apparent. First, the sequence of chapters 7–8 sets off the irony of the request that the elders made. They wanted a king to "fight our battles" (v. 19), but if the battle of Ebenezer taught them anything, it taught them that they already had a King to fight their battles. Second, the literary context also emphasizes the contrast of Samuel and his sons. In 7:15–17, Samuel's circuit court is described, and his administration of justice, as the people later acknowledged, was above reproach (12:1–5). Samuel's sons also became judges, but they took bribes and bent justice, in direct violation of the Torah (Deut. 16:18–19).[5] Samuel was responsible for putting his sons in office (8:1), and the Torah explicitly says those appointed to office must reject bribery. When Moses set up judges and elders in Israel, he selected men who were free from love of money. Thus Samuel must bear some responsibility for the situation. He is often compared to Moses in the early chapters of 1 Samuel, but he failed to imitate Moses' care in selecting rulers and successors.[6] The text issues a sharp warning to Christian leaders: Even leaders who are not Elis, but are as faithful as Samuel, may see their work undone by dishonest "sons."

The wickedness of Samuel's sons provided a pretext for Israel to request a king. Samuel immediately saw the request as "evil" (8:6). The Bible does not condemn monarchy per se, and Yahweh

---

[4] This section expands on my discussion in *A House for My Name*, 133–135.

[5] "Turn aside after" and "pervert" in verse 3 are two forms of the same verb. Samuel's sons "twist" justice because they are "bent" on gain.

[6] Bethel, Gilgal, Mizpah, and Ramah—the stops on Samuel's circuit—were in a central band across the middle of the country, but his sons were in Beersheba, in the extreme south. Perhaps Samuel sent them there to minimize the damage they would do.

had planned for Israel to have a king from the time of the patriarchs and Moses (Gen. 49:8–12; Deut. 17:14–20). What then was
wrong with Israel's request? As the context makes clear, the people
were rejecting Yahweh as King by asking for a human king (1 Sam.
8:7). Further, the people also rejected Samuel; he had been judging
them, but they wanted a king to "judge" them (8:8). They were
"asking for" a king (8:10), but Samuel was the one who had been
"asked for" and received.

Perhaps most crucially, they asked for a king "like the kings
of the nations." In this sense, Israel's request for a king was another
example of the unfaithfulness that had been evident throughout
the period of the judges (8:8). Ever since they entered the land,
Israel had rejected Yahweh in favor of Baal and Ashtaroth, and the
desire for a king was just another idolatrous obsession. And the
Lord threatened to respond as He had during the period of the
judges: When Israel went after other gods, Yahweh sent a nation to
oppress them until they came to their senses and repented. When
they sought to imitate the nations by requesting a king, the Lord
warned that the king would oppress them as the Gentile kings
had. Instead of delivering them from their enemies, the king would
become an enemy.

In rejecting the Lord in favor of the idolatry of political prestige and power, Israel was also renouncing its covenant status. From
the beginning of Israel's existence as a nation, her calling was to
be distinct from the nations, with their national life organized by
the covenant at Sinai. When the elders of Israel said they wanted
to be like the nations, they were saying that they were tired of being Israel. Thus, the final result of this request would be that Israel,
instead of "serving Yahweh" (see 7:4), would become slaves to the
king (8:17). In a reversal of the Sinai covenant, Israel was heading
back to Egypt to be ruled by a king with chariots and horses. As
the people had wanted to return to Egypt in the wilderness days of
Moses, so again in Samuel's time they wanted to return to "Egypt"
instead of accepting Samuel. Israel said, as it would say many centuries later, "We have no king but Caesar."

As the Lord directed, Samuel gave the people a detailed warning about what they could expect from their king, informing them about the "custom" of the king. The word translated as "custom" or "procedure" normally means "judgment" (Heb. *mishpat*) and is related to the word for Samuel "judge" (*shophet*) and the judging activity of his sons (*shaphat*).[7] The elders wanted to replace Samuel's sons, and therefore asked for a king to "judge us" (v. 5), but the king would oppress in far worse ways than Samuel's sons ever did. *Mishpat* also played an important rhetorical role in Samuel's speech. Initially, the word would lead the elders to expect that Samuel was going to discuss how the kingdom would be set up, the "customary law" of the kingdom. As the speech progressed, it became clear that the "custom" of the king would be a lot like the "justice" of Samuel's sons. Through the course of the speech, the meaning of the word shifts from "legal custom" to "customary behavior" to "customary misbehavior." By the time Samuel was finished, the elders should have realized that Samuel was not talking so much about the "judgments" that the king would pronounce as the judgment that the king would *be*. In Samuel's telling, the king would become an instrument of divine judgment on Israel for rejecting the Lord.

Specifically, the king's justice would be like the justice of Samuel's sons in that both were intent on "taking." Samuel's sons "took bribes" (v. 3), and Samuel's account of the king emphasized that he would "take" (vv. 11, 13, 14, 15, 16, 17).[8] The king would take all Israel's fruit: the fruit of their bodies, the fruit of their fields, and the fruit of their vineyards (see Deut. 28:1–6). Samuel emphasized that the king would build up military power, taking the best young men of Israel for chariots and cavalry. In addition, the king would take artisans from their peaceful pursuits and put them to

---

[7] Interestingly, this is the same word used to describe the customary way that Hophni and Phinehas treated worshipers at Shiloh; the sons of Eli did not know the *mishpat* of the priests with the people (2:13). This verbal echo draws out a parallel between the abuses of the priests and those of the future king.

[8] More than one Hebrew word is employed here, but they have similar meanings.

work turning plowshares into swords (v. 12). As he continued taking food, animals, young men and young ladies, his court would become larger and more luxurious, and therefore he would need an even larger supply of food, animals, young men, and women.[9] Lastly, the king would take a tithe. Israel rejected the Lord, who demanded a tithe as her tribute to Him; but rejecting the king did not save Israel from having to pay a tithe.[10]

In spite of this, the Lord allowed the project to go forward. Instead of standing with the old traditional order, Yahweh allowed Israel to move ahead toward monarchy. Though it was a sinful request, it accorded with His plan to set up a new thing in Israel. However sinful the reasons for the destruction of the old world, the Lord intended to move *ahead*, not back. However severe the birth pangs, Yahweh would ensure that barren Israel gave birth.

THE ANNOUNCED ONE, 1 SAMUEL 9:1–10:16[11]

Saul is presented from several different perspectives at the beginning of his story. On the one hand, there are parallels with Samuel. From the beginning of the book, the writer has been punning on the name "Samuel," and that pun came up again when the people

---

[9] James B. Jordan suggested in personal correspondence that, in the light of the association of baking and sexual predation in the Amnon-Tamar affair (2 Sam. 13), Samuel's reference to "bakers" might be an indication that the king would collect a harem to "bake" for him.

[10] As Saul's reign progresses, we see him acting more and more like a Gentile king. One hint of this is in 1 Samuel 22:6–7 where Saul asked the Benjamites whether they could expect a king from Judah to favor them, and the implied question is whether David would "favor you as I have favored you" (v. 6). The setting is in Gibeah, on the "high place," the "Ramah" in Hebrew, and thus connects to Samuel's speech in 1 Samuel 8, which was delivered at "Ramah."

[11] That this is one connected story is evident from the *inclusio* on "donkeys" in 9:1–5 and 10:15–16, as well as by a contrast of Saul's departure from home and his return. Within this *inclusio*, the passage is organized chiastically:

    A   Saul searches for his father's donkeys, 9:1–4
      B   Saul visits the seer, 9:5–14
        C   Samuel announces Saul's future, 9:15–21
          D Feast, 9:22–24
        C'   Samuel anoints Saul, 9:25–10:1
      B'   Saul among the prophets, 10:2–13
    A'   Saul returns to Gibeah, 10:14–16

"asked" for a king and got a king whose name means "asked." Other similarities between the two are also evident. Eli had two defiantly sinful sons, Hophni and Phinehas, but the Lord raised up Samuel as Eli's "adopted" son. The problem of Eli and sons was repeated with Samuel and his sons, and just as Samuel was a replacement for Hophni and Phinehas, so Saul replaced Joel and Abijah. As we shall see below, Samuel anointed Saul as his successor and son. This father-son relationship modulates into a prophet-king relationship: Like later kings of Israel, Saul was supposed to look to the prophet as a son to his father; kings were to listen to the voice of Father Yahweh by heeding the guidance of the father-prophet. Saul, as noted in the introduction, was also like the judges, and as we move forward, we will see that Saul foreshadowed his successor, David.

Saul was from the tribe of Benjamin (v. 1), hardly a commendation in the later period of the judges. Judges 19–21 tells the story of an outrage committed in Gibeah, a Benjamite city, which led to civil war when the Benjamites refused to punish the perpetrators. The result was disastrous for Benjamin, which lost all but six hundred men.[12] Saul was from Gibeah, the very town where this occurred (1 Sam. 10:26), but his father, Kish, was a "mighty man" or a "man of wealth." Despite being in Benjamin, Kish apparently had been able to prosper in a desolate tribe.

Though Saul's origins in Gibeah of Benjamin might suggest a villainous character, other parts of the introductory description leave a more positive impression. Saul was a "choice and handsome man" (9:2), and physical perfection can symbolize the admirable character of the person (e.g., Joseph in Gen. 39:6).[13] Saul was also

---

[12] This occurred early in the period of judges, though it is the last story in the book. Judges 20:28 says that Phinehas, the grandson of Aaron, was priest at the time, and he was already a priest in the wilderness (Num. 25). The period of the judges lasted a couple of centuries, and by Saul's day, Benjamin had had some chance to rebuild.

[13] Associating good looks and good character is not invariable. Absalom was more handsome than any Israelite. By the time the story goes to that point, however, Saul had fallen from his position and that incident had become part of the background. Absalom was a new Saul. See the discussion of the chiastic outline of 1–2 Samuel in chapter 1.

head and shoulders taller than other Israelites (9:2), surely a man who could fight Israel's battles. More than that, the fact that Saul's head rose above the crowd reinforced the parallel between Saul and Samuel, the Nazirite with the dedicated "head." The Benjamite genealogy, therefore, is not an insult to Saul. Rather, as He often does, the Lord chose one of the despised things of the world to confound the wise. Can anything good come out of Gibeah? One might as well ask, Can anything good come out of Galilee?

Besides, the tribe of Benjamin did not begin with this sullied reputation. In Genesis 35:11, the Lord promised Jacob that "kings shall come from you," and shortly after Benjamin was born (35:16–21). In the immediate context, Benjamin was the promised king, and when Benjamin later went to Egypt, Joseph treated him as the superior of his brothers (Gen. 43:34). Yet, Jacob predicted that the scepter would remain with Judah, not Benjamin (Gen. 49:8–12). Genesis, in short, foreshadowed a sequence from a Benjamite to a Judahite king, and this type is fulfilled in the transition from Saul to David (and later, from Israel to Jesus). The distinction between a king from Benjamin and one from Judah is deeper than mere tribal associations; Benjamin was identified as a future king in Genesis 35 without any preparation or training, while Judah was proclaimed the royal tribe only after he had offered himself as a substitute for Benjamin (Gen. 44:18–34). Similarly, Saul became king without ever accepting the cross, while David, the king from Judah, rose to the throne only after a death and resurrection. Despite the limitations of Benjamite royalty, against the background of Genesis 35, Saul's Benjamite genealogy is a royal genealogy.

Saul is introduced into the story while searching for his father's lost donkeys (v. 3). Since "shepherd" was a common metaphorical description of a king in the ancient world, the fact that Saul could not keep track of a collection of large animals foreshadows, in the view of some commentators, his future failure as king. There may be a connection between this search and Saul's later, also unsuccessful, pursuit of David, but the story should be taken in a more

positive way. Saul was a grown man when this event occurred. Early
in his reign, his son Jonathan was already fighting in the army
(13:2), and thus must have been twenty. Saul thus must have
been in his forties. Yet, when his father asked him to go search
for the donkeys, he did so, continuing his search through several
days (v. 20). Against the background of Hophni and Phinehas and
of the sons of Samuel, a man who listens to the voice of his father
marks a welcome and promising change of direction. The donkeys
may also be playing a symbolic role, since donkeys were the beasts
of kings (1 Kgs. 1:33–44; Zech. 9:9). In searching for royal beasts,
Saul was providentially led to Samuel, who anointed him to be one
who rode donkeys. This is not a story about a man who loses something valuable and is unable to find it. This is a story about a man
who uncovers buried treasure while searching for a penny.

Saul's servant suggested that they go to Samuel, who might
be able to "tell" them what had happened to the donkeys (v. 6).
The Hebrew verb for "tell" is a form of *nagad*, and it is used several
times in the rest of the chapter (vv. 8, 18, 19). When he went to
meet Samuel, Saul was anointed as *nagid* (v. 16), a noun related to
the verb "tell" that means "king-designate" rather than king per se.
Saul and his servant hoped that Samuel would tell (*nagad*) them
where the donkeys were; instead, he told (*nagad*) them that Saul
had been designated as king-designate (*nagid*). They were searching for one kind of announcement, but received a much better
announcement. Significantly, these terms are used elsewhere in the
Old Testament to describe a king's designation of a successor. To
nagad a *nagid* is to designate a crown prince, something usually
done by the father whom the crown prince is replacing (1 Kgs.
1:20, 35). Though Samuel was not a king, by anointing Saul he was
"designating" his successor and heir. Saul's progress throughout the
chapter underlines his growing status: He continually went up, being raised up in the sight of Israel. He went "up" to the city (v. 11),
"up" to the high place at the center of the city (v. 14), up to the
"head" of the table (v. 22), up to the roof of a house to spend the

night (v. 25). He ascended to be anointed as a "high one, a great one."

Saul's meeting with the young women at the well was also significant. Well scenes frequently end with a wedding in Scripture, but this one did not, and some commentators have suggested that this throws a shadow on Saul's character. Saul approached the "bride," but the scene was "aborted" before it was consummated.[14] Again a more positive reading is preferable. Samuel already knew that the "prince" (Heb. *nagid*) was coming (v. 16) and had invited thirty men to share a meal, at which Saul was guest of honor and given the favored portion (vv. 22–23). This "feast of the kingdom" celebrated the revelation of Israel's leader, and the brief meeting with the women gives a certain coloring to the feast. The relationship between the king and Israel, we discover in other portions of Scripture, is a covenantal one (e.g., 2 Kgs. 11:17), and marriage is a suitable symbol of this. The man searching for donkeys found a kingdom; the young man at the well married Israel; the feast is a wedding feast between Saul and Israel.

At the feast, Saul was given the leg (v. 24), not merely a large portion but a priestly portion. Samuel was offering a peace offering, which included a meal (v. 13), and according to Leviticus 7:33–34, the leg of a peace offering belonged to the priest who assisted in the sacrifice. Giving Saul the thigh thus announced that the king-designate was receiving an office analogous to the priest's. A priest was essentially a household servant of the Lord, a caretaker of God's house, and the king served in a similar way in the national house, the people-house. Anointing with oil also highlighted the priestly aspects of Saul's position. We associate anointing with kings, but oil was first applied to priests in Israel. The priest was the first "anointed one" or "Christ," and Saul became the first king who was also a "Christ."

---

[14] I first encountered this interpretation in Robert Alter, *The Art of Biblical Narrative* (New York: Basic Books, 1981), 60–61.

A priest would take the leg of a peace offering home to share with his family (Lev. 22:10–16), and by giving Saul this portion Samuel was honoring him as part of his household. Like the rite alluded to in 1 Samuel 1:24–25, this is an "adoption" celebration. Saul was placed at the head of the table, the place doubtless reserved for Samuel. Saul was thus singled out as Samuel's successor, as well as his "son." As part of his "fatherly" guidance, Samuel told Saul to wait seven days before sacrificing to initiate the battle with the Philistines (10:8), just as the people at Ramah waited for Samuel before they began to eat (9:13). Saul was to exercise patience, and this would also show that he was submissive to the word of the prophet, a dutiful son to his adoptive father.

Three signs confirmed Samuel's announcement (10:2–6), each of which was related to Samuel's announcement and anointing and which together laid out a symbolic commentary on the office that Saul was assuming. Going in reverse order, the induction into the company of the prophets was connected to Saul's "adoption" into Samuel's house.[15] When people heard that Saul was among the prophets, they asked what had happened to the "son of Kish." In verse 12, a man asked "Who is their father?" meaning "Who is the father of the prophets?" And the answer is Samuel. If Saul was among the prophets, he was no longer a son of Kish but a son of Samuel.[16] That was what had happened to the son of Kish. But the earlier chapters of 1 Samuel nag us with questions: Would Saul be a faithful son to Samuel, or would he turn out to be another Hophni or Phinehas? Would he remain among the prophets or turn away from them? Would Israel always be able to answer yes when asked, Is Saul among the prophets?

---

[15] Saul was greeted by prophets playing on musical instruments (10:5), similar to the musical band of the prophetess Miriam (Exod. 15:20–21). From this point on, music was a frequent accompaniment of royalty: David played the harp for Saul, and when he became king he organized a musical form of worship on Zion.

[16] This explains why Saul's "uncle" greets him when he gets home (v. 14). This is perhaps a reference to Kish, Saul's father, who is now called "uncle" because Samuel has taken over as Saul's father.

Clearly, this final sign pointed to Saul's association with the prophets, and the other two also indicated features of his office. Above, we noted that donkeys were royal animals in Israel, and therefore the announcement that the donkeys have been found confirmed that Saul was about to assume the kingship (10:2). The third sign was a priestly sign; the bread that the three men gave was intended for a sacrificial rite, since they were "going to God at Bethel" (10:3). In giving Saul a portion of their bread, they were acknowledging that Saul was privileged to receive priestly portions (10:4; cf. 1 Sam. 21:1–6). Though Saul became *king*, in an important sense the Israelite king was also a prophetic and priestly figure.[17] Moreover, Saul's return home progressed through significant points in the history of the tribe of Benjamin. Verse 2 mentions Rachel's tomb which is in the territory of Benjamin, where she died giving birth to Benjamin shortly after the Lord had promised that Jacob would father kings (Gen. 35:16–20). Now, in the same area, Saul was confirmed as king by the three signs. The patriarchal promise that "kings will come from you" is about to be fulfilled.

Through all this and through the power of the Spirit, Saul was transformed into a "new man" (10:6). As the "new man," he soon faced a test.

VICTORY OVER THE SERPENT, 1 SAMUEL 11:1–11
Samuel's anointing of Saul was kept secret even from Saul's "uncle," but soon after Samuel gathered Israel to Mizpah to make a public announcement. The selection of the king proceeded by lot, a procedure similar to the one used to identify the culprit after Israel's defeat of Ai, and also like the procedure later used to identify who had broken the fast during the battle with the Philistines (1 Sam. 14:36–42). Using lots was a way of highlighting the fact that the Lord was choosing Saul as king: "The lot is cast into the lap, but its every decision is from the Lord" (Prov. 16:33). Saul's humility and

---

[17] The encounter with the three men on their way to Bethel also implies that Saul had something like a Nazirite status. They gave him bread, but no wine. Bread is the food of beginnings, giving strength to the heart of man (Ps. 104:15). But wine is to gladden the heart and comes at the end, when the work is done.

meekness were again evident, for when the lot named him as king, he was with the baggage.[18] After being confirmed as king by the people, Saul faced his first test in a battle against the Ammonites, descendants of Lot who lived on the east side of the Jordan. They attacked the city of Jabesh-gilead, which was in the tribal area of the half-tribe of Manasseh in the Transjordan. Philistines were again encroaching on Israel's territory, attacking from the west. The Ammonite threat and the Philistine threat came simultaneously, and it is possible that they were coordinating their efforts and pinching Israel in the middle. In the story of the Levite and his concubine, all the cities of Israel were called to fight against the Benjamites, but the people of Jabesh-gilead refused to join the mustering of the tribes at Mizpah (Judg. 21:8–12). As a result, Israel carried out the ban against Jabesh-gilead after they had defeated Benjamin.[19] Only four hundred virgins from Jabesh-gilead were spared, and these were given to the remnant of Benjamin as wives. Jabesh-gilead was thus full of Benjamites, and Saul had a family connection with them. The theological weight of Saul's test becomes clearer when we note that "Nahash," the name of the Ammonite king, means "serpent." Saul had been raised to kingship as a new Adam. His first test was to be confronted by a serpent. Would he crush the head?[20]

[18] The word for "baggage" is almost invariably used for military gear (1 Sam. 17:22; 25:13; 30:24), and this suggests that the assembly at Mizpah was a military one. The Israelites knew that the Ammonites were on the march, and the Philistine garrison was at Gibeah only a few miles away. Since they were gathering to select a king, Israel played it safe and brought their gear along in case they had to fight.

[19] There's a sobering practical message in this: The Benjamites sinned like Canaanites and were exterminated like Canaanites; the people of Jabesh-gilead did not sin in the same way, but they came under the same punishment. Refusing to fight Canaanites is equivalent to being allied with them.

[20] There is an odd development here. Nahash proposed to poke out the right eye of everyone in Jabesh-gilead (11:2), which would inhibit their ability to fight, especially true if Josephus was correct that ancient shields covered the left eye. As a way of buying time, the elders' request for time was reasonable (11:3), but why did Nahash agree to it? Evidently, he did not think they would be able to find a deliverer. He had marched into Israelite territory without encountering any opposition. Moreover, a siege would be long and expensive, and Nahash apparently preferred to have the whole conquest of Jabesh-gilead over in a week, without a shot fired.

When Saul heard what had happened, he acted like a judge. The Spirit came on him mightily (11:6), as He did on many of the judges (Judg. 3:10; 6:34; 11:29; 13:25; 14:6). The Spirit's descent was always a prelude to holy war, just as the Spirit was poured out at Pentecost to equip the church to prosecute its holy war of preaching. Like the Levite from the book of Judges, he cut up an ox and sent pieces around the territory, threatening those who refused to help, just as there had been an earlier threat against Jabesh-gilead itself (Judg. 21:8–12). This time, there were no reluctant cities in Israel, but all came together because the fear and terror of God was upon them (11:7). When a leader is an instrument of the dread of Yahweh, God's people are afraid *not* to act. Saul gathered 330,000 men, which was not only a very large army but emphasizes the number three, reminding us of Gideon. References to Gideon continue in the following verses, when Saul divided the force into three groups and designed a surprise attack on the Ammonites (11:9–11; Judg. 6:15–23).

After the victory, Saul again showed his humility by refusing to strike out against his opponents, even though he was encouraged to do so by some of his men. Later, David faced similar temptations to take vengeance on his enemies, and, in particular, on Saul. Further, Saul gave Yahweh credit for the victory, presenting it as another Ebenezer in which "Yahweh has accomplished salvation in Israel" (11:13).

After Saul's great victory, Samuel gathered the people to Gilgal to "renew the kingdom" (11:14). There, he addressed Israel for the last time, turned over the kingdom officially to Saul, and formally marked the end of the period of the judges.[21] There are a number of links with 1 Samuel 8, so that these speeches of Samuel form bookends around this section of 1 Samuel. As in chapter 8, legal terminology was prominent and frequent; "bear witness" (12:3, 5), "take a stand," and "plead" are legal terms (12:7, 16).

---

[21] Robert P. Gordon, *I & II Samuel*, 123.

Three parties are on trial in this passage. First, Samuel placed himself in the dock, inviting anyone with a complaint to bring charges against him. Samuel "walked before" the people and had been in the public eye; he had gone "in and out" as their military and religious leader. When Samuel described the "custom of the king," he said that the king's procedure would be "taking, taking, taking." He repeated the same word three times in the speech at Gilgal: He had not taken an ox, a donkey or a bribe (12:3). He had not been like the kings of the nations, nor been a corrupt judge like his own sons. In many ways, Samuel had been a model leader.

The second party to be "tried" was Yahweh Himself. Samuel vindicated God (12:6–11) by telling a story of His "righteous acts" (12:7). Righteousness is conformity to covenant, and the story that Samuel told demonstrated that Yahweh was a covenant-keeping God, a God who kept His promises to protect and bless Israel. The string of deliverances went back to the exodus, and the deliverances during the time of the judges were much like the exodus. Both in Egypt and under the oppression of foreign nations, Israel cried out to the Lord, and the Lord appointed deliverers (12:11), through whom He gave rest to Israel.

This leads to the third phase of the trial, the trial of Israel. Samuel and Yahweh were vindicated, but the righteousness of Yahweh exposed the unrighteousness of His people. Though he reiterated that Israel had sinned in requesting a king (12:12), Samuel assured the people that they were not doomed because of the monarchy. They could still receive the blessing of God. To put it another way, the monarchy was brought under the covenant. The covenant arrangements, with blessings and curses, continued as they had in the past. So long as the people "fear, serve, listen, not rebel, and follow," the king would be established, but if the king or the people failed to listen to Yahweh's word (spoken by the prophet), then the Lord's hand would be against them. Here, the king's standing was dependent upon the people's faithfulness; under the terms of the Davidic covenant, as we shall see, the people's standing turned on the king's faithfulness.

As a sign to confirm the truth of his testimony, Samuel called
on the Lord to thunder and send rain, a rare event during the time
of the wheat harvest (12:17). The Lord thundered and sent rain
from His glory-cloud (see Ps. 68 and 29), and the appearance of
the glory-cloud showed that God was witness to the proceedings.
It also showed that Samuel had an "inside track" with God and
this led the people to request that Samuel continue to intercede for
them. If he could call on the Lord to bring rain in the dry season,
then they could surely depend on him to intercede for their salvation and deliverance.

Samuel's speech was something of a retirement speech. Though
he remained alive for perhaps another thirty years, he no longer led
Israel as judge and military commander. Instead, he led Israel by
speaking the Word of God to the king. Unfortunately, and to the
great sorrow of Saul and Israel, the king rapidly stopped listening.

THE KINGDOM TORN, 1 SAMUEL 13–15[22]

Samuel's speech in chapter 12 ended on a note of warning about
the consequences if Israel sinned against the Lord. In chapter 13,
this apostasy began to occur.[23] The significance of Saul's sins can
be clarified by consideration of the original order of creation. In the

[22] This section expands upon the treatment in *A House for My Name*, 136–140. See
also James B. Jordan, "King Saul: A New Adam and a New Fall," available from Biblical
Horizons, P.O. Box 1096, Niceville, Florida, 32588–1096.

[23] Verse 1 presents an immediate textual difficulty. The verse is a typical formula
that introduces the beginning of a king's reign, stating that the king was X years when he
began to reign and he reigned X years over Israel. Here, the problem is that the Hebrew
says that Saul was "a son of one year" when he began to reign and that he reigned "two"
years over Israel. The first statement is impossible, and the second is contradicted by other
texts. Various proposals have been offered to make the text reasonable. For example, the
New American Standard Bible places "forty" in the first blank and adds "thirty" in the
second to make a reign of thirty-two years. Harmonizing this with Acts 13:21, which says
that Saul reigned for forty years, is possible if the "thirty-two" years refers to the period
between Saul's anointing and the events of chapter 13. Though there may be a textual
problem, it is best to avoid that conclusion if we can make sense of the text in another way.
And we can. As noted above, the anointing of Saul was Saul's adoption by Samuel, through
which Saul became Samuel's designated successor and after which Saul became "another
man" (10:6). Against this background, the "son of one year" refers back to this "adoption"

original creation, the world was divided into three environments.[24] The garden was "east" in Eden (Gen. 2:8), not identical with the land of Eden but a section of Eden in the eastern part of the land. This implies that there was a separate environment called the "land" of Eden. In Genesis 2:10–14, moreover, we learn that there were other lands as well. The original creation was divided into garden, land, and world, and these correspond to the three environments of later biblical history: The garden became the sanctuary, the house of God; the land of Eden corresponded to the land of promise; and the outlying lands were analogous to the Gentile nations.

Each of these environments had a particular relation and a particular task. The garden/sanctuary was the place of worship and the relationship to God as Father; the land was the place of work or the home and highlights man's relation to God the Son and Brother; the world or the nation was the place of witness and in it man related to God the Spirit. In Genesis, these three environments were the locations for the three falls of man: Adam fell in the garden with a sin against God (Gen. 3), Cain sinned in the field by killing his brother and was cast out to wander east of Eden (Gen. 4), and the sons of God intermarried with the daughters of men (Gen. 6). The patriarchal stories match up with and reverse these sins in a rough way: Abraham established worship in the land, Jacob contended with his brother and relatives, and Joseph was a witness in the Egyptian empire. These parallels are summarized in the chart below:

---

into the company of prophets of which Samuel was father. He was publicly made king at Gilgal within a year after his initial anointing, and two additional years passed between his anointing and the battle of Michmash. This means that Saul's first sin comes in the "third year" of his reign, and this links Saul's sin up with other "third-day" and "third-year" events in the Bible. This also helps us to roughly establish Saul's age at the time of his accession. Jonathan, his son, was already fighting with the army at Michmash in the third year of Saul's reign. Saul therefore must have been in his forties by this point.

[24] See the helpful summary of this point in James B. Jordan's *The Handwriting on the Wall: A Commentary on Daniel* (Powder Springs: American Vision, 2007).

Original Creation	Israel's History	Task	Human Relation	Sin in Genesis
Garden	sanctuary	worship	father	Adam: rebellion
Land/field	land	work	brother	Cain: fratricide
World	Gentile nations	witness	stranger	Sons of God: intermarriage

Saul sinned three times, and these match these three environments. Saul's first sin was a sin of Adam, a sin against God as Father and a sin against Samuel as his human "father." During the battle of Michmash, Saul sinned against his men by imposing a foolish oath during battle and against his son by seeking to kill him when he broke the vow; this was a sin in the land against the "Son." Saul's final sin was his refusal to carry out the ban against the Amalekites, a failure in relation to the world and the sin that grieved the Holy Spirit (note 16:14). Every Christian has similar tasks, and those who are in Saul's position of leadership over Israel must be especially careful to listen to be faithful in the garden, the land, and the world.

Saul's first two sins occurred in the context of the battle of Michmash, which he fought with the Philistines. Though Samuel had driven the Philistines out of the land, by the early part of Saul's reign, they were threatening Israel again. Israel had only been able to muster three thousand troops in response (13:2; compare 11:8), which were divided into two companies, one group of two thousand at Michmash, north and east of Gibeah and Ramah, and another one thousand with Jonathan at Gibeah, Saul's hometown (13:2). Jonathan initiated the battle by smiting the Philistine "garrison" ("prefect" may be better) at Geba, which stands between Michmash and Gibeah of Benjamin, three to four miles northeast of Gibeah (13:3). Jonathan's action provoked a massive Philistine response, assembling a force of thirty thousand chariots and six thousand horsemen to attack Michmash, apparently taking over Saul's camp (v. 2, 5, 23). As the word of the Philistine mobilization spread, Saul moved to Gilgal, where the men of Israel gathered, terrified (13:6–7). The dread of Yahweh fell on Israel the last time Saul led them to battle. This time it was terror of the Philistines.

Israel was supposed to be like sand on the seashore, but instead Philistia was (v. 5). Israel, meanwhile, was hiding in caves and pits (v. 6), as if buried. Some Israelites crossed over the Jordan to the region of Gilead, voluntarily going into exile and reversing the conquest. Threatened by a counterfeit Israel, Israel was in danger of ceasing to be Israel. Verse 6 is virtually identical to Judges 6:2, at the introduction to the ministry of Gideon, and fits with the other Gideon references we have noted above. In fact, there are numerous references to Gideon in the account of the battle of Michmash: Like Gideon, Saul faced long odds; like Gideon, he blew the ram's horn (v. 3; Judg. 6:34); and in both accounts, Israel's enemies were compared to the sand on the seashore (Judg. 7:12). Saul had acted like Gideon earlier in his career, and at Michmash he faced a situation where Gideon-like behavior was demanded. Would he continue to act like Gideon in the face of the Philistine attack?

Another question also looms in the background: Would he obey the voice of his "father" Samuel and wait for the prophet to offer the sacrifice? In brief, the answer was "No." Saul waited for most of seven days, but he became impatient, fearing that his army would melt away. Left with six hundred men (v. 15), twice the number Gideon had when he attacked, Saul lost his nerve and acted without faith. Saul had become an anti-Gideon, putting his trust in numbers rather than in the Lord. And note who used the "Gideon" strategy of dividing into three companies in this battle: not Saul, but the Philistines (v. 16). Fearful, Saul offered sacrifice without waiting for Samuel, foolishly seeking the Lord's favor through an act of disobedience. Saul's sin, like Adam's in the garden, was a sin of impatience.[25] From another angle, Saul's sin was a simple matter of disobedience to the "commandment of Yahweh your God" (13:13). In fact, the commandment came from Samuel,

---

[25] Verses 9 and 10 indicate that Saul was prepared to offer the burnt offering but never offered the peace offering. The peace offering was a fellowship offering, an offering that included a covenant meal and feast, but Saul never got to this. The service of worship was aborted in midstream.

but the word of the prophet was equivalent to the commandment of the Lord. This was the one crucial test for a faithful king, as it is the crucial test of the faithful pastor: Did he listen to the voice of the prophet? Was Saul also among the prophets? And who was his father?

Instead of immediately accepting responsibility and repenting of his sin, Saul offered a series of excuses: It was the people's fault for scattering from me (v. 11); it was Samuel's fault for not coming when he said he would (v. 11); it was the Philistine's fault for threatening to attack (v. 11); and, besides, he did it reluctantly, forcing himself to disobey against his will (v. 12). All this dancing around the issue again reminds us of Adam complaining of the woman that the Lord had given him or of Aaron blaming the people (or the fire!) for the golden calf. Samuel's judgment was quick and extremely severe. As a newly anointed king, Saul was under probation, and Samuel's demand that he wait to sacrifice was a test of his faith. Because of this sin, Samuel announced, Saul's kingdom would not endure. The Lord was instead seeking another man, a man after his own heart (13:14). Every leader sins. But those leaders who refuse to accept responsibility for sin and turn from it will find that they have nothing left to lead.

This chapter introduces Jonathan, Saul's son, in an intriguing way. We first learn about him in verse 3, but he is identified only as the one who "smote the garrison of the Philistines that was in Geba." Whoever this Jonathan was, we find him acting with greater boldness than the king, taking Gideon-like initiative against Israel's enemies. Only in verse 16 do we finally learn that Jonathan was Saul's son. By this time, however, we already know that Saul's kingdom was going to belong to another (vv. 13–14). Our first instinct is to think that Jonathan had arrived just in time to replace the fallen king; Jonathan stepped into the books of Samuel as a new Saul. As the story develops, however, Jonathan became less a new Saul and more a prototype of David. The following chapters thus tell a story of double replacement: First, Jonathan began to displace

Saul as the military leader of Israel, and then David more openly replaced Jonathan as the heir to the throne.

Saul's situation got worse after his sin. He marched from Gilgal to Geba to where Jonathan had camped after smiting the garrison/prefect. The Philistines were camped less than two miles away at Michmash, and they were moving to isolate Saul and Jonathan at Geba (13:16). Not only did the Philistines have a superior position, but they had vastly superior technology. They had driven all the blacksmiths out of Israel, so that Israel had to pay the Philistines even to sharpen their farm implements (13:19–20). Among the Israelites, only Saul and Jonathan had swords and spears. This sets up an important motif for the remainder of 1 Samuel: Characters were marked as good or bad by the weapons they used and how they used them.

Jonathan again broke through the impasse. With his armor bearer, he left the Israelite camp to confront the Philistine garrison at Michmash. Between the two camps there was a gulf with a wadi running below. The canyon between the two armies was very steep, with a sharp "tooth" crag on either side. To get to the Philistines, Jonathan had to go down one crag (Heb. *seneh* or "thorn") and up the other on the north (Heb. *bozez*, or "shining"). Among other things, this was a kind "death and resurrection" movement, as Jonathan and his armor bearer went down into the valley and came up again. The Philistines seemed to have discerned this, for when they saw Jonathan coming, they said that the Hebrews were coming up from their tomb-like caves (v. 11). It is also significant that the crags are called "teeth" (v. 4), for Sheol, the place of the dead, is described in the Old Testament as a devouring monster (e.g., Ps. 49:14; 141:7; Prov. 27:20). Jonathan went down into the mouth of Sheol and rose again. The names of the crags reinforce this symbolism, for Jonathan went down the "thorn" and came up the "shining" path; he passed through the curse and emerged to win the victory. Foreshadowing David after him, Jonathan is a dead-and-risen warrior. Because of the "death and resurrection" of the king's son, Israel too was raised from the dead and entered the battle with the Philistines: Jonathan inspired the Hebrews to come out of their caves (13:11, 22), and some Hebrews who had become allies of the Philistines (v. 21) turned against the Philistines and fought on the side of Jonathan and Saul.

The battle of Michmash combined features of the two contrasting battles earlier in 1 Samuel. At the battle of Aphek, with Eli and his sons in charge, Israel was defeated, but with Samuel in charge at the battle of Ebenezer, Israel was victorious. The "son," Samuel, won the victory after the "father's" defeat. At Michmash, father and son were on the field simultaneously. Because of the son's heroism, Israel won the battle, but the victory was almost wasted by the unfaithful father. A striking reminder of Aphek occurs in 14:3: "Ahijah, the son of Ahitub, Ichabod's brother, the son of Phinehas, the son of Eli, the priest of the Lord at Shiloh, was wearing an ephod." With help like that, Saul was sure to fail. Meanwhile, when Jonathan had felled twenty men, the Lord caused the earth to quake with a "trembling of God" (v. 15). This links to the thunder at the battle of Ebenezer (7:10), which, like the Lord's thunder at that battle, threw the Philistines into a panic (14:15).

Saul and his men saw the Philistine army melting away and realized that something odd was going on (vv. 16–19). He mustered the troops and found Jonathan and his armor bearer were missing. Saul had enough wits about him to know that he should not go into battle without consulting the Lord, and so he called Ahijah with the ephod. Verse 18 says that the ark was among the Israelites, but this seems to conflict with what we know from chapter 7, that the ark was in the house of Abinadab being cared for by Eleazar (7:1–2).[26] Further, though Saul called for the ark, the method used involved the Urim and Thummim. The words "withdraw your hand" (14:19) suggests that the priest's hand was within the breastpiece, and verse 41 makes an explicit reference to Thummim (in Hebrew). There-

---

[26] Another oddity is that the Septuagint does not mention the ark, but instead says that Ahijah was bearing the ephod.

fore, it is best to conclude that the actual object on the field was the high priest's ephod with the attached breastpiece. The ark was not actually present, but the priest was consulting the Lord by the normal means, using the Urim and Thummim. But why would the ephod be called the "ark"? From a literary and theological perspective, the reference to the ark links the battle of Michmash with the earlier battle of Aphek. But there was also a functional parallel between the ark and the ephod. The ark was a box containing the tablets of the law, while the breastpiece was a pouch containing the Urim and Thummim, which, on one interpretation, are two stones that are used to consult with the Lord. Thus, the ephod was something like a portable ark.

Saul began consulting Yahweh but then realized that the battle was getting out of his control. So Saul stopped Ahijah in the middle of the consultation, an unparalleled act in Scripture and one that had profound implications for the rest of Saul's reign. At Michmash, Saul silenced the Lord; and in response the Lord became silent. Later, when Saul sought Yahweh, He refused to answer, and Saul went instead to a medium to seek guidance (1 Sam. 28). Rebellion put Saul on the road to divination.

Despite the "life-giving" power that Jonathan gave the troops, they were "hard-pressed" (14:24). Saul had placed them under a curse if they ate anything during battle. Ignorant of this curse, Jonathan reached down and ate some honey, a foretaste of the "land of milk and honey" that Israel would inherit if she drove out the Philistines. By imposing the curse, Saul had prevented Israel from taking best advantage of their military situation, and as a result they could not enjoy the fruits of victory, the milk and honey of the land.[27] Instead, Israel's hungry soldiers fell on the plunder and ate the flesh with the blood (14:32). Blood is the life and the life

---

[27] When Jonathan, in ignorance, tastes the honey his eyes were "brightened." The word here is a pun on the word "curse" (*'or* = brighten, lighten; *'arur* = curse). Saul says that anyone who eats will be *'arur*, but Jonathan is made *'or* by eating. It is an ironic fulfillment of the curse, as Saul's foolish curse is turned into blessing.

belongs to Yahweh; therefore to eat blood is to seize something that belongs to God (Lev. 17:10–13). Horrified by this violation of ritual prescription, Saul set up an altar. Yet, the same Saul, who could not accept men eating the blood of the animals, was shortly intending to shed the innocent blood of his son. He was more ready than anyone to drink hot blood.

Once he had atoned for the offense against blood, Saul decided it was a propitious moment to pursue the Philistines. Again he consulted the Lord, but this time the Lord did not answer (14:37). The situation is reminiscent of the first battle at Ai (Josh. 7). For Saul, it appeared that Jonathan was the "Achan," the "troubler in the camp" who had seized forbidden goods and caused the Lord to turn away. Verse 29 shows us the truth: There was a troubler in the camp, but it was Saul, not Jonathan.[28] This episode also demonstrates the radical change that had overtaken Saul. Earlier, Saul was opposed by sons of Belial, but refused to put them to death (11:12–13). At Michmash, he was ready to put his son to death, though Jonathan was no son of Belial. He was becoming a king like the nations. He was becoming as blind as Eli.

One sign of Saul's growing sense of his own importance was the question he posed to Jonathan: "What have you done?" (14:43). This was Samuel's question to Saul when he sacrificed without waiting for Samuel (13:11). At Michmash, Saul was acting like a prophet challenging Jonathan who had broken his word. Saul was no longer submitting himself to the word of the prophet but trying to replace the prophet. Saul failed to see the answer to his question, though it was lying in front of him: Jonathan "did" this great deliverance and he "did" it with God today (14:45).

The records of the victories of an Israelite ruler are often immediately followed by a reference to either his building projects or the growth of his family. Below, we shall see this pattern repeated a number of times in 2 Samuel 5–8, but the first instance of the

---

[28] The language here also suggests muddying of waters (v. 29). Jonathan's eyes are brightened and he can see how foolish his father has been. His father has made everything murky.

victory-housebuilding pattern occurs with Saul. 14:47–52 help to balance the picture of Saul that the main story has been developing. Despite his sins, Saul was a successful warrior, defeating a number of Israel's enemies who had plundered Israel during the times of the judges and into Saul's reign. He had success against enemies on every side, which made him comparable to Joshua as a warrior (Josh. 23:1). This allusion to Joshua's military successes anticipates chapter 15, where Saul was given a task similar to Joshua and failed to carry it out. The reference to the Amalekites in verse 48 also relates to the following chapter. In 14:48, we learn that Saul acted valiantly against the Amalekites, but chapter 15 shows that Saul actually committed his final sin in the war against the Amalekites. There is no contradiction, however. Chapter 15 records a successful military operation, but this success was immediately followed by disobedience to the Lord.

Saul's wars were not a complete success (v. 52). As noted above, the battle at Michmash was reminiscent in some ways of the battle of Ebenezer in chapter 7. In both, the Lord fought for Israel, and both were victories over the Philistines. But there was also a significant difference between the results of the two battles. The battle of Ebenezer ended with the notice that the Philistines were not a problem for the remainder of the "days of Samuel" (7:13). After Michmash, because of Saul's foolish strategy, the Philistines, though beaten, remained strong enough to continue their assaults against Israel, and they were soon to recover most of the territory they lost to Samuel. Again, Israel's ability to stand against enemies depended on the quality of her leadership: Led by a Samuel, Israel repelled her enemies; led by a Saul or an Eli, Israel was overrun by Philistines.

In Genesis 6, the climactic sin of intermarriage was followed by the flood, which God sent because He was "grieved that He had made man" (Gen. 6:6). Yahweh responded in a similar way to Saul's final sin, grieving that He made Saul king (15:11). The last time God grieved, He cut off all flesh from the earth, but raised up

Noah to start anew. Because Saul grieved the Spirit, Saul's world was destroyed, but by washing away the unfaithful king the Lord was preparing for a new king.

Saul was given the assignment to carry out the "ban" (Heb. *herem*) against the Amalekites. According to this form of warfare, Israel was to utterly destroy her enemies (Deut. 20:16–18). The assignment to ban the Amalekites continued the warfare that the Lord declared on Amalek in Exodus 17:8–16. The Amalekite story was an undercurrent through the rest of the Old Testament, finally coming to resolution in the book of Esther, when Mordecai, a descendant of Saul's father Kish, overcame Haman the "Agagite," a descendant of the Amalekite king who appears in 1 Samuel 15.

The issues in chapter 15 circle around the motif of the "voice." Because Samuel anointed Saul, the king must listen to Samuel as his "father." The Lord spoke to the king through the prophet, so he needed to listen to the "voice" of the prophet to hear the words of the Lord (v. 1). When Samuel got to the camp at Gilgal, however, he heard the "voice" of the sheep and oxen (v. 14), a voice that proved that Saul had not listened to the voice of the Lord (v. 19). Nonetheless, Saul, self-defensive as ever, protested that he did obey the "voice" of the Lord (v. 20).

Samuel's rebuke to Saul was a classic statement of a biblical perspective on sacrifice and rituals of worship (15:22–23). Sacrifice and burnt offerings are no substitute for "obedience to the voice of the Lord." This did not express a divergence between prophetic and priestly forms of religion, as liberal scholars believe, for Samuel himself was virtually a priest. He certainly recognized that sacrifice was supposed to be integrated into a life of obedience. Performing a rite of sacrifice while living in disobedience to the Lord, however, was and is abominable. God departs from an abominable house, no matter how fine the rituals. He had already done this when He abandoned His house at Shiloh, and a short time after this episode the Spirit departed from Saul, despite the fact that he presented himself as a paradigm of piety.

Verse 9 tells us what Saul and the people did and why they did it: Saul and the people *together* spared life and had compassion, which was forbidden in *herem* war. He captured Agag, perhaps because Saul considered Agag as a fellow king like the other kings of the nations. For their part, the people kept the best of the spoils to take back to Gilgal,[29] where they intended to celebrate the victory by sacrificing the animals. They did not utterly destroy them because they were "unwilling to destroy them utterly." This was deliberate and wilful disobedience by both Saul and the people.

When Samuel confronted him, however, Saul refused to repent, as he had done in an earlier encounter with Samuel at Gilgal. Saul said that "the people" had spared the best of the sheep and oxen (v. 15), but we have already been told that both Saul and the people spared the best of the sheep and oxen. Saul then admitted that he had spared the animals, but tried to give a pious reason: He spared them but not because they were "unwilling to destroy them utterly," contradicting verse 9. Rather, they spared the animals because they wanted to "sacrifice to Yahweh your God." This terminology normally refers to a "peace offering," and that implies that Saul was planning to eat animals that were supposed to be devoted entirely to God. Saul apparently thought he was making a good excuse, but it only made things worse. He was admitting that he took some of the Lord's goods for himself; he virtually admitted to being a Hophni.

Finally, after several rebukes, Saul admitted that he sinned and listened to the "voice" of the people (v. 24). Because Saul failed to repent, he would not retain the kingdom, for Yahweh had rejected him (15:26). As Samuel turned to go, Saul seized Samuel by

---

[29] Gilgal was the place where Israel first renewed the covenant when they entered the land. Under Joshua, the men were all circumcised, Israel celebrated the feast of Passover, and then they went out to conquer Jericho and the land. Saul had just violated the terms of the covenant, refusing to carry out the ban, but acted as if he had carried out the Lord's will.

the "corner" or "wing" of his garment and tore it.[30] On the wing
of every Israelite's garment was a tassel that served as a reminder of
the Torah (Num. 15:37–41), and Saul tore this tassel from Samuel's
robe. This represented precisely what Saul had done by refusing to
listen to the voice of the Lord. Elsewhere, the robe is a sign of office
and authority. Ahijah the Shilonite tore his robe to represent the
tearing of the kingdom (1 Kgs. 11:29–39), and Samuel pointed to
this same symbolism when he said that the kingdom had been torn
from Saul. Saul assaulted his "father's" robe of authority when he
refused to listen to his father's voice, and like Ham, who also sought
to remove his father's robe (Gen. 9:20–27), Saul was cut off.

To be sure, Saul's fall was part of God's plan from the beginning. Why, then, did God choose Saul to be king in the first place?
Why not select someone like David immediately? In the context
of 1 Samuel, this was part of God's punishment of Israel for asking for a king. God gave them a king like the kings of the nations,
which is what they asked for. Theologically, the movement from
Saul to David is an almost invariable pattern in the Old Testament. A deliverer is promised, but the first one that appears is not
the right one, and it is only when we get to the second or third or
seventh that we find the true seed. Saul's fall and replacement by
David was an example of this pattern of the replacement of the
firstborn. This is a type of the great "replacement" that is one of
the basic structures of biblical theology—the First and Last Adam.
Saul was made king, but he sinned and lost the kingdom, as Adam
did. But the Lord intended to raise up another king, a type of the
Last Adam, in David.

A final theological question arises in connection with Saul's
fall. After he had been anointed by Samuel and encountered the
Spirit, he was made "another man" (10:6). The language sounds
a lot like what theologians call "regeneration," an act of the Spirit

---

[30] Contrary to my earlier argument (*A House for My Name*, 159, fn. 8), the analogy
between this incident and the incident in 1 Kings 11 leads me to conclude that Saul tore
Samuel's robe, rather than the opposite.

that makes a sinner a new creation. Yet, regeneration is supposed to be irreversible; once changed, always changed, just as once elect, always elect. If we want to preserve our theology, we have to conclude that Saul was not *really* changed into "another man" and did not *really* receive the Spirit.

The problem is, the text says that he "was changed into another man" (10:6), and even claims that "God changed for him another heart" (10:9). If we want to bow before Scripture, we simply have to accept what the text says. Saul became another man through the work of the Spirit, but by persisting in sin, Saul grieved the Spirit, who departed from him. This is a real possibility, not a hypothetical one. We really can grieve the Spirit, He really will depart from those who persist impenitently in sin, God really does withdraw His grace from people who were once changed into "another man." The last state is worse than the first, for those who spurn and offend the Spirit will find their house desolate and will find themselves terrorized by an "evil spirit from the Lord."

CHAPTERFOUR
1 SAMUEL 16-20[1]

SON OF SAUL

Saul was rejected from being king before the battle of Michmash (1 Sam. 13–14), but as we saw, a replacement was immediately introduced, his son Jonathan. Just as Eli was replaced by his "son" Samuel and just as Samuel was replaced by his "son" Saul, so now fallen Saul was to be replaced by his son. And Jonathan was a worthy candidate: Bold and aggressive as a warrior, full of faith in Yahweh's strength, he was what his name suggests, a "gift of God" to Israel. He was everything that Saul had been early in his reign.

According to the pattern of 1–2 Samuel, however, the biological son did not replace the father. Instead, the biological son was himself replaced by an adopted son. As noted in the previous chapter, Jonathan was introduced as the "son of Saul" only after Samuel had already cut Saul off from the kingdom (13:16). No sooner do we learn that he was a son than we learn that he was a disinherited so. Instead of being the replacement for Saul, Jonathan functioned in the story as a preview of the true replacement, David, and the similarities between the two were marked:

---

[1] The rest of 1 Samuel divides into three large sections, the first having to do with David's rise and his life in Saul's court (16–20), the second recording his life as a fugitive (21–27), and the last focusing on Saul's final battle at Gilboa (28–31). David Dorsey (*The Literary Structure of the Old Testament* [Grand Rapids: Baker, 1999], 131) has suggested that the first of these sections, the subject of the present chapter, is structured as a chiasm:

A   Samuel anoints David, 16:1–13
 B   David plays harp for Saul, 16:14–23
  C David defeats Goliath, 17:1–58
   D Jonathan acknowledges David as crown prince, 18:1–5
  C' Saul is jealous and tries to kill David, 18:6–30 (jealous about Goliath)
 B' Saul tries to kill David and Michal saves him, 19:1–17
A'   David flees to Ramah to Samuel; Jonathan helps David depart, 19:18–20:42

Jonathan (1 Samuel)	David (1 Samuel)
Son of Saul, 13:16	Son-in-law of Saul, 18:26
Fights Philistines single-handedly, 14:1–15	Fights Goliath single-handedly, 17:41–51
Leads Israel to victory, 14:16–42	Leads Israel to victory, 17:52–54
Twice attacked by Saul, 14:43–46; 20:30–34	Twice attacked by Saul, 18:10–11; 19:8–10
Trusts Yahweh, not numbers, in battle, 14:6	Trusts Yahweh, not weapons, in battle, 17:47

Doubtless many more analogies could be found, but these are sufficient to establish the point: Jonathan foreshadowed David, and David's career was modeled on Jonathan's.

In a stream of stimulating books, René Girard has offered a theory of culture that focuses on the phenomenon that Girard calls "mimetic rivalry." According to Girard, human desire is not purely instinctual or purely individual. Rather, desire is "mimetic," that is, imitative; we want things because we see others wanting them, especially others whose lives serve as models for ours. Frequently, the desires of children are formed by the desires of their parents. A father's passion for sporty cars is passed to his sons, and daughters pick up their mother's delight in sewing. Mimetic desire, though

---

The whole section is framed by passages in which Samuel played a prominent role, and by David's arrival to and departure from Saul's house. At the center, significantly, is Jonathan's acknowledgment that David is the true crown prince, the true firstborn and elder brother.

The passage also cycles through a series of similar events three times. David's role is emphasized, then there is a threat to David, and then a member of Saul's household acknowledges or loves David:

```
A       Samuel anoints David, 15:34–16:13
  B     David ministers to Saul with music, 16:14–23
    C   Triumph over Goliath, 17:1–58
      D Jonathan acknowledges David as crown prince, 18:1–5
A       Saul is suspicious about David, 18:6–9
  B/C   Saul raving in house, and David cast out of Saul's house, 18:10–16
      D Saul and Michal: she loves David, 18:17–30
A       David returns to court, 19:1–7
  B/C   Saul tries to kill David again, 19:8–10
      D Michal saves David, 19:11–17
      D David escapes to Ramah, and Saul follows, 19:18–24
      D David and Jonathan make a covenant and part, 20:1–42
```

pervasive in human life, is fraught with danger. After all, if I want something because I see you desiring it, we are setting ourselves up to compete for it. The more closely we mimic the desires of others, the greater the danger of violent rivalry. The more sons mimic their fathers' desires, the greater the danger of strife between fathers and sons.

Girard's insights highlight some important aspects of the story of Saul, David, and Jonathan in these chapters. For each to some degree the object of desire was the crown of Israel. As soon as Jonathan appeared in the story, he was a rival to his father, performing all the heroics that his father should have been performing. David was even more obviously a rival, since he was anointed as soon as he showed his beautiful eyes and handsome face (16:12–13). In fact, David was a potential rival to both Saul and Jonathan: He was designated as Saul's replacement, and that meant he was also destined to usurp the place of Jonathan. Saul certainly viewed David as a dangerous opponent, becoming envious of David's exploits (18:6–8), suspicious of David's popularity (18:9), and fearful of David's success (18:12, 15, 29). Saul even became suspicious of Jonathan, seeking to kill him when he defended David (20:33–34) and blaming him for turning David against him (22:8). Saul was a case study in the violent tendencies of mimetic rivalry.

Jonathan, however, provides a dramatic example of a godly man who resisted envy and the violence that accompanies it. Instead of fearing or hating David, Jonathan loved him (18:1; 20:17). Instead of clinging to his privileges as the king's son, Jonathan acknowledged that David would be the next king (23:17). Instead of cringing when he heard David's exploits praised, Jonathan lent his own voice to that praise (19:4–5). This is all the more striking when we consider the age difference between the two men.[2] David was thirty when he became king (2 Sam. 5:4), and Saul reigned forty years (Acts 13:21). Thus, David was born in the tenth year of Saul's reign. Jonathan, however, was already fighting with Saul in

---

[2] Thanks to James B. Jordan for pointing this out to me in private correspondence.

the third year of his reign at the battle of Michmash (1 Sam. 13:1, 3), and therefore must have been at least twenty at that time. By the time David was born, Jonathan was at least thirty and perhaps even older; though David and Jonathan are in a sense brothers, Jonathan was certainly old enough to be David's father. Instead of treating the dashing warrior from Judah as a young upstart, Jonathan recognized his qualities, conceded that the future belonged to him, and voluntarily gave up his own ambitions for David's sake. Jonathan decreased so that David could increase.

The life of Jacob provides another kaleidoscope of perspectives on the early history of David. In the following chapters, I will make much of this analogy, because it is the theological backbone of the story of David. For now, it will suffice to point out how this analogy adds further luster to the character of Jonathan. Some of the parallels between Jacob and David are summarized in the chart below:

Jacob (Genesis)	David (1 Samuel)
younger son, 25:26	younger son, 16:10–11
chosen by God, 25:23	chosen by God, 16:12
opposed by hostile father, 25:28	opposed by hostile father-in-law, 18:20–29
flees Isaac's house, 27:42–43	flees Saul's house, 19:11–24

Against the background of these parallels, Jonathan's love for David stands out as all the more astonishing; for Jonathan was the "Esau" of this story. It would be hard to imagine a man less suited to the role of Esau.

Finally, we can overview the early life of David by referring again to the three zones of the original creation. We saw in the last chapter that Saul sinned in the garden, the land, and the world. David became king after proving himself faithful in all three areas, and in each David had to prove himself in relation to both allies and enemies:

Creation	Corresponding Area in David's Story	Allies	Enemies
Garden	King's house	Michal, Jonathan	Saul
Land	Wilderness/dealings with Israel	Jonathan, Joab and warriors	Saul, Nabal
World	Philistia	Achish	Amalekites

With enemies, David had to be shrewd and patient; with allies, he had to be both faithful and firm. Insofar as he was successful in these tasks, he was reversing the effects of Saul's sins. Insofar as he failed, he was laying treacherous groundwork for his kingdom. Meditating on the life of David through this grid would be a healthy exercise for anyone aspiring to leadership in the church, and we should expect rulers to prove themselves faithful in each area before they take their places as "clan chiefs" or "kings." It is important to see again that ultimately it is Yahweh who trains David for his office by throwing various sorts of obstacles in his way that stretch his wisdom, strength, and ingenuity.

IN THE KING'S SERVICE, 1 SAMUEL 15:34-16:23[3]

Yahweh Himself grieved over Saul's failures (15:35), and so did Samuel. But there is a time for mourning and a time for action, and Yahweh came to Samuel to tell him that things had to move on. Yahweh again shows He is not a God who dwells in the past, but one who draws Israel into the future.

Understandably, Samuel was afraid of Saul's response if he were to fill his horn with oil and tramp off to Jesse's home. Samuel

---

[3] The story of chapter 16 actually begins with 15:34-35, since the references to Ramah in 15:34 and 16:13 form an *inclusio* around this section. Further, there is a contrast between the Lord's regret regarding Saul and the Lord's choice of David. Thematically 15:35 introduces the key word "see": Samuel did not see Saul again until the day of his death. In itself, this was a forceful judgment on Saul and Israel, for when Saul was cut off from Samuel, he was cut off from the Word of the Lord. The word "see" (along with "eyes") is used throughout the chapter. In 16:1, the Lord said that He had "seen" a king for Himself; Samuel "saw" Eliab and was sure he was the Lord's anointed (16:6), but the Lord said that He does not "see" the "eyes" but the heart (16:7). Along the same lines, the text says that David had beautiful "eyes" (16:12). This emphasis on sight contrasts human sight with Yahweh's and also connects back to the story of the priests, especially Eli, whose sight was failing as he grew old.

knew that Saul had changed radically from his earlier modesty and humility, and that the king was ready to kill his rivals. For Samuel's protection, the Lord ordered Samuel to cover his intentions by claiming to offer a sacrifice at Bethlehem (16:2). Samuel *was* going to Bethlehem for a sacrifice, but that was not the whole truth. This was the first of many deceptions that David and his allies used in their struggle with Saul, and it is important to notice that this strategy was first proposed by Yahweh Himself. When David later employed deception to parry Saul's thrusts, he was just following Yahweh's cunning example.

The sacrificial context connects the anointing of David with the anointing of Saul, which was also performed at a sacrificial feast (1 Sam. 10:12–13). Jesse paraded his sons before Samuel, and Samuel initially thought that Eliab would make a good king. Eliab was, after all, a tall man, a young Saul (16:7). But like Saul, he had been rejected (16:7). David, by contrast, was the "smallest" of Jesse's sons (16:11), but God had chosen the small things of this world to confound the large. David too looked like a king, handsome and with beautiful eyes, (16:12) but what made Him the Lord's choice for king was not his external beauty, but his heart. Yahweh's choice was not based on what men could see of David but upon His view of David's heart.[4]

When Samuel anointed David, the Spirit of Yahweh came on him (16:13). Throughout the Old Testament, the Spirit equipped people with strength to fight, for prophetic ministry, and with wisdom to rule. In receiving the Spirit, David was receiving a "down payment" on the kingdom. Like Saul, he was anointed as king-designate, as *nagid*, the announced one. Though he would not become king for another decade or more, he was already the bearer of the Spirit of the kingdom. At the same, the Spirit abandoned

---

[4] David was the seventh son of Jesse (1 Chr. 2:15). Seven is the number of the creation week, and particularly of the Sabbath. David is being presented as the one who would bring rest to Israel (like Noah). In 1 Samuel 16:6–8, only three other sons are mentioned: Eliab, Abinadab, and Shammah. David is the fourth son named. Perhaps this connects him to Judah, who was the fourth of Jacob's sons, and the royal son.

Saul, leaving him terrified, anxious and paranoid (16:14). Because Saul persisted in rebellion, he grieved the Spirit, driving Him out and leaving room for seven demons to come in to torment him. Saul still had a "spirit" from the Lord; but instead of the Spirit of Yahweh, it was an "evil spirit" who brought only anguish. Before we see David as a warrior or general or king, we see him as a musician and exorcist. In a sense, as soon as the Spirit came upon him, David had already replaced Saul. Though Saul was still king, David was superior spiritually and Saul was dependent upon him.

This exchange of spirits (vv. 13–14) led to an invitation to the royal house: The spirit that tormented Saul was relieved by the man bearing the Spirit of God. David eventually became a permanent member of the royal household. Not only did he play the harp during Saul's fits of madness, but he became his armor bearer, "standing before" Saul as a personal attendant (16:21). When he first moved his residence to Saul's house, he brought a donkey laden with bread and wine (16:20), reminding us of the rite that Samuel's family performed when he was "adopted" into Eli's house. As with Samuel, David transferred from his father's house to the king's house. This story brings out a different sort of comparison between David and Jacob, one in which Saul fills the role of Laban rather than of Isaac. We shall point to other details of this analogy as we move through the next few chapters of 1 Samuel.

GIANT KILLER, 1 SAMUEL 17:1–58

After being anointed and acclaimed as crown prince, Saul had to fight a battle against Nahash, king of Ammon. David's test was a man-to-man battle with Goliath. As noted above, David proved himself another Jonathan, and the passage that follows the story of Goliath shows that Jonathan recognizes this (18:1–5). Though the story of David and Goliath is popularly known as an example of a great underdog triumphing over great odds, the accent in the biblical account is not upon David's heroism or his glory.[5] Of course,

---

[5] I have treated this incident briefly in *A House for My Name*, 141–143.

he did receive honor, as the women sang his praises on his return from battle (18:7). But David's heroism was not like the heroism of an Achilles or an Odysseus. David did not fight because his honor had been violated, but to vindicate the honor of the Lord.

Earlier in 1 Samuel, there have been a number of allusions to the book of Joshua, and here, again, we find a number of allusions to Numbers and Joshua. Doubtless encouraged by reports of Saul's madness, the Philistines encroached deep into Israelite territory (17:1), reversing the conquest and undermining the gains Samuel had made (7:13–14). The Gittite giant Goliath terrorized the Israelites morning and evening, blasphemously taunting Israel at the very time that sacrifices were being offered (17:16). Most of the Israelite army cowered before him, just as the Israelites in the wilderness were afraid of the "giants" in the land (Num. 13:25–33). Goliath's family origins in Gath are significant: The Anakim were conquered by Joshua and relocated to Gaza, Gath, and Ashdod, three Philistine cities (Josh. 11:21–23). Goliath was possibly descended from the Anakim that Joshua conquered. Faced with a giant from Gath, Israel needed another Joshua and another Caleb, and they found one in David. Saul, of course, had been selected as king to fight giants and such things, and being something of a giant himself, he was fully equipped for the task. Because the Spirit had departed, however, he sat idly sharing the dismay of his troops (17:11). David, unlike Saul, remembered that he lived in a nation of giant-killers and knew that he served a God greater than the giants. The fact that Goliath taunted Israel for "forty days" (17:16) was analogous to Israel's wilderness experience; but David was about to bring Israel out of the wilderness and into the land of milk and honey.

Goliath's armor is given unusually detailed attention. We never learn anything about David's armor after he became king.[6] Verse 5 says that the Philistine giant was wearing "scale armor,"

---

[6] By contrast, most of Book 18 of the *Iliad* describes Achilles' armor and the process of arming.

and the Hebrew word simply means "scales." This sort of armor is attested throughout the ancient Near East, but the fact that he is described as wearing "scales" indicates that Goliath was a serpent. Once again there is a serpent in the garden-land of Israel (see 1 Sam. 11). Israel needed not only a Joshua, but a true Adam, a seed of the woman, to crush the serpent's head.

Meanwhile, the hero was back in Bethlehem caring for his father's flocks and moving back and forth between Bethlehem and Saul's home in Gibeah.[7] His father sent him with food for his brothers (17:17–19), and Jesse's instructions are almost verbatim the instructions that Jacob gave to Joseph in Genesis 37:12–17, and this brings out a series of analogies between Joseph and David. Joseph, a younger brother chosen by God to be preeminent over his brothers, was mistreated and sold into slavery, and David received similar treatment from Eliab (17:28–30). Most importantly, the parallels with Joseph foreshadow David's future: Just as Joseph was faithful and patient until the Lord exalted him, so David would have to show the same patience under affliction before coming to the throne.

When he heard Goliath's blasphemy, David inquired about rewards and spoke boldly against Goliath's defiance of Israel, and word of the brash young man got back to Saul. David told Saul that he was prepared to face the Philistine because he had already fought and defeated a bear and a lion (17:37). To David's mind, when Goliath started defying God, he almost ceased to be human and became no more than a bear or lion. And David was confident that the Lord would deliver him from Goliath's "hand" as He had delivered him from the "hand" of beasts. David was the new Adam that Israel had been waiting for, the beast-master taking dominion over bears and lions and now fighting a "serpent."

[7] David was probably not quite twenty years old at the time. Twenty was the age of enlistment in the army (Num. 1:3), and if David were old enough he would probably have accompanied his brothers to the battle. There may, however, have been other reasons for David to remain at home. In the chronology offered in chapter 1, I have estimated that David was seventeen.

Saul attempted to clothe David with his "gear," his royal armor (17:38), which brings out a striking parallel between Saul and the well-armed Goliath. Further, Saul's action appears to have been something like an investiture: The king offered his armor to David, just as Jonathan gave his garments to David after the battle (18:1–5), in an implicit acknowledgment that David was now the one who would go in and out before Israel. Saul's offer also revealed something about his strategy for fighting Israel's enemies. Since Goliath was wearing armor, Saul thought, it was necessary for Israel's hero to wear armor. David had very different ideas about how to fight the Lord's battles. Saul believed he had to become like a king of the nations to fight the kings of the nations, but David went out to fight the Philistine dressed as a shepherd, bearing a stick and a sling, the same gear he used to fight the other beasts. Goliath had committed blasphemy, a capital crime, and David was going out to stone him to death.[8] David's choice of a sling was significant for another reason. In Judges, Benjamites were known for their prowess with the sling (20:16). Israel had a Benjamite king, but David out-Benjamined the Benjamite; he was the true "son of the right hand."

In some respects, David's weapons gave him a tactical advantage. Weighed down by his gear, Goliath moved slowly, and his impressive spear would have been hard to hurl more than a few yards. Goliath was made for close hand-to-hand fighting, while David could move quickly and attack from a distance. Of course, David was not relying on his tactics. Knowing that the Lord did not deliver by sword or spear (v. 47), he fought in the fear of Yahweh. David's statement about weaponry becomes an important theme verse. Throughout the rest of 1 Samuel, Saul consistently will be seen holding a spear. He had become almost a Philistine king, relying, as Goliath did, on armor and weapons.

Goliath was dressed like a serpent with his scale armor, and he died like a serpent, with a head wound, just as the Philistine

---

[8] Bergen, *1, 2 Samuel*, 195.

god Dagon had his head crushed. As the Psalm says, all those who worship idols will be like them (Ps. 115:1–8). And by crushing the head of the Philistine army, David began a rout, driving the Philistines down the valley to the coastal plain and back to Ekron. The heroism of one warrior inspired the whole Israelite army to battle. David plundered Goliath's weapons, and they were later in the tent of the Lord (21:9). Yahweh received the spoils of the battle, since David acknowledged that He was the true Victor. Meanwhile, Goliath's head was sent to Jerusalem, an odd decision since Jerusalem was still controlled by Jebusites. Perhaps David sent the head to Jerusalem to give the Jebusites a glimpse of their future. In any case, Goliath's severed head was sent to the city where one of David's descendants would many centuries later win a great victory at Golgotha, the place of the skull.

The end of chapter 17 has long been a puzzle.[9] Why did Saul fail to recognize David when he was one of his favorites earlier? The best resolution is to notice carefully what went on in the exchange between Saul and David. Saul asked about David's family, and nothing in 17:55 necessarily implies that Saul failed to recognize David. Earlier in the chapter, David had been informed about the rewards promised to the man who killed Goliath (17:25). First, the victor would marry the king's daughter; as in the fairy tales, whoever defeated the dragon would win the bride and become the king's heir. Second, the victor's family would be made "free" in Israel, which meant that the family would be exempt from tribute, taxes and royal service. Since David defeated Goliath, he received these rewards, and Saul, who apparently could not recall David's family background, asked about David's origins so that he could reward David's family.

In the valley of Elah, David proved himself a giant-killer. But Goliath was not the only giant around. Saul was also a giant, and

---

[9] Thematically there is an interesting play on Saul's name in the final verses of chapter 17. He demands that Abner go and "ask" (*sha'ul*) about the boy. David was now the asked-for one, as, previously, were Samuel and Saul. Indeed Saul himself was "asking for" David.

like Goliath he would come against David with a spear. David was to find that fighting an Israelite giant was a trickier affair than killing a lion or a bear, or slinging a stone at a Gittite's head on the battlefield.

A SWORD IN SAUL'S HOUSE, 1 SAMUEL 18:1-30

Chapter 18 is built around a contrast, not so much between David and Saul (as in chapter 17) as between reactions to David. David "prospered" wherever he went (vv. 5, 14–15), and the word for "prosper" can also be translated as "act wisely" (v. 30). His prosperity and wisdom was a sign that the Lord was with him (vv. 12, 14, 28). These statements allude to descriptions of Joseph. When Joseph was in the house of Potiphar, the Lord was "with Joseph" and made him "prosper" in everything (Gen. 39:1–6, 21–23). Again, the analogies between Joseph and David indicate a similarity in their life's story: The story line of Joseph moved "from suffering to glory," and this was David's life's story as well. It was also, of course, the life story of Jesus, and of all disciples of Jesus.

David's prosperity and the Lord's presence with him made him an attractive, charismatic figure. People fell in love with him, and love is a key theme of chapter 18. Jonathan loved David as himself (v. 1), which was hardly surprising since David was another Jonathan. Jonathan's love for David led to a covenant, a formal bond that gave order and permanence to a relationship based on love. A covenant is not merely a legal structure, but proceeds from love and gives structure to love. Some commentators have seen Jonathan's relationship with David as a homosexual one, but this is incredible for many reasons. The Torah thoroughly condemned sodomy as an "abomination" worthy of death (Lev. 18:22; 20:13). If David and Jonathan were homosexual lovers, they were in flagrant rebellion against Israel's law, hardly what one expects from a man "after God's own heart" (1 Sam. 13:14). Either the writer of 1–2 Samuel was ignorant of David's sin or cynically brushed it aside. Neither option is plausible. A writer who knew the inside

story of David, Bathsheba, and Uriah would have known about a
youthful homosexual fling, and a writer willing to present David's
adultery without evasion or excuse would not be willing to treat
sodomy as a peccadillo. Jonathan and David, like many men who
have shared battlefield adventures, were strongly devoted to each
other. But there was not a hint that their love included homosexual
intercourse.

As part of Jonathan's covenant-making, he formally designated David as his replacement. Jonathan voluntarily removed the
robe and armor of the crown prince and gave them to his younger
brother. Not only did this demonstrate Jonathan's devotion to David and his superhuman humility, but also showed that David's
claim to the throne was not revolutionary or based on sheer power.
Instead, David's pursuit of the kingdom was based on Jonathan's
relinquishment of his position. David had rejected Saul's armor,
refusing to act like a king of the nations; but he accepted the armor
of Jonathan, who fought, like David, in the power of the Lord.

All the people and servants of Saul also loved David, in part
because he was filling the role that Saul had abandoned. David
went out and came in before the people (v. 13), language used to describe the military leadership throughout the Old Testament. Saul
was supposed to "go in and out" before the people, but his rebellion
turned him into a shadow of the king he had been. David thus took
over Saul's role as the military leader. Michal, Saul's daughter, also
loved David (v. 20), and she was the only woman in the Old Testament who is said to have loved a man. David, who said that he was
"lightly esteemed" (18:23), became "greatly esteemed" (18:30). His
name was becoming great, and as a "son" of the king, he was rising
as Samuel rose during the time of Eli, Hophni, and Phinehas.

But David brought a sword to the house of Saul, dividing a
son from his father and causing dissension between a father and
his daughter. Though Saul's whole house loved David, Saul's hatred
only increased. Saul first became suspicious of David when he heard
the songs of triumph that the women sang to the returning hero

(18:6–9). David was a true husband to Israel, a true Adam who had defeated the serpent, and the brides of Israel came out to praise him. The description of the women singing is also reminiscent of the song after the Exodus when the women sang and danced to the Lord (see Exod. 15:20–21). Led by David, Israel again passed from death to life, and the women rightly praised the one whom Yahweh used as an instrument to bring them up from bondage to the Philistine-Egyptians. Saul, however, had changed drastically from the Saul we met at the beginning of the book. After defeating the Ammonites, Saul refused to put his rivals to death, showing restraint in the face of enemies. But he was suspicious of David, showing hatred in the face of friends.

The complexity of David's situation should be noted. When he faced Goliath on the battlefield, there was little need to contemplate the ethics of the situation; in open war, the goal is straightforward: Inflict whatever damage on the enemy as is necessary to win. Confronted by the Israelite giant, however, things were not so obvious. David had to discover a way of faithfully serving a man, an *anointed* man, who was his master, and at the same time avoid and deflect the hostility of the same man, a *demon-possessed* man, who was trying to kill him.

Several practical points emerge from David's example. First, with one exception (see 24:1–7), David did nothing to harm or attack Saul in the slightest degree. He never returned evil for Saul's evil, but instead did good service to Saul even when he was being attacked, hounded and harassed. He always did homage to "Yahweh's anointed." Long before Jesus preached the Sermon on the Mount, David had discerned that the Lord required love for enemies. Second, David frequently simply avoided Saul; he escaped from the room when Saul was chucking spears, he jumped out a window when Saul sent thugs to capture him, and he fled into the wilderness and eventually into Philistia so that Saul would stop chasing him. At several points, David did verbally confront Saul, but he never picked a fight, never pushed things to a pitched battle.

Third, David also used a variety of deceptions, stratagems, and ruses to avoid the pitched battle. David acted like a madman when he was recognized in Gath, Michal arranged his bed and lied to her father's (!) soldiers, David asked Jonathan to deceive Saul about his whereabouts to discover whether Saul was still hostile. David has been attacked for centuries for these actions, but they are righteous acts, illustrating a love of enemies that is as shrewd as a serpent. Finally, David was able to maintain this demeanor toward Saul not because he thought Saul's hatred might be justified; you will find little false guilt in David. He loved his enemy because he knew that the Lord would eventually intervene and vindicate him. He knew that the Lord would judge rightly, so long as he was patient.

The story of David and Goliath has been the subject of innumerable inspiring sermons. Inspiring, uplifting, exciting—but are such sermons helpful? Very few of us face situations where a sling and a stone can be much help; we might crave for the opportunity to crush the head of an irrationally demanding boss, an abusive spouse, a faithless pastor, but the opportunity rarely presents itself. We are much more apt to be faced with Israelite giants than with Philistine giants. And therefore we need to spend as much time considering David's conflict with Saul as we do considering David's conflict with Goliath, and we should be inspired by his wiliness as much as we are by his courage.

Saul first tried a direct assault on David (vv. 10–16), while he was "raving" in his house. The word for "raving" is the same word for "prophesying" in 10:10–11. Is Saul among the prophets? Perhaps, but he was inspired not by the Spirit of Yahweh, but by an evil spirit; he had become a mouthpiece for false prophecy. It is significant that Saul used a spear against David; in fact, the text says "*the* spear," and the only spear mentioned so far is Goliath's. Even if it is not the same spear (and the size of Goliath's spear suggests that it was not), it is certainly associated with Goliath's. Like Goliath, the Israelite giant came after David with spear and sword; but David had already proven himself a giant-killer. Saul had a spear in his "hand" while David played a harp "with his hand," and the phrase in Hebrew is identical. Saul's power came from the spear, for Saul had turned into a king like the kings of the nations. David's power was the power of the Spirit, the power of the harp and music, of poetry and praise.

David's escape no doubt rattled Saul (18:11–12). Saul was the great warrior-king of Israel, and he could not even hit a target sitting across the room, unsuspectingly playing the harp. For his part, David apparently forgave Saul's first assault, chalking up the attack to Saul's madness. But Saul was not finished and decided to get rid of David more indirectly. He made him a commander of a thousand, sending him from his court in the hope that the Philistines would do his work for him (18:13–16, 21). Saul used the spear like a Philistine, and wanted to use the Philistines themselves.

When a frontal assault failed, Saul turned to more seductive methods. He first offered his daughter Merab, apparently as a reward for David's service, but this offer was withdrawn when David protested that he was unworthy to be the king's son-in-law (18:17–19). When Saul realized that Michal was in love with David, he decided to use her as a "snare" (18:21), a word often used to describe entrapments to idolatry. Saul apparently hoped that David would be undone by a woman, which, much later, turned out to be a sound intuition. Saul hoped Michal would be a snare in one of two senses: Either David would be killed trying to win Michal, or once they were married Michal would draw David away from the Lord. Saul may have had some basis for this hope for Michal had household idols (19:13). If David were enticed to turn from Yahweh, the Lord would withdraw from him, and the contest between Saul and David would be evened out with no inconvenient imbalances produced by a divine "third party." Saul had become a serpent, seeking to employ the bride as a snare; but David had already fought and defeated a serpent.

Saul's offer of two daughters to David is linked to the Jacob-David typology discussed at the beginning of this chapter. At this point, however, Saul was filling the slot of Laban rather than of Isaac. The parallel plots may be outlined as follows:

Jacob (Genesis)	David (1 Samuel)
hated by Esau, 27:41	hostility from brothers, 17:28
leaves father's house, 28:5	leaves father's house, 16:22
in Laban's house	in Saul's house
prospers, 30:43	prospers, 18:5, 14, 29
Rachel offered/withdrawn, 29:13–31	Merab offered/withdrawn, 18:17–19
becomes son-in-law, 29:21–30	becomes son-in-law, 18:20–29

David, like Jacob, was learning wisdom as he struggled with his relatives.

Saul demanded a hundred Philistine foreskins as dowry for Michal, and this picks up on an implicit theme that has been running through several chapters. Saul was at Gilgal on both occasions when Samuel announced that he was being cut off from the kingdom (13:8–14; 15:12, 34). Gilgal was the place where Israel was circumcised when they entered the land, and this circumcision removed the reproach of Egypt from them (Josh. 5:1–9). Saul's sin brought reproach on Israel again, as did the continuing threat of the Philistines. For David, the problem was that an "uncircumcised Philistine" could mock the living God without being challenged. Saul did nothing to remove that reproach, but David did, not only by defeating Goliath but by circumcising the Philistines. Again, the hero kills and strips the enemy to win the bride and to renew the land.

ESCAPE FROM HARAN, 1 SAMUEL 19-20
These chapters describe the beginning of David's life as a refugee and outlaw, and as this story opens the language of hiding, escape, deceit and flight becomes prominent in the repeated use of the verbs "hide" (19:2), "elude" (19:10), and "escape" (19:10, 11, 12, 17). David exercised godly wisdom in avoiding an all-out confrontation

with his "father," which would have been disastrous no matter who "won." As noted above, Saul was like a Laban toward David, and this connection with Jacob is even more prominent in chapter 19. Connections with the exodus are also evident, and crucial for understanding the theology of this section of 1 Samuel. Like Israel before him, David escaped from a murderous king (another Pharaoh), fled into the wilderness, and later fought against the Amalekites before returning to the land to take control.

These chapters also trace the continuing decline of Saul. David had acted "wisely," and according to Proverbs 14:35, a king takes delight in a wise servant. Initially, Saul did; not long before, he was sending messengers to David to say "the king delights in you" (18:22). Even then it was a cover for his hostility, but his hostility became more and more open as he sent his servants to kill David (19:1). Saul was also deliberately trying to separate David and Jonathan. He knew of their attachment to each other and attacked Jonathan as a co-conspirator with David. Saul's whole world was turned upside down. While David was out fighting Philistines, Saul stayed behind, though he was made king precisely to fight Philistines. Ironically, though he did not go out onto the battlefield to fight, he made his house a battlefield. He spent his days sitting in his house with that spear in his hand, frothing himself into a frenzy of mimetic rivalry with David. Because Saul did not obediently fight God's enemies, he could not be at peace at home. David, however, knew that there was a time for war and a time for singing. And because he did his fighting on the field, when the Lord required, he could also rest and worship when God gave him victory.

Despite his father's pressure, Jonathan remained loyal to the covenant he made with David. As noted at the outset of this chapter, Jonathan was a wonderful example of sacrificial discipleship, for he gave up everything to attach himself to the Lord's anointed. He treated his father as an enemy and gave up his own position and future out of love for David. And, out of love, Jonathan attempted to repair David's relationship with Saul (19:1–7). He arranged for a meeting with Saul to dissuade him from pursuing David and hid David in the field so that he would be able to overhear the conversation for himself. Jonathan's plan was to stand "at the hand of" his father (v. 3), a phrase that elsewhere describes the position of a highly placed and trusted adviser (1 Chr. 18:17; Neh. 11:24). Jonathan served as intermediary for David for David's sake; but he also believed that reconciliation with David was in his father's best interests. He was not merely acting as a friend, but as a royal counselor.

In speaking to Saul, Jonathan used the word "sin" several times (19:4–5) and specifically warned Saul that he was "sinning against innocent blood" by trying to put David to death without cause. Deuteronomy 19:10–13 required that anyone who shed innocent blood by deliberate and planned murder be put to death to "purge the blood of the innocent from Israel." From Jonathan's perspective, Saul was setting himself up as an object of vengeance if he continued to attack David. Jonathan also reminded Saul of the service that David had done, especially his victory over Goliath (19:5). Ironically, this was precisely the incident that made Saul so insanely jealous. Jonathan reminded Saul that through David the Lord brought "great deliverance for all Israel," the same phrase Saul used when he refused to put his opponents to death because "the Lord has accomplished a great deliverance in Israel" (11:13). Jonathan was perhaps reminding his father of his own words, hoping that this would spark some repentance. Saul listened to Jonathan and swore that David would not be killed. Through Jonathan's efforts, David was brought back into the royal house.

The truce lasted only until David won another victory over the Philistines (19:8). Gripped by mimetic rivalry, Saul could not see David as anything but a dangerous opponent who had to be removed. As David played the harp, Saul again tried to pin him to the wall (19:8–10). Saul had sworn in the name of Yahweh that David was safe (19:6), yet he immediately turned back on his oath, showing that he had as much contempt for the name of God as he did for the commandment of God. Again David's success, the faithful service he rendered to the king, became the occasion for hatred and envy. Throughout the story, it is only the *good* things that David did that aroused Saul's hatred. Peter tells us that Christians should expect the same kind of treatment: When we do good, the Sauls of the world reach for their spears.

After his second failure to kill David, Saul sent messengers to his house to watch it, so they could kill David in the morning. During the night, however, Michal deceived the messengers and her father to help David escape through the window (19:11–17).[10] It is again noteworthy that Michal lied in order to protect David. This was no sin, but an act of loyalty to Yahweh and His future king.

There are a number of typological dimensions to this event. David's escape was a kind of Passover. Like the Passover, it was a nighttime deliverance, and David was delivered through the use of a "substitute," the skin of a goat. From this perspective, Saul was in the place of Pharaoh. A more direct connection was with the escape of the spies from Jericho, which was also a kind of Passover. Like Rahab, Michal lied to the king's men, sending them out the wrong way, which allowed the spies to escape through a window (Josh. 2:1–24). This comparison puts Saul in the place of the king of Jericho and also suggests that his "city" was doomed to fall before David, a new Joshua. Further, the teraphim remind us of Rachel (Gen. 31:34–35). Michal, another Rachel, deceived her father with respect to teraphim, and this extends the analogy between Saul and Laban that we have been examining.[11] These further analogies with the Jacob story are summarized below:

[10] It is unlikely that the "teraphim" that Michal used (19:13) were man-sized idols, which would be unusual to have in a house. Even in the temples of the ancient world, the images of the gods were not normally full-sized. Michal apparently arranged the bed covers to make it appear that someone was in bed, with a goats' hair quilt at the head to look like hair, and then set the teraphim beside the bed (the Hebrew preposition can mean "at"), implying that they were set up to assist in healing David of his alleged sickness.

[11] The text places emphasis on the "quilt of goat's hair" (vv. 13, 16), which is not a stray detail but connects this incident with Jacob's deception of Isaac, in which he covered himself with the skin of a kid (Gen. 27:16).

Jacob (Genesis)	David (1 Samuel)
escapes from Laban, 31:17–21	escapes from Saul, 19:12
pursued by Laban, 31:22–23	pursued by Saul, 19:11, 18–24
Rachel lies about teraphim, 31:33–35	Michal lies using teraphim, 19:13–16
Laban asks why he was deceived, 31:27	Saul asks why he was deceived, 19:17

Jonathan and Michal both protected David, but behind them was the work of the Spirit of God. In the following episode, the Spirit came to the foreground as David's Advocate and Protector, the Paraclete. After escaping from Saul, David went to Samuel at Ramah, and then both escaped to Naioth (19:18). "Naioth" means "dwellings" and may not be a place name but a reference to a prophetic community over which Samuel presided. Saul, again, was not content to let David go. He sent three groups of servants, but in each case, they were caught up in the spiritual worship of the prophets and did not fulfill Saul's instructions.

Eventually, Saul decided to go himself and first headed toward Ramah (19:22). This was not the first time Saul had been on the road to Ramah. He went to Ramah to consult with Samuel about his father's donkeys, and this second trip to Ramah was similar in many respects to the first: In both cases, Saul stopped and asked where Samuel could be found, and in both cases it was close to a well (9:11; 19:22). When he left Ramah after being anointed, he came upon a company of the prophets (10:5; 19:20), and in that case as in this, he was gripped by the Spirit (10:6, 9–10; 19:23). In both cases he prophesied (10:10; 19:23–24), and in both cases, the same question was asked, "Is Saul among the prophets?" (10:10–12; 19:24).

But how different this encounter with the Spirit![12] In this second visit to Ramah, he was approaching Samuel with intentions of murder, not to honor his father but further to violate the word

---

[12] There is an interesting variation in terminology that describes the activity of the Spirit. In chapter 10, the Spirit "came upon" Saul, and the verb often means "succeed." But here, the Spirit merely "was" on Saul.

of his "father." In the first incident at Ramah, Saul's prophesying confirmed his status as king-designate, showing that he had been transformed by the Spirit into a "new man." Here, his prophesying confirmed Samuel's judgment against Saul, for his robe is stripped from him (19:24). Is Saul among the prophets? The last time this question was asked, the answer was Yes. Clearly, Saul had abandoned the prophets. The Spirit that departed from him had become his enemy. Because the Spirit no longer "clothed" him, he was left naked.

The story of David's final departure from Saul's house is one of the longest chapters in 1 Samuel, and length is often an indicator of importance. Structurally, this is the final subsection of this part of 1 Samuel, which began with David's entry into Saul's service. It thus brought to an end this phase of David's life and work. He had undergone a testing by fire in his father's house, and he was ready to take over leadership of his own band, the seed and root of a renewed Israel.

This chapter also brings to an end the story of Jonathan, who has been a prominent figure in the story since chapter 14. Jonathan was the first "son of the king" whose glory shone by contrast with Saul, and in that way he foreshadowed David, the "son of the king" who would replace the king. As noted above, the typology of 1 Samuel runs through the "replacement" theme again and again. Though Jonathan did not lose his place due to his own sin, he was removed, as Cain, Ishmael, and Esau were. Unlike Cain and Esau, however, he gave up his position willingly; Jonathan was an anti-Cain and an anti-Esau, who willingly did homage to Abel/Jacob. Significantly, much of this episode took place in a "field" (20:5, 11, 24), the same location where Cain killed Abel (Gen. 4:8). The anti-Cain helped a new Abel escape from the real Cain, king Saul.[13]

---

[13] Structurally, the sections of the chapter are marked by changes in setting:

A	Jonathan and David, somewhere near the palace, vv. 1–11a	
B		Jonathan and David in the field, vv. 11b–23
A'	Saul and Jonathan at new moon feast, vv. 24–34	
B'	Jonathan and David in the field, vv. 35–42	

David's plea to Jonathan was like a formal protest before a member of the court. David was willing to consider the possibility that he had sinned, but whatever the reason, David knew for sure now that Saul was still trying to kill him. Jonathan denied that David was in danger. He did not want to believe that his father was capable of swearing in the Lord's name and then turning back on his oath. Jonathan's statement in 20:2 ("It is not so") echoed the words of the people when Saul intended to kill Jonathan (14:45). The allusion is ironic: Jonathan should well know how murderous his father could be, for he himself was nearly a victim. David's plan, therefore, was not so much an effort to gauge Saul's attitude as an effort to persuade Jonathan.

David proposed a plan involving a new moon feast (v. 5). The fact that this is a two-day feast meant that David's farewell to Jonathan took place on the "third day," which is repeated throughout the passage (v. 5, 12, 19). David fled from the house of Saul on the "third day," a day of transitions and resurrections. This was the first resurrection, but not the last, for David. David told Jonathan to let Saul know that he was at home, and this excuse might well have been intended to provoke Saul. Elsewhere, kings were proclaimed king at feasts (2 Sam. 15:7ff; 1 Kgs. 1:5–10). Though David did not intend to foment a revolt, he knew that Saul would put the worst possible construction on his every action. The last time David was at a sacrificial meal with his brothers, he was anointed king, something that Saul had perhaps discovered in the meantime. He hoped that Saul's suspicions would be provoked by news that he was back in Bethlehem and convince Jonathan that Saul intended harm.

David pled for *hesed,* or "covenant loyalty," at the beginning of the chapter, asking Jonathan to be loyal to the covenant they had made earlier. In that earlier covenant, Jonathan, as the superior to David, was the initiator, but as they parted Jonathan pled for *hesed* from David (vv. 14–15), not only for himself but also for his house. He knew that David's enemies would be cut off, and he would find out in the next day that his father was David's main enemy (vv. 15–16).

Although Jonathan gave up His own position, he secured a future for his house by allying with David. Jonathan's plea for faithfulness was not just a plea for personal kindness. It was another acknowledgment that the kingdom was being transferred.

On the first day of the feast, Saul suspected that David was absent because he was ceremonially unclean, but on the second day Jonathan told him the lie about David going to the annual feast. Enraged, Saul referred to David with evident contempt as a "son of Jesse" (vv. 27, 30),[14] a sign that he no longer considered David his own son. Indeed, he even called David a "son of death" (20:31). Jonathan's story had the desired effect of provoking Saul, which proved to Jonathan that Saul still wanted to kill David. Saul's attack, however, was not directed against David himself but against Jonathan, and he threw his spear at Jonathan, as he had at David. Jonathan loved David as himself and suffered the same persecution from his father. If Saul hated and persecuted the master, he would also hate and persecute the disciple. Jonathan himself becomes angry at his father, for David's sake. Saul thinks that Jonathan has shamed himself, but Jonathan thinks only of the shame and dishonor that Saul has done to David.

The Bible, usually so succinct, tells about the parting of Jonathan and David in considerable detail (vv. 35–42), and the scene lingers on the page and in the mind. Two sons of Saul, twins in their devotion to Yahweh and in their courage, separated. Even in this last major scene, the character of Jonathan glows; he returned to his father's doomed house, virtually disappearing from the text, not thinking equality with David something to be grasped but making himself of no account and leaving the stage to another son of Saul.

---

[14] At another level, Saul paid an unintentional compliment to David by calling him "son of Jesse." Jesse, after all, was a member of the royal tribe of Judah and the grandson of Boaz (Ruth 4:21–22), whose name means "strength" and whose demeanor in the book of Ruth was royal through and through.

CHAPTERFIVE
1 SAMUEL 21–26[1]

IN THE WILDERNESS

The last section of 1 Samuel ended with David's "exodus," his escape from the house of a hostile king. Before he came into the "promised land" and began to rule, however, he had to go through a wilderness experience. In Exodus and Numbers, the wilderness was a place of trial, but more particularly a place of death. The Israel that left Egypt died and a new Israel came into being before the conquest. David's sojourn in the wilderness resembled Israel's in a number of respects:

Israel	David (1 Samuel)
pursued by Pharaoh, Exod. 14:1–31	pursued by Saul, 23: 15 –29
Yahweh provides manna, Exod. 16:1–21	priest provides bread from tabernacle, 21:1–6
opposed by Edomites, Num. 20:14–21	Doeg the Edomite, 21:7; 22:11–19
Ammonites and Moabites give no bread or water, Deut. 23:3–4	Nabal gives no bread or water, 25:11

David, like Israel, passed through the realm of death before entering the land to take the throne.

Typologically, David's wilderness period points forward to Jesus' sufferings. As noted several times above, 1 Samuel draws attention to similarities between David and Joseph, both of whom

---

[1] Chapter 21 starts a new section of 1 Samuel, one that stretches to chapter 27. These chapters fall out rather nicely as a chiastic pattern:
  A   The priests at Nob, chs. 21–22
    B   Deliverance of Keilah, ch. 23
      C   David spares Saul's life, ch. 24
        D David and Nabal, ch. 25
      C' David spares Saul's life, ch. 26
  A/B' David moves to Gath for his protection, ch. 27
The connections between the beginning and end sections (A and A/B') need further comment. In both, David fought against Israel's enemies and on behalf of the cities of Israel, and in both, David had an encounter with Achish, king of Gath, in which he deceived the king.

rose to great prominence only after great trials and afflictions, and in this respect both foreshadowed the life of Jesus. Like Jesus, David was opposed by the established rulers of Israel. Like Jesus, David gathered "disciples" who formed the foundation of a new nation. Like Jesus, David was a man of sorrows and acquainted with grief.

As noted in the previous chapter, David's training for the leadership of Israel involved the reversal of the three sins of Saul by showing faithfulness in the garden, the land, and the world. In chapters 16–20, David struggled with his "father" Saul, showing wisdom and prospering while being persecuted by one in authority over him. Once David left Saul's house, their relationship shifted significantly. David was no longer subordinate to Saul in a direct way; with his growing band of warriors, he was becoming much more an equal. David's farewell to Jonathan in the "field" thus opened a new phase of his experience, one that focused on his relations with his "brothers" in the land. But Saul was only one of the brothers that David encountered during his wilderness period. David also dealt with his relatives in Moab (22:3–4), his fellow-Judahite, Nabal (25:2–3), the men of Keilah, a city of Judah (23:10–14; Josh. 15:44), and his cousins, the sons of Zeruiah. More broadly, he had to learn to handle opposition from fellow Israelites. While he was in Saul's house, everyone loved him (18:5, 16), but as soon as he fell out of favor, they searched for opportunities to betray him (23:19; 26:1).

While in Saul's house, David rendered faithful service when Saul was not throwing spears at him and escaped from Saul's presence when he was. In the wilderness, David no longer served Saul, and he was faced with the temptation to use his power against the Lord's anointed. He was tempted to kill his hostile "brother" in the wilderness. But David had learned an important lesson from his elder "brother" Jonathan, and he (generally speaking) treated Saul with the same deference that Jonathan had shown to him. At the same time, David had to restrain the brothers who were allied with him, the six hundred men who gathered to his stronghold. Dealing with fraternal friends and foes prepared David to take the throne of a deeply divided nation and to complete the "revolution of the elites" that Hannah had longed for.

BREAD FROM HEAVEN, 1 SAMUEL 21-22[2]

After fleeing from Saul's house, David came to Nob where the priests were living. These descendants of Eli's house had apparently taken the tabernacle to Nob following the destruction of the Shiloh sanctuary at the battle of Aphek. Though there was no ark in the tabernacle, the rest of the tabernacle was functioning. At least, the shewbread on the golden table was being changed every week, as the law required (1 Sam. 21:6).

When David arrived, Ahimelech the priest came out "trembling" to meet him (21:1). Ahimelech knew that Saul was pursuing David and feared association with him. Earlier, the elders of Bethlehem came out "trembling" when Samuel came to anoint David (16:4). This similarity prepares us to see other correspondences between the two incidents. In chapter 16, David was anointed, and another kind of "coronation" occurred in Nob—not unlike one of the "coronation" signs given to Saul in 1 Samuel 10.

Noting the priests' fear, David attempted to allay them by saying that he was on a secret mission from the king (21:2). Again, David used deceit as a way of avoiding direct conflict with Saul. David accomplished two things with this deception. First, it gave Ahimelech the impression that David was still doing the king's

---

[2] These two chapters clearly form a single unit, which is chiastically arranged:
  A   David and the priests of Nob, 21:1–9
    B   David feigns madness in Gath, 21:10–15
      C   David's movements, 22:1–5
    B'   Saul plots against the priests, 22:6–10
  A'   Saul carries out the ban against Nob, 22:11–23
One of the intriguing effects of this structure is to bring out a parallel between Saul's court and the royal house of Achish of Gath. Though both were at this point hostile to David, the Gentile Philistines at least acknowledge David as "king of the land" (21:11), while Saul viewed him only as "the son of Jesse" (22:7).

business, and thus relieved Ahimelech's fears about helping. Second, David's lie also protected Ahimelech by providing deniability. If Saul showed up and demanded to know why Ahimelech helped David, Ahimelech would be able to plead ignorance: "I thought he was on a mission from you." Of course, things did not turn out that way. David underestimated the lengths to which Saul would go.

David's two questions were syntactically parallel and emphasized the "hand": "What is under your hand? What can you give into my hand?" (v. 3). The emphasis on the hand continues into verse 4, and David later asked if Ahimelech had a spear or sword "under hand," which he needed because he had no weapon in his "hand" (v. 8). This emphasis on the "hand" provides a clue to the significance of this incident. According to the Hebrew phrase, when priests were ordained, they had their hands "filled." During the ritual, there was a literal "filling of the hands," when the flesh of a sacrificial animal was placed in the ordinand's hand as a sign that he could henceforth offer sacrifices and also eat from the sacrificial meat (Exod. 29:19–25; Lev. 8:25–28). In 1 Samuel 21, the repetition of "hand" suggests that something like an ordination was happening. Of course, David was not ordained as a priest, but, as we have seen, there was a priestly aspect to the kingship in Israel. When Saul attended the feast where Samuel anointed him, he received the priestly portion of the sacrifice, and one of the signs that confirmed his appointment was the gift of bread. Similarly, the priests at Nob filled David's hands with bread, a sign that the kingdom was shifting to him.

According to Leviticus 24:5–9, the bread of the presence was changed out on the Sabbath, and thus it is clear that David arrived at Nob on the Sabbath day (1 Sam. 21:6). According to Leviticus, however, this bread was "most holy" food reserved for the priests and had to be eaten in a holy place. Normally, commentators see David's action as an exceptional case, an illustration of the principle one can violate the details of ceremonial law for the sake of charity. But if the priest was bending the ceremonial law for a humanitarian reason, why did David and his men have to be "holy" (v. 5)? David insisted that his men had been "kept from women," a reference to Leviticus 15:18, which informs us that sexual intercourse caused uncleanness. David did not, however, merely say his men were "clean," but that they were "holy," and the two terms are not identical. An Israelite was clean simply by avoiding uncleanness and by washing himself when he became unclean; to become "holy," a man had to undergo a consecration rite. David's statement thus suggests that his men had "consecrated" themselves as part of their preparations for war (see Josh. 3:5; Is. 13:3), putting themselves under something like a Nazirite vow until their holy war was concluded. Because they were consecrated as "temporary priests," David's men were qualified to eat the bread of the sanctuary.

This episode also continues the exodus pattern that has been running as a subtext in 1 Samuel. When Israel escaped from Pharaoh into the wilderness, the Lord provided miraculous bread from heaven. David also received bread from heaven, for the tabernacle was an architectural representation of God's heavenly dwelling. We saw in the last chapter that David was a new Jacob, and we are beginning to see that he was also a new Israel.

David asked for a weapon and was given the sword of Goliath. Saul had been holding a spear almost continually since he turned against David (one imagines him putting it under his pillow at night), and this symbolized the fact that Saul had become a king like the kings of the nations. David also took a Philistine weapon: Did this mean that he, too, was becoming a ruler like the rulers of the Gentiles? No. Instead, the story presents two ways in which the righteous can use the weapons of the wicked. On the one hand, one can use the weapons of the wicked in such a way as to become like them; that was what Saul did, using Philistine weapons as the Philistines did, i.e., to attack David. On the other hand, one can use the weapons of the wicked to fight the Lord's battles, and this was what David did. Just as he used Goliath's sword to decapitate Goliath, so he continued to use Philistine weapons against the Philistines.

From Nob, David traveled to Gath (21:10–15). This seems an odd choice, especially since David fought and killed the hero of Gath and rolled into Gath carrying Goliath's sword. When he went to Gath later and became a vassal to Achish the king of Gath, Saul gave up searching for him (27:1–4). Perhaps David was hoping that Saul would not go into enemy territory to capture him. Whatever David's reasons, Achish's men recognized him, recited part of the song about David, and called him the "king of the land." Though perhaps based on a mistake, the Gentile Philistines showed better insight than Israel's king. Having been recognized, David again acted deceptively, disguising himself as a madman. In part, this deception intended to make him appear harmless before Achish, but it also made him resemble Saul.

Nob was not safe, but neither was Gath. David went to the cave at Adullam, a town between Gath and Bethlehem. Caves are associated in the Bible with death, since caves were used as tombs. When Lot and his daughters thought that the world had come to an end, they went to live in a cave (Gen. 19:30). David had been driven out of Saul's house, from his home and safety. Utterly deprived, he went to live in a cave at Adullam. Though he lived in a tomb, it was not to be permanent. David would rise from this grave.

While David sojourned as an outlaw, like the judge Jephthah (Judg. 11:3), men began gathering to him, forming a core for a new Israel. The fact that four hundred fighting men joined David in the wilderness indicates that a significant portion of the nation had lost confidence in Saul and was turning to David (22:2). David's was a considerable force (compare 13:15), but this blessing brought intense temptation. Some of these men had no doubt been mistreated by Saul and were seeking vengeance, and others were sons of Belial, men who were willing to join up with any militia that seemed capable of creating havoc in Israel. With a growing force, David was tempted to take things into his own hands and overthrow the Lord's anointed. To qualify as leader of Israel, David had to learn how to resist these temptations and continue honoring the Lord's anointed. Among the men that joined David was a seer,

Gad (22:5; see 2 Sam. 24:18; 1 Chr. 29:29), through whom David consulted with the Lord.[3] Not only did Gad provide guidance, but his presence in David's camp indicated that David was taking on the trappings of a king, since a prophet was a royal advisor.

The scene shifts to Saul, holding court (and his spear) beneath a tree on a high place (22:6). It is not a pretty picture. Saul had been giving lands to members of his own tribe (22:7), becoming the kind of king Samuel had warned about (1 Sam. 8:11–18). Saul was appealing to his Benjamite warriors' tribal loyalties, an ugly appeal that contributed to the divisions among the tribes that would break out even more after Saul's death. From Saul's perspective, however, in spite of his gifts, his men were disloyal, since none of them was willing to "uncover his ear" to report on David. In addition to David's four hundred men in the wilderness, there were evidently many within Saul's house and army who had some attachment to David, who at least refused to aid Saul in tracking David down. Saul believed he had figured out what was going on: There was a conspiracy against him (vv. 8, 13). But Saul was now so paranoid that he no longer thought of David as the main conspirator, but Jonathan. Jonathan, he charged, was trying to seize the kingdom and had turned David against him.

Though the men of Israel were not willing to inform on David, Doeg the Edomite was only to happy to offer a report. When Saul learned that the priests had helped David, he ordered his men to destroy them (22:16–17), but Saul's men were faithful to Yahweh and refused. Doeg the Edomite had no such scruples. His attack on the priests was one episode in the lengthy warfare between Israel and Edom. Though Israel was forbidden to "detest the Edomite" (Deut. 23:7), there was centuries-long hostility between the two nations. It began, of course, with Jacob and Esau, Esau being the

---

[3] Gad had the name of one of the tribes of Israel. Intriguingly, as James B. Jordan pointed out to me, Jacob blessed the tribe of Gad by saying that "raiders shall raid him but he shall raid at their heels" (Gen. 49:19). It was thus fitting that a prophet named Gad should appear at the same time that David became a raider in the wilderness.

first of the Edomites. When Israel came out of Egypt, they requested passage through Edom but were denied (Num. 20:14–21). In a number of places, the Edomites were associated with stronger nations. According to Psalm 137:7, the Edomites are pictured as joining in taunting Jerusalem when she fell to Babylon, and in Obadiah 10–14 Edom gloated over Jerusalem's fall and entered the city gate on the day of disaster to loot the city.

Doeg not only killed eighty-five priests but carried out the ban against the city of Nob (v. 19).[4] Saul was unwilling to carry out the ban against the Amalekites, the enemies of Yahweh, but utterly destroyed the Lord's own priests. Having refused to carry out Yahweh's holy war, Saul ended up making holy war against Yahweh. According to the law, the ban could be carried out against an Israelite town if it went astray after other gods (Deut. 13:12–18), but Saul destroyed a city that he thought had been unfaithful to him. Like the kings of the nations, Saul had put himself in the place of God. Terrible as the slaughter of priests was, however, Saul was carrying out the Lord's threat against the house of Eli. Like the Philistine destroying Shiloh, Saul's attack on Nob was a further fulfillment of the prophecies of Samuel and the man of God.

AND HIS OWN DID NOT RECEIVE HIM, 1 SAMUEL 23[5]

One interesting literary feature of these chapters is the repetition of the word "hand." As we have noted, this has already begun in chapters 21–22, and in chapter 23, the word "hand" is used mainly as a figure for power. Saul was hoping that David would be delivered into his hand (v. 7); the men of Keilah planned to give David

---

[4] Possibly, Saul's attack on the Gibeonites took place at about the same time (see 2 Sam. 21:1–14). The Gibeonites were, after all, assistants at the altar (Josh. 9:27), and some may have been stationed in Nob.

[5] This passage can be divided into three sections. Verses 1–13 have to do with Keilah, which is mentioned in verse 1 and again in verse 13. Verse 14 refers to the wilderness of Ziph, where David fled, and this section closes in verse 24a, where Ziph is mentioned for the last time. Then verses 24b–29 describe David's movements from Maon to Engedi (which means "spring of the wild goat").

into Saul's hand (vv. 11–12), but the Lord did not "deliver David into his hand" (v. 14). This theme carries over into the next chapter as well. David had an opportunity to kill Saul, and his men encouraged him by claiming that the Lord had given Saul into his hand, but David refused to stretch out his hand against the Lord's anointed (24:6). Earlier, Saul and David were contrasted by what they held in their hand: Saul held the spear, while David held the harp. The hand that holds the spear cannot grasp the harp player. And eventually, the one holding the spear would be left empty-handed, while the one with the harp would grasp a kingdom.

David was inheriting all the symbols of Israel, as his rag-tag band in the wilderness, now swollen to six hundred (23:13), was being constituted as the remnant of Israel. This is part of the significance of David's inquiry of the Lord, which is emphasized in the Keilah episode. David consulted the Lord twice before going to rescue Keilah from the hand of the Philistines (23:2, 4), and he then inquired of the Lord again to find out if he was in danger in Keilah (23:9–12). Abiathar, the sole survivor of Saul's attack on Nob, had the ephod with him when he escaped to David (v. 6),[6] and the ephod was equivalent to the ark, a sign of the Lord's presence in the midst of Israel. Yahweh had moved camp, from Gibeah of Saul to the wilderness hideout of David. Saul slaughtered eighty-five men wearing the linen ephod, but the ephod that gave divine guidance ended up with David. David's reliance on God's direction contrasted with Saul's reliance on messengers and others who were willing to betray David's whereabouts (vv. 7, 19, 27). The punning on Saul's name continues into this chapter; the verb for "inquires" in verse 2 is *sha'ul*. David is the true "Saul," not only the one asked for but the one who asks the Lord.

[6] Abiathar reached David after David had taken the city of Keilah (23:6), and this meant that the slaughter of the priests by Saul and David's attack on Keilah must have taken place nearly simultaneously. This fact heightens the contrast of David and Saul, for David was attacking Philistines at the same time that Saul was using Gentiles to attack the priests. At the end of 1 Samuel, David's battle with the Amalekites and Saul's final war with Philistia also took place simultaneously.

David was also continuing to be a more successful warrior than Saul. Chapter 23 begins and ends with a Philistine attack. When the Philistines attacked Keilah, David went to help and became the city's savior. Saul, however, gathered his men to march to Keilah only after he learned that David was there (23:7). A Philistine attack was not enough to get Saul out of the house; he was only willing to mobilize against David. There is an ironic twist at the end of the chapter. David was in the wilderness of Maon in the Arabah, in the south. When Saul heard that David was there, he pursued him into the wilderness. David was retreating further into the wilderness and in danger of being boxed in as Saul's men surrounded him (v. 26). At the last moment, Saul received a message that the Philistines were attacking and left the wilderness. Previously, Saul had sent David out to fight Philistines, hoping he would be killed. But in the Arabah, the Lord used the Philistines to *save* David from the hand of Saul.

David was the true Israel and the true savior, but he was a rejected savior and deliverer.[7] The men of Keilah, after being delivered from Philistines, turned on David and were ready to give him over to Saul. Perhaps the men of Keilah retained some loyalty to Saul, or perhaps they were merely afraid of reprisals. The news concerning the slaughter at Nob no doubt made headlines, and the men of Keilah were willing that one man, David, should die to save the city. The Ziphites likewise offered Saul information on David's whereabouts, willing to surrender David into the king's hand (23:19–23).

David responded to these hostilities in the way he responded to Saul's: by flight and escape, but not by attack. And the Lord blessed him for his restraint. Chapter 23 ends with David going to "Engedi." The word "En" or "ein" means "spring" or "eye," and

---

[7] The episode at Keilah is reminiscent of Samson, especially the reference to being locked in the city with "double gates and bars" (v. 7). According to Judges 16:1–3, Samson was in Gaza with a harlot, and the Gazites surrounded the city and planned to ambush Samson. Samson also was a rejected deliverer (Judg. 15:9–13), fighting not only Philistines but enemies in his own nation.

Engedi was a well-watered place in the wilderness, an oasis. David had to flee from Saul and from the fertile promised land, but even in the wilderness the Lord fed him with heavenly bread and brought him to still waters.

OF FOOLS AND KINGS, 1 SAMUEL 24–26[8]

Chapters 24–26 record a series of David's encounters with abusive opponents. Two of the encounters were with Saul (chapters 24, 26), and the central one was with Nabal, a wealthy landowner living near Carmel (chapter 25). In each of these episodes, David was tempted to strike out against his enemies. He had plenty of opportunity and plenty of provocation. Saul was a tyrant who was willing to destroy an entire city of priests on the suspicion that they cooperated with his supposed enemy. If anyone deserved to be overthrown, it was Saul. David, furthermore, was not a private person, but a commander of Saul's army with an armed force of his own. If anyone had the resources and the right to overthrow Saul, it was David. But he did not. Practical considerations entered into his decision, for David was still heavily outnumbered, but the reason David always gave was that Saul was the Lord's anointed. The encounter with Nabal highlights another aspect of these chapters: David came close to taking vengeance against Nabal but was dissuaded

---

[8] The clearest indication of the chiastic arrangement in chapters 21–27 (see above, footnote 1) is the parallel between chapters 24 and 26. Chapter 24 is organized as a basic chiasm, ABA':

    A   Saul enters the cave and David "cuts off" the corner of his robe, vv. 1–7
      B   David confronts Saul, vv. 8–15
    A'   Saul responds and asks David not to "cut off" his descendants, vv. 16–22
The first section is likewise organized chiastically:

    A   Saul enters the cave, 24:3a
      B   David and his men in the cave, 24:3b
        C   David's men urge him to kill Saul, 24:4a
          D   David cuts Saul's robe, is conscience-stricken, 24:4b–5
        C'   David replies to his men, 24:6
      B'   David and men in the cave, 24:7a
    A'   Saul leaves the cave, 24:7b
I have covered chapters 24–26 more briefly in *A House for My Name*, 143–144.

by his beautiful wife Abigail. Her argument, as we shall see below, was that David ought not to ascend to the throne with the blood of his subjects on his hands. As Robert Gordon has pointed out, the avoidance of blood guilt is a central theme of these chapters.[9]

But the theological background to these chapters is deeper. Gordon points out that one-third of the eighty or so uses of the words "good" and "evil" in 1 Samuel are found in chapters 24–26.[10] In several places, the two words are used in combination (24:17; 25:15, 21). This creates a penumbra around the text that forms a link to the "tree of knowledge of good and evil" in Genesis 2–3. From this perspective, the temptations that David faced while in the wilderness were Adamic temptations: He was tempted to impatience, to seize the forbidden fruit and take a juicy bite. One of David's chief qualifications for kingship was the fact that he resisted these temptations. Any leader of the church today must have his senses trained to resist similar temptations—power-grabs, taking advantage of opportunities to embarrass one's opponents, mounting symbolic assaults.

The first encounter took place while David was hiding out in the strongholds of Engedi (24:1). Verse 3 mentions sheepfolds near the cave, which hints that the issue in the chapter has to do with revealing the true shepherd of Israel. While David and his men hide in the recesses, Saul entered the cave to "cover his feet," a euphemism for defecation. The only other place where this euphemism is used is Judges 3:24, where Ehud killed Eglon, king of Moab, while Eglon's servants waited outside the room, thinking that Eglon was "covering his feet" in the cool room. Saul was something of an Eglon, and he came close to being attacked in the cave by an Ehud. Coming into the cave, Saul was doubly exposed. He was separated from his men, since it was unlawful for Israelites to have a toilet in

---

[9] Robert P. Gordon, "David's Rise and Saul's Demise: Narrative Analogy in 1 Samuel 24–26," *Tyndale Bulletin* 31 (1980), 43: "Nabal, no less than Saul, poses the question, Will David incur blood-guilt on his way to the throne?"

[10] Ibid., 48.

the war camp (Deut. 23:12–13). Also, obviously, he was exposed because he was using the toilet. Saul's vulnerability, and the allusion to Ehud, heightens the emphasis on David's restraint.

David was surrounded by a band of self-appointed Ehuds. His men concluded that Saul had been given into his hand (v. 4), citing a promise that the Lord would deliver David's enemy into his hand. No specific promise to this effect is found in 1 Samuel, though perhaps they were applying general promises that the Lord would eliminate the enemies of David. That may be too generous, for it is certainly possible that they made up the promise on the spot to encourage David to slaughter the king. David sharply rebuked his men. The verb translated as "rebuke" in verse 7 is actually much stronger, meaning something like "tear apart." David verbally tore into his men to keep them from tearing into Saul.

David did, however, cut off the edge of Saul's robe. As we have seen earlier, clothing was a sign of office, and tearing the robe was a sign of the kingdom being taken from Saul. The chapter ends with Saul admitting that David would eventually receive the robe (24:20). Saul accepted that David deserved the corner of the robe that he cut off. Because the robe was a sign of office, however, an attack on the robe was an attack on the king himself. After cutting the robe, David realized that even this kind of symbolic attack was a sin.[11] Another dimension emerges when we consider this event in the light of the tearing of Samuel's robe in 1 Samuel 15. There we noted that Saul had torn his "father's" robe, committing the sin of Ham. David did the same, cutting the wing off the robe of his "father." When Ham grasped for his father's robe, he was cut out of his inheritance; when Saul tore Samuel's robe, he lost his kingdom; if David had not repented, he would have faced the same grim future.

But David did repent, and more. When Saul left the cave, David called to him. David, of course, could have remained in the

---

[11] Perhaps this says something about the legitimacy of public demonstrations such as, say, burning a ruler in effigy.

cave with his men. Saul would have eventually discovered that he was missing part of his robe, but he would not have known that David had taken it. Staying in the cave would have been far safer. Going out of the cave meant taking the risk that Saul would call his men to attack David. David's desire for reconciliation did not, however, allow him to stay in the safety of the cave. His love for his enemy was active and bold. Perfect love casts out fear.

David's love was also shrewd, as reflected in the rhetoric of his appeal to Saul (24:9–15). He addressed Saul with respect ("My lord the king") and bowed to the ground. This gesture was an acknowledgment that he was lower than Saul, subordinate and vulnerable to him. David also called him "father." Though this may have been a general term of respect, it would surely remind Saul of their earlier relationship. David, moreover, wisely avoided charging Saul directly and attributed Saul's hostility to "men" who falsely accused David. As we know, Saul's men had in fact been loyal to David, but David was speaking words that would be sweet enough to catch Saul's ear. David also knew that he could do more than talk about his innocence. He had evidence, which he emphasized by repeating the verb "see" (vv. 10, 11), a word associated with judgment in Scripture. David was calling on Saul to judge the visual evidence, the corner of the robe that David still had in his hand. Though cutting the robe was a sin, it also provided proof that David had not harmed Saul, despite having the opportunity to do so.

Not that the speech was all sweetness and light. It included an element of rebuke. In verse 12, he appealed to the Lord to judge, and this doubtless expressed David's confidence that he was in the right. But his faith in the Lord's judgment was the reason David could be patient under affliction. Since he entrusted Himself to the Lord who judges rightly, he did not have to return evil for evil. David could return good for evil in the confidence that Yahweh would vindicate him in the end. David's speech included an implicit warning as well: The Lord would avenge David, so Saul had better watch out. The same note of warning might be intended by the questions in verse 14. David might have meant that Saul was wasting time and resources, since David was nothing more than a dead dog and, even less, a flea on a dead dog. But David might also have implied that Saul should not think that David was nothing: "You may find that you've taken on more than you can handle. I'm no dead dog, no flea."

David's words had a profound effect on Saul. Throughout the last several chapters, Saul implicitly disowned David, pointedly calling him the "son of Jesse" rather than acknowledging him as a son of the king. After David's speech, Saul, weeping, called him "my son" and "David" (24:16). This was not only a sign of renewed personal affection toward David but was a political statement as well: If David was Saul's son, he was again a member of the royal household and legitimately in line for the throne. In fact, Saul explicitly recognized that David would become king (v. 20). This recognition was confirmed by a glance at David's hand: They were not filled with blood but with the corner of the robe, the symbol of royal office. David's hands had been filled with bread and a sword, and were now filled with a clear emblem of the kingdom. As a result of this encounter, David added Saul's endorsement to Jonathan's acknowledgment that he would be Saul's successor. Just as David refused to "cut off" Saul, but only "cut off" his robe, Saul asked him not to "cut off" his seed (24:21).

SAUL'S ALTER EGO, 1 SAMUEL 25

A moving scene it was, but there was no reconciliation. Saul returned to "his home," while David returned to his mountain hideout (24:22). Soon Saul was back chasing David, and the two had a very similar encounter. Before that, however, the lengthy story about David's encounter with Nabal and his wife Abigail intervenes. Saul is mentioned toward the end (v. 44), but otherwise is completely out of the picture. One of the key questions concerning this chapter is its placement in the midst of the story of David's flight from Saul. Historically, it is placed here because this event happened during David's wilderness years, but many events that happened during this period are not recorded at all.

The central placement of 1 Samuel 25 in the structure of these chapters gives us a hint of its significance. With his story nestled between two stories of Saul, Nabal was Saul's "alter ego." Nabal was very rich and feasted like a king (25:2, 36). In the next chapter, Saul confessed that he had acted like a fool (26:21), and Nabal's name means "fool." Though the Hebrew word was not the same, they are close synonyms, and Saul might as well have admitted that he was acting like Nabal. When we look at Nabal's treatment of David, the parallels with Saul become clearer. David had been serving Nabal (v. 7), his men had not insulted Nabal's servants nor stolen anything from them, but instead had been like a wall to Nabal's house and goods (vv. 16–17, 21). David had performed similar service for Saul, but both Nabal and Saul were completely ungrateful and refused to do good in return. Instead, both returned evil for David's good (v. 21). Nabal gave David nothing, contemptuously called him the "son of Jesse," as Saul had been doing, and treated him as a rebel.[12]

The Nabal episode rings further changes on the Jacob-David connection. From this angle, David's flight from Saul's house corresponded to Jacob's flight from Isaac's house, and this places Nabal in the position of Laban. Nabal was a "Calebite," a descendant of the heroic Kenizzite who was incorporated into the tribe of Judah, and that meant David and Nabal were related, as were Jacob and Laban. David cared for Nabal's flocks and herds, as Jacob did for Laban's. Neither Jacob nor David received anything like adequate compensation for their efforts. There may even be a hint of this

---

[12] This is a masterfully written story. Structurally, it works out as a neat chiasm:

A		Samuel dies, v. 1
	B	David comes into Nabal's area, vv. 1–3
		C	Nabal rebuffs David, and David prepares to attack, vv. 4–13
			D	Abigail prepares food for David, vv. 14–19
				E	David and Abigail, vv. 20–35
			D'	Abigail returns home; Nabal dies, vv. 36–38
		C'	David praises God for avenging him, v. 39
	B'	David takes Abigail as wife, vv. 39–43
A'		Saul treats David as dead, v. 44

parallel in Nabal's name, for in Hebrew as in English, "Nabal" is "Laban" spelled backward!

Chapter 25 opens with a notice of Samuel's death (v. 1). Why is this mentioned here? Though not officially high priest, Samuel had been the chief religious leader of Israel for many years. In the Old Testament, the death of the high priest cleansed the land and enabled those who were in cities of refuge to return to their ancestral lands (Num. 35:25). The death of Samuel was theologically parallel; David had been a fugitive in the wilderness, but after Samuel died he entered the land and eventually inherited Nabal's land by marrying the widowed Abigail. This property includes a portion of "Carmel," a place name that means "vineyard, orchard or garden." By the death of the high priest, David reentered the land and the garden.[13] David would not be able to remain in the land, but after the death of Samuel he got a foretaste of what it would be like to live like a king in Judah.

To give this a more psychological spin: Samuel was a father figure for both Saul and David.[14] As noted in chapter 2, Saul was "adopted" into the company of prophets and became a "son of Samuel" at his anointing, and Samuel also guided and advised David. The death of Samuel had two related effects on the contest between Saul and David. First, with the "father" removed, Saul and David began to function more as "brothers." In chapter 24, David was deferential to Saul, feeling conscience-stricken about an assault on his "father's" robe; in chapter 26, David did not address Saul as "father" but treated him more as an equal. Second, the death of Samuel meant that David lacked the prophet's guidance, and this was perhaps one reason for David's near disaster with Nabal.

[13] There's a geographic difficulty. The Massoretic Text says that David was in the wilderness of Paran, while the Septuagint (LXX) says he was in "Maon." If David was truly in the wilderness of Paran, he was rather far away from the other areas associated with his wilderness period, since Paran was in the Sinai peninsula. Still, the MT should be followed rather than the LXX. "Paran" included the Negev at the south and thus was located at the edge of the land, and therefore David could go there to avoid Saul. Also, this was the place where Israel wandered in the wilderness, and the mention of Paran connects David with Israel. Maon and Carmel are far enough south to be within reach of the Negev.

[14] Thanks to James B. Jordan for suggesting this perspective.

If Nabal was an Adam living in Edenic Carmel, this "Adam" had become a fool. "Nabal" means "fool," and Abigail said that his name was appropriate since he was full of "folly" (v. 25; *nebalah*). Further puns on "Nabal" are sprinkled throughout the story. The Hebrew name puns with another of Abigail's descriptions of her husband: He was a "son of Belial" (Heb. *ben-beli'al*), a phrase that includes the consonants of Nabal's name (v. 25). On the morning after his feast, the "wine went out of him," and another pun is hinted at, since the word for "wineskin" is *nebel*; wine poured into Nabal out of a wineskin, and wine poured out of Nabal as if he had become a wineskin. When Abigail told him what had happened, his heart became like a stone (25:37). In Hebrew, "heart" is *leb* and the phrase "as a stone" is *l'aben*, both of which employ consonants from Nabal's name. Further, Nabal was a Calebite (v. 3), which means he was a descendant of Caleb, the spy who faithfully said that the land was Israel's for the taking. This descendant of Caleb was not cut from the same cloth as his illustrious ancestor, and "Calebite" probably also puns on the Hebrew word for "dog" (*keleb*).[15]

Abigail was everything her husband was not. Where he was a Nabal, she was wise (v. 3). She is described in terms that remind us of Rachel, "lovely in form" (cf. Gen. 29:17), and it was no wonder that David-Jacob found her attractive. Interestingly, the word used for "intelligent" was also used of David (18:5, 30). Wisdom is a royal virtue and Abigail was the virtue of a very regal woman. Abigail was a female David, wise and shrewd and bold.

The occasion of David's encounter with Nabal was a sheep-shearing festival in Carmel. Sheep-shearing was accompanied by great feasting (25:36; see 2 Sam. 13:23ff) and would be an ideal time for a rich landholder to extend hospitality to strangers. David made a very humble and polite approach to Nabal. He pronounced peace three times (25:6), reminded Nabal of his service to him (25:7–8), and requested "whatever you find at hand" (25:8). Nabal's response shows that he was indeed "harsh and evil in his dealings."

---

[15] I have discussed the significance of Nabal's canine tendencies in somewhat more detail in "Nabal and His Wine," *Journal of Biblical Literature* 120/3 (2001), 525–528.

David approached Nabal as a "son" (v. 8), yet another allusion to David's relation with Saul and an indication of the respect he was showing to Nabal. Nabal, however, dismissed him as the "son of Jesse." In verse 10, Nabal referred to David as a fugitive from Saul, one of many slaves who have abandoned their masters; ironically, Nabal was the master from whom servants, and even his wife, were going to break away. In a single verse, Nabal managed to use first person pronouns ("I" and "my") eight times (v. 11, in the Heb.). Like a spoiled child, Nabal could only speak of what was his, and we can detect the nasal whine in his voice as he says it: *my* bread, *my* water, *my* meat, *my* shearers, *I* take, *I* slaughter, *I* give, *I* know. It is no accident that Nabal's property was described before the owner was named (v. 2).[16]

Nabal's refusal to help David is part of the exodus typology that we have noted several times. David was in the wilderness like Israel, but, as in the period after the exodus, some refused to help. Israel requested to pass through Edomite territory, but the Edomites did not permit them (Num. 20:14ff), and the Moabites and Ammonites were cursed because they did not meet Israel with food and water as they came up from Egypt (Deut. 23:1–6). By refusing to help the true Israel, Nabal became the moral equivalent of an Edomite, a Moabite, and an Ammonite, excluded from the congregation of Israel.

But Nabal is not really the focus of attention in chapter 25. David is. Uncharacteristically, he reacted to Nabal's insult by launching an attack. He took four hundred men, leaving two hundred behind at the baggage, and went out to destroy Nabal's household (25:13). As he made his way to Carmel he uttered an oath (v. 22): Though refusing to use Nabal's name (as Saul has refused to use David's), he vowed to wipe out every male in the house for an insult (as Saul wiped out the priests at Nob). With Samuel dead, David needed restraint, and Abigail came to fill that role. David was beginning to act like Saul, and he needed a "David" to confront

[16] J. D. Levenson, "1 Samuel 25 as Literature and as History," *Catholic Biblical Quarterly* 40 (1978), 15.

and bring him up short. Fortunately, a "David" would soon be on her way.

When she heard of David's impending attack, Abigail acted quickly and in complete defiance of her husband. Her husband had refused to share "my" food and insulted David, but Abigail took a load of food from Nabal's house and brought a blessing (25:18). Like Rebekah, another heroic woman who defied her husband's wicked plan, Abigail foiled her husband's folly. Whatever we might say about the husband's headship in the home has to include consideration of these passages. These women were great heroes of faith, and they were heroic precisely when they treated their husbands as the fools they were.

Abigail prepared a generous gift of food (v. 18) and sent it on ahead. Like Jacob meeting Esau (with four hundred men! Gen. 32:6), Abigail knew that a gift softens wrath. When Abigail met David, she treated him with great deference and won him over with a shrewd speech reminiscent of David's speech to Saul in chapter 24. She fell on the ground before David (v. 23), as David had to Saul. For a single woman standing before an angry and hungry army of four hundred men, this was an act of considerable courage and cunning. She addressed David with respect, calling him "my lord" in nearly every sentence of the speech. There is a curious twist to this, since "lord" (*'adonai*) is often used of a husband. Implicitly, Abigail was transferring her loyalty from the foolish son of Belial to David. In this, Abigail represented the loyal remnant of Israel, the bride, who was turning from her "fool" of a husband and declaring loyalty to her true master, the true anointed of the Lord, the true Christ.

Abigail's first word was "mine" (v. 24), but instead of asserting her ownership, as her husband had done, she accepted responsibility for her husband's folly and took the blame for the evil treatment that David received (v. 24, cf. v. 28). Knowing Nabal was a moron, it was her duty to prevent him from dealing with anyone from the outside world (25:25). This was a significant opening argument. If Abigail was guilty as she claimed, then David had to carry out his vengeance against her, which would be, to put it mildly, a very difficult thing to do. Further, and more subtly, in the same speech that she admitted that she failed to protect Nabal from his own folly, she was doing *exactly* the same thing for David. David was acting rashly, and she was intervening to save David from his folly.

Abigail went on to argue that it was in David's self-interest to leave off this escapade. She reminded him that he was the future king and that it would be disastrous for his rise to power to be sullied by an attack on Nabal's house (v. 31). If evil was found in him, then he would end up like Saul, abandoned by God and unable to fight the Lord's battles effectively. Related to this, though not explicitly mentioned, was the fact that bloodshed on this scale would provoke resentment and anger against David. He would have difficulty keeping the loyalty of his troops or people if he came to the throne along a trail of blood. When he rose to take the kingdom, moreover, he would suffer grief and a troubled heart if he had killed Nabal and his household for an insult. Again, this would destroy his effectiveness as king: If he was burdened with a bad conscience, he would not rule well. Wise advice from a wise woman: But this last statement goes beyond wisdom and becomes prophecy. What Abigail warned about was exactly what happened with Bathsheba: David removed Uriah as an obstacle and spent the rest of his life virtually paralyzed by guilt. Abigail's words also offer important counsel to any would-be Davids: Do nothing on your way up that will bring you down later.

David had originally pronounced peace on the house of Nabal (v. 6), and after hearing Abigail he reiterated his peace and urged Abigail to go to her house in peace (v. 35). He had taken an oath that he would destroy everyone in Nabal's house that urinated against the wall (v. 22), but after hearing Abigail he took an oath that he *would have* destroyed the house of Nabal *if* Abigail had not intervened. His second oath reversed the first, with a direct allusion to it, and he assured Abigail that he had left off his plan for vengeance.

Soon, however, vengeance was carried out, for Nabal died. The writer tells of Nabal's last hours by emphasizing his heart. Nabal's heart was merry with drink (v. 36), but his merry heart turned into a stone when he was told how close David came to attacking him (v. 37). Nabal the fool was given a heart of stone to replace his heart of flesh, and the Lord killed him ten days later. The message to David was clear: If he refrained from stretching his hand against Saul, the Lord would deal with him as he had dealt with Nabal.

In the flush of this great deliverance, David sinned by taking another wife. Contrary to the law, David was beginning to multiply wives, and by the time he became king in Hebron, he had six sons, each of which had a different mother (2 Sam. 3:2–5). This sin of David had enormous ramifications for Israel's future history. By the time of the Bathsheba episode, David had an ingrained habit of taking whatever woman attracted him and adding her to his collection. He had begun to "take" (25:40, 43; cf 1 Sam. 8:11–18), and why not take Bathsheba also? Further, David's sons all followed his example: Amnon raped Tamar, Absalom started a rebellion that included taking David's harem, and Solomon took one thousand wives and concubines. At the same time that David took Abigail as his wife, Saul took away Michal and gave her to Palti. By doing this, Saul cut off David from the royal household and treated him as dead. After Saul's tearful confession in chapter 24, this is surprising, but the juxtaposition of David taking and losing a wife may indicate that the Lord was punishing David for his polygamy.

WHO IS SAUL'S HELPER? 1 SAMUEL 26

Chapter 26 closely matches chapter 24.[17] In both, David had an opportunity to kill Saul; in both his men urged him to do so, in almost exactly the same words; in both, David refused; in both, David took a token from Saul, which later served as proof of David's

---

[17] Chapter 26 is structured as follows:

    A   Saul pursues David, David seeks out Saul
     B   David and Abishai in the camp
     B' David rebukes Abner
    A' Saul and David converse: Saul-David-Saul-David-Saul

loyalty; in both, David refused to flee but chose to confront Saul; and in both, Saul repented after a certain manner. There are also more subtle situational and verbal echoes between the two stories. In both passages, the Ziphites were involved in directing Saul to David's location (23:19; 26:1). In chapter 24:4, David's men said, "Today the Lord has given your enemy into your hand," a statement that Abishai echoed (26:8). In 24:6, David refused to "stretch out his hand" against Saul because he was the "Lord's anointed," and he protested in the same way to Abishai (26:9). Both 24:14 and 26:20 used the image of "chasing down a single flea."

The similarities are so marked and obvious that even slight differences become significant. One difference is that the first story reports a "chance" encounter in a cave, while in chapter 26 David deliberately sought Saul out and snuck into his camp. David was the "aggressor"; he had been the prey throughout the preceding chapters but for a moment he became the hunter. Another difference was that David's men are not unnamed. A specific soldier, Abishai, urged him to kill the king, an important foreshadowing of the violent exploits of Abishai and the other sons of Zeruiah, most notably Joab. David's ability to control the "brothers" who are with him faced its most severe testings, and its most important failures, in relation to these men. Most importantly chapter 26 focuses less on David's relation to Saul than on David's relation to Abner, the commander-in-chief of Saul's army. Abner was lying next to Saul (v. 5), and when David began to speak, he spoke first to Abner, not to Saul (v. 14).

The text is unusually detailed about the setup of the camp (v. 5). Saul was lying at the center, literally in the "circle," which perhaps refers to some kind of embankment or even rudimentary fortifications. The early chapters of Numbers tell us that the Israelite wilderness camp was organized around the tabernacle in the center, where the divine King of Israel was enthroned above the cherubim. Saul arranged his camp in a similar way, with the important difference that Saul, the Lord's anointed, rather than Yahweh Himself, was at the center. The king was Yahweh's representative and thus was appropriately stationed at the center of the camp. The organization of the camp, and its similarity to Israel's camp in the wilderness, symbolizes what was at stake in this episode. Saul was Yahweh's anointed, and like the Lord's tent, Saul's tent and person were inviolable. To enter the Most Holy Place was a sacrilege, and to attack Saul was a similar sacrilege. David was already anointed and knew that he would someday be in Saul's position in the circle of the camp. The description also suggests a continuation of the Edenic motif. David was being tempted to "seize forbidden fruit." This is perhaps why the spear in the ground and the water jug are emphasized, a tree of knowledge beside the waters of Eden.

Abner was the "son of Ner" and Saul's uncle (compare 1 Sam. 14:50–51 with 1 Chr. 8:33). Abner was therefore older than Saul (by a generation), apparently a venerable soldier. Abner's position as Saul's right-hand man is important for understanding the drama of this incident. Some time before, David had been rising in Saul's service and was known, by some at least, to be the heir apparent to the throne. He seems destined to be the commander of the army, but at present Abner had this position. The parallel between Abner and David is an important feature of the story.

Saul, Abner, and the rest of the men were asleep, and we are told later that the Lord had brought a "deep sleep" on them (v. 12). This is a rare phrase, and one use is in Genesis 2:21, where it describes the sleep that came upon Adam when God built Eve.[18] Given the hints of a garden setting in the story, the "deep sleep" suggests that Saul was an Adam sleeping in the garden, waiting for his "helper" to be revealed. The issue in this passage is, Who is the true "helper fitted to Saul"? Is it Abner or David?

Saul's spear stood beside his head, stuck in the ground (v. 7). Practically, it was nearby so that he could grab it if anyone came into the camp to kill him; though surrounded by three thousand men, paranoid Saul still slept with his spear close at hand. The spear was near his head, a foreshadowing of his eventual death, for

[18] It is also used in Genesis 15:12, when Abram, in a deep sleep, saw the cloud move through the parted sections of the animals.

the Philistines would cut his head off. The spear was the symbol of Saul's oppressive rule. He tried to kill David with it, and his possession of the spear shows that he was like a king of the nations. It was a symbol of his authority and also of his abuse of authority.[19]

Having taken the spear and the water jug, David crossed over opposite the camp of Saul and called to Abner, mocking the commander because of his failure to guard his king. Especially when the king slept, Abner should make sure that the king was guarded, and he deserved to suffer the death penalty for his negligence. "Someone" had been able to sneak into the camp and take the spear and water, and "one of the people" came near to destroy the king (vv. 15–16). This was literally true: Abishai had come into the camp intending to kill Saul. Perhaps David knew that Abishai would behave as he did and arranged the whole drama so that he could bring a charge against Abner. In any case, David challenged Abner with the question, "Who guarded the king?" And the answer was, Not Abner, but David. Who was the helper suited to Saul? Not Abner, but David.

Though David's initial challenge was to Abner, Saul awakened and recognized David's voice. The rest of the chapter records the final exchange between Saul and David. This is the second time that David stood before Saul, the chief magistrate of the land, and for the second time Saul admitted his own guilt and conceded David's innocence. Several details of this conversation are reminiscent of Samuel's confrontation of Saul (1 Sam. 13). Samuel said that Saul had "played the fool" (13:13) and failed to "guard the commandment of Yahweh." In chapter 26, David charged Abner with a failure to guard the king, and Saul admitted his folly. In short, this incident replayed the prediction that Saul would be deprived of the kingdom. Because David had guarded the Lord's anointed, he would soon become the Lord's anointed.

---

[19] Abishai wanted to pin Saul to the ground (v. 8), and he used the same expression that described Saul's attempts to "pin David to the wall." It may well be that Abishai knew about David's escapes, and Abishai was claiming to be a better soldier than Saul, since, unlike the king, he would not have to make two attempts. Pinning Saul to the ground might also appeal to Abishai's sense of eye-for-eye justice.

INTO EGYPT, 1 SAMUEL 27

Throughout the story of David, the story of Jacob has been lurking in the background. At times, the parallels have worked like this: David = Jacob, Saul = Isaac, and Jonathan = Esau's good twin. At other times, the story has been more like this: David = Jacob, Saul = Laban, Michal = Rachel. To this point, whatever the shufflings of other characters, David has always stood in the role of Jacob. And he still plays that role in chapter 27, for near the end of his life, Jacob journeyed to Egypt. Jacob, however, died in Egypt, and so after David has gone into Philistia (related to Egypt, Gen. 10:13–14), he can no longer play the role of the individual Jacob. Instead, the narrative analogy changes; for the remainder of 1 Samuel and into the first half of 2 Samuel, David recapitulates not merely the life of Jacob but the whole history of Israel. In the latter part of 2 Samuel, the David-Jacob connection returns to the foreground.

David's exile also recalls the exile of the ark at the beginning of 1 Samuel, for David was the Lord's anointed going into exile. The return of the ark held out a promise that David would also one day return to the land to be enthroned. Further, as noted above, exile always means death. The Babylonian exile cut Israel off from the land, which was the source of all good to the people of Israel, the source of their life before God. Whenever Israel was in sin, they were punished, but the sentence against Israel, like the sentence against Adam, was always a sentence of death. When Israel sinned, Israel had to die; and if Israel hoped to continue, the only hope was resurrection. Israel underwent a death and resurrection in Egypt, in the wilderness, and later in Babylon. The same happened to the true Israel, David: He went into the grave of exile before he was raised up to return to the land and become king.

After fleeing from Saul for some time, David determined that going to the Philistines was the only way to save himself from Saul. It worked (v. 4). David took six hundred men, with their households, as well as his own household with him. All told, he led a company that probably numbered several thousand people. David's was a large-scale exodus from the land into the land of the Philistines. The Philistines evidently knew what was going on in Israel. They knew something about Saul's madness and that he was occupied with chasing David. In 23:27, the Philistines timed a raid on Israelite territory to be simultaneous with Saul's pursuit of David. This background helps to explain why the Philistines would receive David. Achish had no way of knowing that David had remained loyal to Saul throughout his flight from Saul, and David had no reason to tell him. Achish believed that David was a disaffected Israelite warlord, and David was content to let Achish continue believing that. There may be a reason beyond this as well. Situated on the border with the tribal area of Judah, Gath remained an ally of David and the house of David throughout the history of Israel. In prophetic passages that condemn the cities of Philistia, Gath is absent (Amos 1:6–8; Zech. 9; 2 Sam. 6:10). Several residents of Gath returned from Philistia with David when he became king (e.g., 2 Sam. 15:18ff). 1 Samuel 29:6, 9 indicates that Achish himself was a convert, since he swore in the name of Yahweh. Like Jesus, David was rejected by his own but found a welcome reception among the Gentiles.

Given his large retinue, David's request for a city was reasonable. He claimed that he did not wish to be a burden to Achish (27:5), but he also hoped that living outside of Gath would give him freedom of movement outside the surveillance of Achish. Ziklag, the city given to David, was some twenty-five miles southeast of Gath, in territory that was intended for Judah (Josh. 15:31) or Simeon (Josh. 19:5), but was never conquered. David occupied Ziklag, which later became a part of the inheritance of the kings of Judah.

Even while he was in exile, David was beginning to complete the conquest. Using Ziklag as a base for operations, David launched a number of other attacks on unconquered areas of the land (1 Sam. 27:8).[20] There is an explicit contrast with Saul in the fact that David fought against the Amalekites, and the contrast

---

[20] The Girzites, mentioned here, are otherwise unknown. Possibly the text should read Gizrites, inhabitants of Gezer, a city mentioned in Joshua and in Judges 1:29 as a people that the Ephraimites failed to conquer.

with Saul is also brought out by the fact that David carries on his wars with six hundred men (see 27:2; 13:15). Though he was doing Joshua's work, David's method of this conquest differed from Joshua's. David did not carry out the ban, which would require that he slaughter not only the men and women, but also all the animals. David, by contrast, took animals for plunder. In sparing the animals, David did not break the law; certain territories were under the ban, but the conquest was not to be carried out entirely by the ban. Deuteronomy 20:10–18 required the ban against the Hittites, Amorites, and several others, but not against the Geshurites, for example. David did not leave any women alive for pragmatic reasons, since he did not want Achish to discover where he had been raiding. Verse 9 suggests that he was bringing tribute to Achish, and if he brought women, they might well talk.

As he did in his first visit to Gath, David again deceived Achish by saying that he was raiding Judah and its associated territories (v. 10). This was not an outright lie. Geographically, verse 10 describes areas in the southern regions of Judah that David really did attack. Yet, his words were deliberately ambiguous. When David talked about attacking the "Negev," he did not actually say *whom* he was attacking in the Negev, but he deliberately left the false impression that he was "making himself odious" among Israelites. Achish already believed that David was a traitor to his people, and David fed that impression by giving him deceptive reports. In this way, David maintained the illusion that he was loyal to Achish, while actually demonstrating loyalty to Saul and above all to Yahweh.

Ziklag never became the center of Israel or even of Philistia. But for sixteen months, Ziklag was the center of world history, because it was the place where seeds of a new Israel were germinating. The God who began the "revolution of the elites" with a poor barren woman in the hill country of Ephraim was bringing her hopes to fruition in the land of the Philistines. Who knows in what Ziklags He is at work today?

CHAPTER SIX
1 SAMUEL 28-31[1]

APHEK AGAIN

David proved himself faithful in the house of his father and in the land with his brothers. He did not take vengeance on his hostile father, using deception and escape to avoid confrontation, and he successfully restrained his more violent allies. Beginning in chapter 27, he entered a new zone of responsibility, as he left the land to live among the Philistines in Ziklag. Just as David's farewell to Jonathan (1 Sam. 20) introduced the brother-brother thematic of the following chapters, so David's escape to Philistia (1 Sam. 27) prepares for the concerns of the final chapters of 1 Samuel. When he moved to Ziklag, David had to deal with a new set of temptations and questions, pertaining to his relations with the Gentile world. The temptation in the "field" was fratricide, a temptation to yield to the urgings of his bloodthirsty men by taking up arms against treacherous brothers—Saul, Nabal, and the men of Keilah and Ziph.

David's task in the "world" was twofold: On the one hand, he had to render faithful service to his Philistine benefactor, Achish, while resisting religious and cultural "intermarriage" with the Philistines; he had to resist the temptation to *become* a Philistine, fighting Philistine wars and worshiping Philistine gods. On the other hand, David had to fight hostile Gentiles (Geshurites,

[1] The final section of 1 Samuel begins at chapter 28:3, and the section is unified by its focus on the battle of Mount Gilboa, where Saul died (note the *inclusio* on "Gilboa" in 28:4 and 31:1). There is a basically chiastic arrangement here:

> A   Saul at the witch of Endor: his death predicted, 28:1–25 (vv. 15–19)
> B   David goes out with Philistines and returns to Ziklag, 29:1–30:6
> C   David defeats the Amalekites, 30:7–25
> B'   David returns to Ziklag, 30:26–31
> A'   Saul's death at Gilboa, 31:1–13

David's victory over the Amalekites is at the center of the passage. Saul's loss of the kingdom turned on his treatment of the Amalekites, while one step in David's ascension to the throne was his victory over Amalek.

Girzites, Amalekites, and others). This was a tricky balance, but one that David was shrewd enough to pull off, with a good deal of providential aid from Yahweh. And, just as David's dealings with brothers prepared him for rule over Israel, so David's dealings with Philistines and Amalekites prepared him for his international role as Israel's king. He was shaped into a leader of Israel by training in the garden, the land, and the world.

Clearly, too, these chapters continue the exodus typology that has been so prominent in the account of David's life. Recalling that the Philistines were an Egyptian race (Gen. 10:13–14), we can see that chapter 27 marks the beginning of David's "Egyptian" sojourn, and a number of the features of Israel's Egyptian experience were recapitulated in David:

Israel	David (1 Samuel)
left land because of threat (famine)	left land because of threat (Saul)
accepted warmly by Pharaoh, Gen. 45:16	accepted warmly by Achish, 27:1–3
given Goshen, Gen. 47:1–6	given Ziklag, 27:5–6
Pharaoh converted, Gen. 47:7–12	Achish converted, 29:6
Passover meal, Exod. 12	Saul's counterfeit Passover, 28:24–25
death of firstborn, Exod. 12:29–30	death of Saul, 31:1–13
exodus from Egypt, Exod. 13–14	exodus from Philistia, 2 Sam. 2
fought Amalekites, Exod. 17:8–16	fought Amalekites, 30:1–31

By the end of 1 Samuel, with the firstborn dead and Israel delivered from Egypt, everything is prepared for a new conquest, and a new king.

REBELLION IS AS DIVINATION, 1 SAMUEL 28:1–25

The Philistine crisis had again become severe. They invaded the land, assembling at Aphek (29:1) and then marching to Shunem, some ten to fifteen miles southwest of the sea of Galilee. Apparently, they were attempting to maintain control of the valley of Jezreel, a strategically important valley that cut east-west across the northern portion of the land. As long as the Philistines controlled Jezreel, they would be able to cut off the northern tribes from those to the north, interrupt communications and supplies between the two sections of Israel, and attack both north and south. As judgment for Saul's sins, the Lord was using the Philistines to cut the land in half, in anticipation of the later division of the kingdom after the reign of Solomon. To prevent the Philistines from gaining this advantage, Saul sent Israel to camp on Mount Gilboa, on the opposite side of the Jezreel valley from Shunem (28:4).

Frightened by the Philistine invasion, Saul set off on a quest for guidance. Fear is one of the important themes of the chapter. Saul was afraid (v. 5), the woman he consulted was frightened when Samuel appeared (v. 12), and Saul assured her that she had nothing to fear (v. 13), though Saul himself admitted he was distressed (v. 15). When Samuel told Saul he would die, Saul became "very afraid" (v. 20) and "terrified" (v. 21). Saul's fear had been growing in him since his initial sins (chs. 13–15). When Goliath taunted Israel, Saul and his men were "greatly afraid" and "dismayed" (17:11), and when Saul tried to kill David and failed, he began to fear David (18:12, 29). Faced with another Philistine assault, Saul was again fearful. Courage, especially courage in battle, is a gift of the Spirit, but now that the Spirit had departed, Saul was afraid of everything. The repetition of "fear" and the intensification of the language to "afraid" to "very afraid" to "terrified" shows us the "progression" of sin and unbelief.[2] And a king gripped by fear is not the man you want fighting Israel's battles.

Saul consulted the normal means of guidance. Dreams were often given to kings: The Lord appeared to Solomon in a dream, and Nebuchadnezzar and Pharaoh both had dreams that required

---

[2] Not only does the chapter describe Saul's increasing fear, but in the Hebrew there is a play on the word "fear" and the word "see." "See" is *ra'ah* in Hebrew, and fear is *yarah*, and in certain forms the two words are even closer. A common form of "see" is *yarah*, and the same form of "fear" is virtually the same word. What causes fear throughout the chapter is what people see. Saul "sees" and "fears" (v. 5), and the woman fears when she sees Samuel, and Saul recognizes her fear and asks what she has seen.

interpretation. "Urim" was a priestly method of revelation, and of course prophets were a third means by which the Lord guided His people. Saul thus employed the royal, priestly, and prophetic media for consulting Yahweh. Nothing worked.

And no wonder. No prophets could help, for, as verse 3 reminds us, the chief prophet, Samuel, was already dead. When Saul first became king, he was among the prophets, but since he refused to heed the word of the prophet, he had been cast out and could no longer be found among them. Urim means "lights," and Saul's inability to get priestly guidance shows that he had been deprived of light; as before the battle of Aphek, the lampstand was going out. The lack of priestly guidance was Saul's own fault, for he slaughtered all the priests who might have helped, and the ephod had gone to the side of David. The passage includes yet another ironic twist on the punning with Saul's name. Verse 6 in the Hebrew begins with *yish'al Sha'ul*, which are both variations on the verb "ask." Saul was no longer the one that Israel was asking for, and Saul was no longer able to receive an answer to what he asked. Again, the effects of Saul's persistence in sin issues a warning to Christians, and to Christian leaders in particular; those who reject the word of the Lord will find themselves stumbling here and there without light, without guidance. Like Saul, they may become an unanswered question, a living question mark. *Sha'ul* indeed.

Having exhausted the legitimate means for consulting Yahweh, Saul sought out illegitimate means. Even these were hard to find, because Saul, following the requirements of Torah, had removed the "mediums and spiritists" (v. 3; cf. Lev. 19:31; 20:27; Deut. 18:10).[3] When Saul learned that there was a woman who had escaped his edict, he went to Endor to consult with her. Endor was in the tribal area of Manasseh, and the word means "spring of dwelling" or "spring of generations." The fact that there was a

---

[3] This was a real consultation with Samuel, but the woman was surprised by his appearance (v. 12). This suggests that she was not used to getting the sort of response she gets here.

spring suggests a gardenlike setting, but if this was Eden it was a very fallen Eden.

A number of details of the meeting with the witch are noteworthy. Saul disguised himself by taking off his royal robes (28:8). Like King Lear, he had progressively divested himself of his royal garb, and with it his authority. Saul's consultation further exposed his contempt for the Lord's name. He not only sought guidance from a medium, which violated the law, but he also swore in Yahweh's name that the medium would come to no harm (28:10)—swearing in the Lord's name that he would not obey the Lord's word! When Samuel appeared, the woman described him as a "god." The word is *'elohim*, and it occurs in a number of places in the Old Testament in the sense of "judge" or "ruler" (Exod. 21:6; 22:8; Ps. 82:1).

Samuel was recognized by his robe (1 Sam. 28:14), which marked him as a prophet. Saul also should have been recognized by his robe, but he had taken it off. The last time Samuel's robe was mentioned, Saul tore it, a sign that the kingdom had been torn away (1 Sam. 15:27–28), and he reiterated this message when he appeared at Endor. The Lord was treating Saul as His adversary (28:16), and therefore Samuel could give him no aid. Samuel's reference to Amalek was significant (28:18), for David would soon be fighting the Amalekites. The most devastating news, however, was that Saul and his sons would fall in the coming battle (28:19). There is a link here with the earlier battle with the Philistines, the battle of Aphek (1 Sam. 4); what happened to the priestly house of Eli was about to happen to the royal house of Saul. Intriguingly, Samuel's first and last prophecies were both predictions of disaster on a ruling house. Perhaps this was a message Samuel first heard from his mother (1 Sam. 2:1–10).

Saul had been fasting, perhaps in preparation for the consultation with the dead Samuel. When the medium offered food, he at first refused but eventually accepted it. The emphasis on "listening to the voice" is deliberate and pregnant (28:21–23). Samuel chided Saul for not listening to the voice of the Lord (v. 18), the medium listened to the voice of Saul, she asked him to "listen to the voice of your maidservant" concerning the food (v. 22), and he finally relented and listened to their voice (v. 23). Saul was condemned for not listening to the voice of Yahweh, and then he turned around and listened to the voices of a medium and of his servants. Ultimately the roots of this scene go back to Eden, for Adam was also condemned "listening to the voice" of a woman and accepting the food she offered, rather than listening to the voice of Yahweh (Gen. 3:17).

Saul's meal at the medium's house is a good Old Testament example of a "table of demons," and Saul was there participating in a feast at the house of the dead. Is Saul among the prophets? Not anymore. He was among the witches, feasting at their table. He shared in a counterfeit Passover, a meal of "unleavened" bread (28:24), which, like Passover, took place at night. This Passover was no benefit to him, but it was still preparation for an exodus. During the following day Saul died in battle; the Lord destroyed the "firstborn," Saul, and thereby enabled the true Israel, David, to come up out of Egypt.

DAVID AND THE PHILISTINES, 1 SAMUEL 29:1–11

The focus of attention throughout these final chapters of 1 Samuel is on the Philistine threat and the preparations for Saul's final battle. The Philistine mobilization was mentioned in 28:1–2, and now it is brought back to our attention in 29:1. Though part of the same sequence of events, chapters 28–29 are not in chronological order. We should avoid coming too quickly to the conclusion that events are recorded out of chronological order, but here it is evident from several factors. First, in 28:19, Samuel told Saul that he and his sons would die "tomorrow," so the visit to the witch at Endor happened on the night before the battle of Mount Gilboa (31:1–6). Second, according to 28:4, the Philistines "gathered" and then "came and camped in Shunem," where they were camped when Saul visited the medium. Thus, the night before the battle, the Philistines were already at Shunem. Yet, 29:1 tells us that the Philistines gathered at Aphek, a considerable distance south and west of Shunem and Gilboa. Thus, 29:1 identifies the "gathering place" mentioned in 28:4 as Aphek, and this means that the events at or near Aphek in chapter 29 come before the Philistines marched to Shunem. If chapters 28–29 were in chronological order, then the Philistines must have been at Aphek during the night that Saul is at the medium or on the morning after, but that would contradict 28:4.

In general, then, the sequence of events is:

> Philistines gathered at Aphek, 29:1
>
> David was sent home from Aphek to Ziklag, 30:1
>
> The Philistines arrived at Shunem, 28:1, 4
>
> Saul became fearful and visited the witch at Endor, 28:8–25
>
> On the next day, Saul was killed at the battle of Mount Gilboa, 31:1–13

It is possible that David's victory over the Amalekites was actually simultaneous with Saul's defeat at the hands of the Philistines. This cannot be established with absolute certainty, but it is a plausible account of things. Consider: David left the Philistines at Aphek on what we will call Day 1 and got to Ziklag on Day 3 (the "third day," 30:1). That same day, he went off in pursuit of the Amalekites, found their camp, waited through the night (30:17),[4] and attacked the following morning. After his victory, he returned to Ziklag on the same day, Day 4. Another three-day period is mentioned in 2 Samuel 1:2. On the third day after David's return from slaughtering the Amalekites, an Amalekite arrived at Ziklag to report Saul's death. If we count inclusively, the first day of this three-day period (mentioned in 2 Sam. 1:2) was the day of David's return from defeating the Amalekites and the fourth day after he left Aphek. The third day after his return to Ziklag from fighting the Amalekites was the sixth day after he left the Philistine army at Aphek. Thus, we have the following sequence:

---

[4] The phrase is translated as "from twilight until the evening of the next day," but the word translated as "twilight" elsewhere means "dawn." David stayed the night and attacked early on the morning of the following day.

David	Day	Saul
left Aphek (morning)	1	
	2	Philistines arrived at Shunem?
arrived in Ziklag	3	Philistines arrived at Shunem?
chased down Amalekites		visited the medium of Endor, 28:19
defeated Amalekites	4 (1)	Battle of Mount Gilboa; messenger left Gilboa
returned to Ziklag		
heard of Saul's death	6 (3)	Amalekite slave reports Saul's death

If this chronology is correct (and there is little room for alternative chronologies), a couple of intriguing insights emerge. First, the contrast of David and Saul is considerably sharpened. While David was combating the Amalekites successfully, Saul was falling on his own sword on Mount Gilboa. This chronology also suggests that the whole sequence of events took the better part of a week, in the middle of which David won a great victory and Saul suffered a crushing defeat. The week or seven-day pattern always takes us back to creation. This was the final week of Saul, but a new week began with David taking over leadership of Israel. The death of the old Adam was announced on the sixth day, and a new Adam was on his way to the throne on the seventh day. And the new Adam, the seventh son of Jesse, would bring Sabbath rest to the land.

The reference to Aphek in 29:1 is significant. Philistines and Israelites had already fought once at Aphek, on the day that the priests died and the ark was taken. The reference to Aphek foreshadowed what would happen in this coming battle. At Gilboa, Israel again became Ichabod, deprived of her royal glory. The Lord's promise concerning the priesthood applied equally to the kingship, however: Though he removed Saul, He was at work to raise up a faithful king.

When the Philistine commanders recognized David,[5] they insisted that he be sent back to Ziklag. They were afraid that David

---

[5] Achish was something of a blunderer here. The commanders asked about the "Hebrews" that were among them, apparently not recognizing David. But Achish said, "Oh, that's David, the servant of Saul the king," which was not, shall we say, very rhetorically effective. Achish had something to learn about tact from his Hebrew bodyguard.

and his men would form a fifth column of Israelite warriors within the Philistine army (see 1 Sam. 14:21) and that they would begin to fight for Saul once the battle began (v. 4). David could thereby regain Saul's favor: Philistine heads would be a perfect gift to Saul, and perhaps David could even get Michal back, whom he won with two hundred Philistine foreskins. Hebrews had, after all, betrayed the Philistines once before (cf. 14:21). Achish objected and defended David, three times declaring him guiltless (vv. 3, 6, 9). The commanders were afraid that David would become an adversary (Heb. *satan*), but Achish insisted that he was an angel.[6] Ironically, David had been deceiving Achish during the sixteen months that he had been in Ziklag, yet it was true that David had done nothing to harm Achish. In any case, Achish formed an intriguing contrast to Saul: Achish defended David's loyalty when David was deceiving him, while Saul believed that David was an enemy and rival, though David had done no harm to Saul. Achish made David his "bodyguard for life" (28:2), while Saul dismissed David from his service.[7] Like the Gentile Pilate, Achish pronounced that David innocent, while the Jewish king was sure that David was a traitor and demanded his crucifixion.

Would David have done as the Philistine commanders feared? The answer is surely Yes. Throughout his period in the wilderness, David refused to stretch out his hand against Saul, and he had refused not for tactical or pragmatic reasons, but because Saul was the Lord's anointed. Even after Saul's death, David was defending the "Lord's anointed" (2 Sam. 1:14). Further, joining with the Philistine attack on Israel would have been political suicide. David was close to becoming king, and he knew he would be king,

---

[6] The Shunemite woman would later say that David was "like an angel of God, knowing good and evil" (2 Sam. 14:17), a compliment to David's wisdom, discernment, and good judgment as king. Achish recognized the same royal qualities in David, as the rest of the Philistines did in David's first flight to Gath (1 Sam. 21:11).

[7] The phrase translated as "chief bodyguard" means something like "protector of my head." David had been associated with another "head" from Gath—Goliath's—and this phrase also contributes to the "headship" motif that has come up several times in 1 Samuel.

even if he did not know how close he was. If his last battle before becoming king were a battle against the Israelites, he would have trouble convincing his countrymen that he was suitable successor to Saul. David had difficulty enough as it was, given the divisions within Israel. Being an Israelite, David was required to submit to the Lord's anointed so long as he remained in power. Achish, by contrast, though a believer, did not have to submit to Saul in this way. He could do the Lord's will by attacking and killing Saul, something that David could not do. As with Nabal, David could stand back, defend and protect Saul, while waiting for Yahweh to strike him.

If this was indeed David's intention, his conversation with Achish was full of unnoticed ironies. David responded to the Philistines by saying that he wanted to go out so that Achish could see what he was able to do (28:2). Did he mean that Achish would see what David could do to Saul, or does it mean that Achish would see what he could do to the Philistines? The same ambiguity attaches to David's words in 29:8. David wanted to go out and fight the enemies of "my lord the king." He consistently used this title for Saul (24:8, 10; 26:17–18). The Philistine soldiers were right to suspect that David would "show them" where his true loyalties lay.

David was sent back "in the morning" (29:10–11), a phrase that occurs three times in two verses. We are near the dawning of a new day, after the night of Passover, when Israel would be released from the Philistines and enter into a new covenant.

WAR AGAINST AMALEK, 1 SAMUEL 30:1–31

Though chapter 30 records David's victory over the Amalekites, that story is over by verse 20, and the rest of the chapter is devoted to a strangely detailed account of the distribution of plunder. By its structure, the chapter emphasizes not so much David's military prowess as the gifts he gave. There are, as we shall see, several reasons for this emphasis, but one reason is typological. David won the battle, plundered his enemies, and gave gifts; in this, he foreshadowed Jesus, who won the victory at the cross, plundered the strong man's house, and distributed gifts to His church, preeminently the gift of the Spirit. 1 Samuel 30 would be a good text to preach at Pentecost.

This battle with the Amalekites must be seen in several contexts. Most immediately, David's victory contrasted with Saul's defeat at Gilboa. Threatened by the Philistines, Saul went to the Lord, but He did not respond, and Saul ended up seeking guidance from a medium. Threatened by the Amalekites, David went to the Lord, and the Lord gave direction (30:7–8). David carried out a great slaughter, fighting almost as a one-man army (vv. 17–20). Saul failed not only to carry out the slaughter against the Amalekites (1 Sam. 15), but also failed to defeat the Philistines at Gilboa.

As noted at the outset of this chapter, David's battle with the Amalekites was part of his exodus story, and the exodus background also throws light on the emphasis that the chapter places on plunder. Like the spoils of Egypt, the spoils of Amalek and Philistia became the inheritance of the cities of Judah.[8] With Israel, the exodus and conquest were separated by forty years of wilderness wanderings. With David, these events were telescoped together, so that his battle with the Amalekites corresponded to the various battles that Israel fought before entering the land. In particular, since this was the final battle before David's "invasion" and "conquest," it corresponded to the battles that Israel fought after the death of Aaron, when they began to conquer the Transjordan (Num. 20:22–35). In this sense, David's victory over Amalek was the beginning of a new conquest of the land, and again the emphasis on plunder is appropriate: David won the favor of the elders of Judah by sending plunder to their cities, setting himself up to subdue the land and receive the kingdom.[9]

---

[8] The opposition from David's soldiers fits with the exodus typology. Moses brought Israel from Egypt but was threatened several times by the people (e.g., Num. 14:10). Strikingly, they sought to stone him shortly before the battle with the Amalekites (Exod. 17:4).

[9] David is also being compared to Gideon. He launched a surprise attack on the enemy, and the four hundred men on camels are reminiscent of Judges 7:12 where the Midianites were known for their innumerable camels.

After being sent away from Aphek, David arrived at Ziklag on the third day to find the city burned and the women and children missing (1 Sam. 30:1–6). Attacking defenseless cities was typical Amalekite behavior; when they attacked Israel as they came from Egypt, they focused on the weak and stragglers (Deut. 25:17–19). Like Israel, David had no sooner been delivered from a tight difficulty with the Philistines than he had to fight Amalekites. It is always dangerous to relax after a big victory, after an exodus; there are always Amalekites just around the corner.

Verse 5 specifically mentions that David's wives were taken, but this was already obvious from verse 3. Why repeat this? The emphasis on David's family brings out an analogy between the Amalekite attack and other attacks on the bride and the seed that occur throughout Scripture. Ultimately, the theme goes back to Genesis 3, when the serpent sought to seduce the bride (2 Cor. 11:3) and Adam failed to guard her. In Genesis 3 as elsewhere, the issue was the future of the woman's seed. The serpent sought to "seduce" the bride to raise up seed for himself, and the bride had to be protected because she would give birth to the seed who would bring redemption. With David this was especially true. He did not know it yet, but *the* seed would come from him, and attacking the bride was part of Satan's strategy to prevent this. By immediately going out after the raiders, David showed himself a faithful Adam who rescued the bride and seed and crushed the serpent's head.

In the light of this typology, the emphasis on the "third day" is significant. Jesus, of course, was raised on the third day, and Paul said that this fulfilled the Scriptures (1 Cor. 15:4), but the Scriptures normally brought forward as prophecies of "third day" do not help explain what Paul meant. Paul's point becomes clearer when we recognize that the "third day" was not prophesied in one or two isolated texts but was a frequent motif in the Old Testament. On the third day of creation, dry land emerged and plants sprang from it, our first glimpse of life coming from the ground (Gen. 1:11–12). Abraham and Isaac arrived at Mount Moriah on the third day of their journey, and Isaac died and rose again that day (Gen. 22:4). At Sinai, the Lord came to the mountain on the third day to cut a covenant with Israel (Exod. 19:11, 15–16), and in the rite for cleansing from corpse defilement, the defiled Israelite had to be sprinkled on both the third and the seventh days to be delivered from the living death of uncleanness (Num. 19:12).

In all these passages, a transition from death to life occurred on the third day, but we need to be more specific. Some transitions from death to life occur on the "first" or "eighth" day. Circumcision was administered on the eighth day of an infant boy's life, marking his transition from the world into Israel, and several other rites of cleansing involved an eighth-day washing (e.g., Lev. 15:14, 29). In fulfillment of this, Jesus rose on the day after the Sabbath, the first day, which is also called the eighth day, the beginning of a new week. By contrast with the "eighth day," the "third day" symbolizes a transition from old to new that comes before the end of the old, a transition from life to death in the *middle* of the week. Thus, Christ's resurrection on the third day offers a symbolic theology of history: History is moving toward "Sabbath" or to the "eighth day," just as the first week moved toward Sabbath, but in the middle of this week of history God intervened in Christ to begin His new creation on the "third day."

There is a cluster of three-day periods in these chapters of 1–2 Samuel: David arrived at Ziklag on the third day (30:1), the servant of the Amalekites had been without food or drink for three days (30:12), and David was back in Ziklag for three days before he received word of Saul's death (2 Sam. 1:2). By this repetition, the writer was emphasizing that these events mark a crucial transition, a "resurrection." For instance, David experienced a personal revival. When David discovered what had happened at Ziklag in his absence, he and his men wept until they "had no strength" (v. 4), but then David strengthened himself in the Lord (v. 6). He was revived on the third day, and what a revival it was! David's name is used twenty-five times in chapter 30, four times in verse 21 alone: David smote. David recovered. David brought back. David took sheep and cattle. When the spoil was taken, it was David's spoil (vv. 16–21). Nearly every verse sings the name of David. Suddenly David was everywhere doing everything. Perhaps David had this battle in mind when he wrote, "By the Lord I can run against a troop."

These chapters also record a major transition in the life of Israel. On this same day, David's "third day," Saul died and David emerged victorious and enriched with plunder. In this "Passover," the Egyptian prince, Saul, fell before the Philistines, while the Israelite prince passed through the doorways to inherit the land. Judgment fell on the third day, and because this judgment fell on the wicked king, the whole nation was "raised from the dead." The king is dead; long live the king. Israel has died; long live the new Israel. The large-scale structure of 1–2 Samuel reinforces the importance of these chapters. As explained in chapter 1, they form the structural hinge of the whole of 1–2 Samuel. Everything pivots on the death and resurrection of the king—on the third day.

David, in fact, had already begun to act like a king, and, as we have been led to expect from the earlier chapters, David had a very different conception of what being a king meant than Saul had. When his troops reached the brook Besor, a third of David's men were incapable of going on. They had marched for three days from Aphek to Ziklag, where they found a devastated city, and marched off with little rest to pursue the raiders. When David discovered that two hundred men were exhausted, he did not push them, but left them in charge of gear at the brook (30:9–10). Saul, by contrast, imposed a fast on his men, forcing them to fight despite their exhaustion and hunger, and even threatening to kill Jonathan because he ate some honey (1 Sam. 14). David attacked the Amalekites with only four hundred men, a much smaller force than the Amalekites had (1 Sam. 30:17). David showed himself another Gideon by launching a surprise attack despite being greatly outnumbered (see 1 Sam. 13:15).

When David first set out, he did not know who had raided Ziklag. That information came from an Egyptian he found in the field, having been abandoned by the Amalekites (30:11–15). Before he found out anything about the Egyptian, David gave him bread, water, figs and raisins. In the midst of pursuing an enemy, David stopped to show kindness to a Gentile, again a sharp contrast to Saul's conduct in battle and a glaring contrast with the Amalekites, who had left the Egyptian to starve in the desert. Again, we see the face of Amalek clearly in its brutal treatment of the weak and ailing. David was a thoroughly un-Amalekite leader, nothing like the kings of the nations. And as it turned out, the Egyptian was of enormous help to David, since he had been with the raiders who had attacked the Cherethites (allied with Philistines), Judah, Caleb, and Ziklag (v. 14). Ziklag was the climax of the attack, and perhaps the purpose of the whole raid was to avenge David's attacks on the Amalekites (see 27:8).

Revived by food on the third day, the Egyptian led David to the Amalekite camp, where they were eating, drinking, and dancing. The word for "dancing" is connected to the Hebrew word for a festival (*hag*) and may indicate that the Amalekites are in the midst of a religious celebration, giving thanks to their gods for the conquest of Ziklag. David's victory over the Amalekites was thus also Yahweh's victory over the gods of Amalek. David attacked on the morning after their drunken party, so that they, like Nabal, were destroyed at morning light.

David took spoils from the Amalekites, the same action that caused Saul to lose the kingdom. Why was David not condemned for this? Most obviously, Yahweh had given him no command to carry out the ban against the Amalekites, as He had given to Saul (15:3). David was not required to carry out the ban because he was not yet officially king. In the Old Testament, the ban was always carried out by a ruler of all Israel. Joshua brought the Canaanites under the ban, but after Joshua Saul was the next leader who is commanded to wage *herem* war. Between Joshua and Saul, judges operated in a smaller arena and none of them was ordered to utterly destroy their enemies. Thus, because David was still more a judge than a king, he was not required to destroy Amalek.[10]

Because there was no specific command, David applied the general rules of the Torah regarding plunder, which were given to Israel during their wilderness wanderings. According to Numbers 31:25–31, plunder was divided between those who fought and the rest of the congregation, and then a portion for the Lord was levied from both halves (.2% for warriors and 2% from others). After the Lord's portion was removed, the remainder was distributed evenly. Those who fought received a greater share of spoil, but everyone shared the fruits of victory. In David's application of these rules, the warriors who went to battle and those who stayed with the baggage shared equally (1 Sam. 30:23–24), since, in terms of the distinction from Numbers 31, both of these groups were among those who entered the field for battle. Thus, David's distribution of plunder proved he was a law-keeper. Beyond that, verse 25 says that David made this application of Torah a "statute and ordinance," language normally used for the Lord's laws. As the King of Israel, Yahweh promulgated statutes and ordinances, and David, the Lord's anointed, began to do the same after the battle with the Amalekites. He was acting like a king who had been given the prerogative to legislate. He was a lawmaker as well as a lawkeeper.

Among David's band were "wicked and worthless men" who complained that the men who stayed behind guarding the baggage should get nothing more than their own goods and families. The word for "worthless" is "Belial," which has been used several times already in 1 Samuel. Eli's sons and the men who opposed Saul when he was first announced as king were "sons of Belial." Both the "sons of Belial" and the mention of "baggage" reminds us of 1 Samuel 10:17–27, and this brings out a parallel between the

---

[10] Much of the plunder David collected consisted of goods that had been taken from his people and himself. There is, however, also some plunder from the Amalekite raids on Philistia and Judah (v. 16).

initial revelation of Saul as king and the revelation that David was becoming king. In both cases, the new king faced not only external enemies but divisions and evil men within Israel. In both cases, the new kings acted wisely and firmly toward the "sons of Belial" in their midst. Leaders of the church can expect the same range of attacks and difficulties.

David spread the plunder to thirteen cities or groups of cities in the southern territory of Judah. In part, this was simply a matter of returning goods that the Amalekites had stolen, but David's action was also politically astute. Sooner than he realized, David would one day rule these cities, and he established good relations with them through gift-giving, a common method for forging political and social bonds in the ancient world. In this respect, it is significant that the list of cities culminates with Hebron (v. 31), for that became David's initial base of operations. David was looking more and more like a king, but less and less like the king described by Samuel (1 Sam. 8:11–18). Samuel warned that the kings of Israel would rule by taking. David did the opposite. He established his rule by giving.

PASSOVER, 1 SAMUEL 31:1–13

Before examining 1 Samuel 31, it is necessary to address the question of how it relates to 2 Samuel 1, where an Amalekite offered his own version of Saul's death. Clearly, there are differences between the two accounts. 1 Samuel 31 records nothing at all about the presence of an Amalekite and says that Saul fell on his own sword (31:5). The armor bearer was a witness, and seeing that Saul was dead, immediately fell on his sword. In 2 Samuel 1, however, the Amalekite was on Gilboa, Saul was still alive, and Saul asked the Amalekite to finish him off.

Josephus, among others, attempted to harmonize the two stories. He suggested that Saul fell on his sword but did not quite kill himself ("I'm not dead yet!"). His armor bearer, thinking that Saul was dead, fell on his sword and really did die. While Saul was wallowing around in the throes of death, the Amalekite wandered by and Saul asked him to finish the job. There are several problems with this harmonization. First, according to 1 Samuel 31:4, Saul did not want the Philistines to kill him because he did not want to become sport for the "uncircumcised." Why, then, would Saul ask an Amalekite to kill him? Further, the Amalekite claimed that he found Saul "leaning on the sword," an odd description if Saul had already made one attempt to kill himself. 2 Samuel 1:6 is also suspicious for the Amalekite said that he happened on Gilboa "by chance." How does one "happen" upon a battle?

The other option is to conclude that the Amalekite lied. Of course, he did not lie about everything. He knew that Saul was dead and he had Saul's crown and arm band as proof (2 Sam. 1:10). But he lied about the manner of Saul's death. According to this interpretation, Saul died as described in 1 Samuel 31, by his own hand, but then the Amalekite came on the body while doing a bit of post-battle scavenging. 31:8 tells us that the Philistines did not strip the bodies until the day after the battle, so there was plenty of time for a bold and shameless Amalekite to take what he could find from the field—and this was one bold and shameless Amalekite. If the Amalekite lied, what was his motivation? No doubt, he hoped to be rewarded by David. It was well known that Saul had been persecuting David, and it was widely assumed, by Achish for example, that David was responding in kind. The Amalekite expected David to rejoice at the news that his rival was dead. Of course, he got things badly wrong and was convicted out of his own mouth.

Saul fell in the battle of *Mount* Gilboa. Mountains were associated with worship in the Bible and ancient world. Normally, temples were built on high places and they were always symbolically high places. Saul was punctured by arrows, his belly was split open with a sword, he was beheaded, and finally he was burned. The sequence of events in Saul's demise suggests a sacrifice and fits with the idea, mooted above, that Saul's death was a kind of Passover. Saul died and David took his place, and this process of sacrifice and renewal brought renewal to all Israel. Saul's death removed the curse from the land and made way for blessing, just as the death of a murderer cleansed the land and renewed it.

A couple of earlier stories come into play in the story of Saul's death. As noted several times already, this battle recapitulated the battle of Aphek.[11] The parallel between the first and last battles of 1 Samuel suggests something about the structure of 1–2 Samuel. Though part of a larger literary structure that includes 2 Samuel, 1 Samuel has its own internal structure, beginning and ending with battles in which a leader dies with his sons. One detail further strengthens the link with Aphek. Eli died by "falling" off his chair, and the word "fall" is used repeatedly in chapter 31: Saul fell on his sword (v. 4), the armor bearer followed Saul's example (v. 5), and verse 8 tells us that Saul and his sons were "fallen" on Mount Gilboa. In the next chapter, David's "song of the bow" begins and ends with the phrase "How have the mighty fallen" (2 Sam. 1:19, 27). This was Saul's final fall, and it made him look a lot like Eli.

Saul's death is also reminiscent of the death of Abimelech, the first king of Israel (Judg. 9). When Abimelech attacked the tower at the center of Thebez, a woman dropped a millstone on his head, crushing his skull. Abimelech asked his armor bearer to run him through so that the word would not spread that Abimelech had been killed by a woman (9:54), just as Saul asked his armor bearer to kill him to prevent an uncircumcised Philistine from getting to him. It is ironic that Saul should end like Abimelech. His first battle against the Ammonites showed that he was a potential Gideon, but he ended his life like Gideon's wayward son, Abimelech.

Interestingly, Saul's armor bearer refused to kill him, unlike Abimelech's armor bearer, who seemed all too ready to finish off his

---

[11] A ruler with three helpers is a very common pattern in the Bible. We learn at the end of 2 Samuel that while David was king, he had three mighty men who were particularly close to him. Jesus had Peter, James, and John. The ruler and his four close aids are like the four corners of a house, and the death of all of them at Gilboa shows that the house of Saul was being destroyed. When the foundation stones crumble, the whole house cannot be far behind.

king. Like Macbeth in the final scenes of Shakespeare's play, Saul barked out orders but no one listened; he refused to listen to the word of Yahweh, and in the end no one listened to him. In the armor bearer's refusal, moreover, we see a snapshot of the whole story of David and Saul. David was Saul's original armor bearer (16:21), and throughout David's dealings with the king, he steadfastly refused to run Saul through, despite provocation and opportunity. Saul decided to destroy himself, which again provides a perspective on Saul's whole decline. Though he found many different people to blame, Saul was thoroughly self-destroyed.

The extent of the Philistine victory can be gauged in a number of ways (vv. 1, 3). Saul's body was still around the next day when the Philistines plundered the corpses (v. 7). Normally, protecting a fallen fellow-warrior was an essential demand of honor in battle, and protecting the body of the king would have been a high priority. Homer's *Iliad* has dozens of scenes where a hero falls, and the whole army gathers around his body to protect it. Saul had no such help. Either there were no Israelites left to give him a decent burial, or they were all scared or they did not care enough for their king to prevent his body from being desecrated. Saul had become completely isolated from his army and died completely alone. Verse 7 further tells us that the Philistines came in and took over cities that belonged to Israel. According to 1 Samuel 9:16, Saul was chosen king because of the Philistine threat (see 7:14). After forty years of Saul's rule, Israel was right back where they were when Saul began. In Joshua's day, Israel destroyed the Canaanite peoples but retained their cities and lived in them. When the Philistines did the same to Israel, a reverse-conquest was taking place.

When the Philistines plundered the next morning, they found more than they had hoped: Saul and his sons. While David was plundering Amalekites and sending gifts to men, Saul was being plundered. The Philistines cut off Saul's head, another of many head wounds in the Bible. Within 1 Samuel, both Dagon and Goliath have had their heads removed, and there are several additional decapitations in 2 Samuel. Saul's head was cut off because he had become a Satan, a false accuser and a persecutor of the true Israel, David. One is tempted to wax proverbial: Live like a Philistine, die like a Philistine; use your spear like Goliath, lose your head like Goliath. Saul did not, however, die from a head wound but from a belly wound.[12] This too becomes a theme in 2 Samuel.

Saul's weapons were taken to Philistia and went on a tour of the land, so that the Philistines could display the trophies of war. Saul's weapons, like the ark earlier, were put in a Philistine temple, this time the temple of Ashtaroth (31:10). The "gospel" of Saul's demise was carried to all the houses of the Philistines' idols. Of course, the Philistines were not merely celebrating a military victory. As in the battle of Aphek, they were making a theological statement: The gods of Philistia had triumphed over the God of Israel. Saul had been the bearer of the Spirit, the anointed of the Lord, who had fought against the Philistines and other enemies of Israel. He was the bearer of the Lord's presence, like the ark, but the Lord had departed from him. With the fall of Saul and the capture of his armor, the glory has departed from Israel. Israel was again Ichabod.

The Philistines exposed Saul's body on the walls of Beth-shan (v. 10), left to be devoured by birds and beasts of prey, one of the curses of Deuteronomy (28:26). To prevent further desecration of the Lord's anointed, men of Jabesh-gilead came to save the body. These were the people first delivered by Saul, and they were still grateful to Saul (1 Sam. 11). The reference to Jabesh-gilead brings up a reminder of the glory of Saul's early reign, a reminder of how the "mighty have fallen."

After the bodies were burned, the bones were buried under a tamarisk tree. The last time we saw Saul under a tamarisk tree, he was holding a spear in his hand and complaining that everyone

---

[12] The Septuagint (LXX) of 31:3 says that the arrows wounded Saul "under the ribs." Even though this has no basis in the Hebrew Massoretic Text, the fact that Saul fell on his sword indicates that he was wounded in the belly.

was conspiring with David (22:6). The place where he exercised his paranoid, self-destructive rule was the place where his body was buried; he ruled with a spear in his hand, and he died by the sword. Doubtless, the men of Jabesh-gilead intended to honor their king. They buried him beneath a tree because trees were understood as ladders to heaven. A grave beneath a tree was a fitting symbol for a king who once stood head and shoulders above Israel, seeming to connect heaven and earth, but who was now cut down by the Philistines.

CHAPTER SEVEN
2 SAMUEL 1–4[1]

THE HOUSE OF DAVID AND THE HOUSE OF SAUL

The "revolution of the elites" that Hannah hoped for was accomplished in phases. The priests of Israel had been removed, and the Lord was working to raise up a faithful priest. Judges had been replaced by a king, and now the first king was being replaced by David, a man thoroughly trained for his office. He had learned obedience by what he suffered, for suffering in righteousness was David's path to glory and kingship. Saul, importantly, never went through this "death" prior to becoming king; he was a king of the earth, earthy, but David had been through death and back. As noted above, this contrast of two types of royalty is rooted in Genesis, where Benjamin was simply declared the royal tribe (Gen. 35:9–18) while Judah won approval as king by his willingness to die for the sake of Benjamin and out of respect for his father (Gen. 44:18–34; 49:8–12). David had been prepared by passing tests in the garden, the field, and the world. He proved his wisdom with allies and enemies in Saul's house, his patience with his brothers in the wilderness, and his service to his Gentile master in Philistia. In the early chapters of 2 Samuel, David operated in each of these zones once again, this time as king:

---

[1] Dorsey (*The Literary Structure of the Old Testament*, 133) offers this chiastic outline of these chapters:

A		David executes Saul's "murderer," 1:1-16
	B	David's lament over Saul and Jonathan, 1:17-27
	C	War between David's house and Saul's, 2:1-3:1 (Abner/Asahel)
	D	David's household, 3:2-5
	C'	Abner/Joab, 3:6-30
	B'	David's lament for Abner, 3:31-39
A'		David executes Ish-bosheth's murderers, 4:1-12

Environment	Task (2 Samuel)	Ally	Enemy
Garden	establish ark in Jerusalem, 6:1–19	Obed-edom	Michal
Land	reunite tribes of Israel, chs. 2–4	Joab/Abner	Ish-bosheth
World	secure Israel, 5:6–25; 8:1–18	Hiram of Tyre	Philistines and others

When we evaluate David's performance in each of these areas, we must judge it mixed. In chapters 1–4, the main issues have to do with the "land," with relations with "brothers" in Israel and Judah. David had to build the foundations of his kingdom, and within this large effect there were two subordinate goals. One issue was continuity with the reign of Saul. Throughout 1 Samuel, David had remained loyal to Saul, refusing to return evil for evil, and David continued this attitude toward Saul's house even after he had achieved the throne. He did not gloat, made no effort to use his power to settle scores, and did not remove Saul's house because they posed a political threat. In fact, chapters 1–4 begin and end with David defending the house of Saul: He executed the Amalekite who claimed to have killed Saul (1:14–16), and he executed Rechab and Baanah, who assassinated Ish-bosheth (4:9–12).

The other related issue had to do with the internal workings of David's house and administration. Much of what David did was very wise, but two main failures haunted his reign: Joab and polygamy. Joab was a violent, vengeful man, and David failed to deal with him firmly; though David was gentle with the enemies among his "brother" Israelites, he failed to restrain the brothers who were allied with him. Polygamy is highlighted by the structure of chapters 1–4: At the center of the passage is a list of the sons of David who were born to David at Hebron (3:1–5). These births demonstrated that God was building the house of David, but this same section also emphasized that David was multiplying wives. His polygamy created fissures in the royal house that were never worked out, and these fissures eventually broke out in open civil war.

David continues to be presented as Israel in these chapters. The story of David's reign was one of conquest, rise, fall, division, exile, and restoration, and the specific analogies that occur in the early chapters of 2 Samuel are summarized in this chart:

Israel	David (2 Samuel)
exodus from Egypt, Exod. 14–15	exodus from Philistia, 2:3
war with Canaanites, Josh. 1–12	war with Ish-bosheth (3:1–4:12) and Philistines, 5:17–25
conquest of land, Josh. 1–12	conquest of Jerusalem, 5:6–10
Yah rules the land, Josh. 13–17	David rules the land, 5:1–5
ark at Shiloh, Josh. 18:1	ark in Jerusalem, 6:1–19

Thus, David's reign recapitulated the whole history of Israel to his own day, and after 2 Samuel 11 David's life was a preview of her future history.

THE MIGHTY FALLEN, 2 SAMUEL 1:1–27[2]

Beginning a section with "after the death of Saul" reflects a common device in the Old Testament (see Josh. 1:1; Judg. 1:1). The death of a leader like Moses, Joshua, the judges, and Saul, was a moment of crisis in Israel's life. Without effective leadership, Israel was in danger of going after other gods and failing to fulfill her calling. In Joshua, God reassured Israel about the continuity of leadership by enabling Joshua to perform some of the wonders that Moses had done. Under Joshua, the waters of the Jordan parted and Joshua led Israel through (Josh. 3:1–17), and later, Joshua encountered the

---

[2] Chapter 1 has a chiastic outline:
- A   David strikes Amalekites, v. 1
-   B   David questions the Amalekite, vv. 2–10
-     C   Mourning, vv. 11–12
-   B'   David questions the Amalekite, vv. 13–14
- A'   David orders the Amalekite killed, vv. 15–16

Intriguingly, the whole narrative begins and ends with David killing Amalekites, highlighting again that David proved himself faithful in carrying out the commission against the Amalekites in a way that Saul was not. David and his men's reaction to Saul's death is at the center, and thus the structure of the passage highlights David's mourning and lament over the fallen king, and his protection of Saul's status and memory.

captain of the Lord of hosts, as Moses met with the Lord on Sinai (5:13–15).[3]

With David, God did not work directly to establish continuity. Instead, David did the work. Nearly everything David did in the early years of his reign was an effort to heal the breach between his house and the house of Saul, and thereby to heal Israel. He honored the dead king's memory by executing the Amalekite and chanting a lament (1:14–27). He rewarded the men of Jabesh-gilead who had honored Saul with a decent burial (2:4–7), and he mourned for Abner (3:31–39). Later, he executed the men who killed Saul's son, Ish-bosheth, who succeeded his father (4:9–12). Though Saul's "sacrificial" death created a new world and a new dynasty, David tried to smooth over the transition. David was being politically shrewd by showing respect for Saul. He knew that a public display of mourning for Saul and Abner would send a message that David did not have a hand in their deaths, and he discerned that respect for Saul's son would pacify groups in Israel who were unhappy that the kingdom had passed out of the tribe of Benjamin. But David's grief was also a sincere expression of respect and even love for the Lord's anointed, consistent with David's behavior throughout his dealings with Saul. Despite his sins and failures, Saul was a great warrior, and Jonathan was even closer to David's heart. David praised Saul also as a generous "husband" to Israel (vv. 22–24). Though David had been living among the Philistines, his loyalties were always with Israel and Israel's God, and he did not want the Philistine daughters to rejoice at the fall of Saul and Jonathan (v. 20). Kindness, loyalty, and political expediency all gave David reason to follow this course. Faithfulness and loyalty, far from being politically impractical, were good policy.

In the previous chapter, I argued that the Amalekite lied about his responsibility for Saul's death, hoping that David would reward him (2 Sam. 1:1–16). Yet, a few details of his story are intriguing.

---

[3] I have developed this point at somewhat greater length in *A House for My Name*, 108–109.

He claimed that he saw Saul leaning on his spear, something he may actually have observed during the battle (v. 6). Whether or not the Amalekite saw it, it was a telling detail and very true to Saul. Saul had been leaning on his spear from early in his reign, relying on its power and using the weapons of the kings of the nations. Saul's spear was no more help on the mountains of Gilboa than it had been when he tried to pin David to the wall. It is, furthermore, ironic that an Amalekite claimed to have killed Saul, for in a very real sense the Amalekites destroyed Saul's kingdom, removing his "crown and bracelet" long before Saul had fallen on his sword (1 Sam. 15). Saul lost his kingdom because he took plunder from the Amalekites, and in the end the symbols of his kingship were plundered *by* an Amalekite. If the chronology suggested in the previous chapter is correct, the Amalekite was plundering Saul while David was plundering the Amalekites.

Saul's crown and bracelet were tokens of kingship. The connection of the crown with royalty is obvious, but the arm band was in all likelihood also a royal symbol. Thus, the Amalekite plundered Saul and brought David the visible signs of royalty. David could add these to his collection of royal insignia: the prophet and priest, the ephod, the sword of Goliath, bread from the priests, and the corner of Saul's robe. Of these, he had seized only one, the robe of Saul; all the others Yahweh had placed in his hand. This was the third time Amalekites helped bring the kingdom over to David: Because of Saul's sin with the Amalekites, Saul lost the kingdom; David's victory over the Amalekites was the last of his battles before becoming king; and the Amalekite brought Saul's crown to David.

During the interrogation, David discovered that the Amalekite was an alien living in Israel as a sojourner or "stranger" (v. 13). This was the basis for his sentence, for it meant that he understood exactly what he was doing. The Amalekite knew that Saul was Yahweh's anointed, and he did not fear to stretch out his hand. David, moreover, was now the Lord's anointed and his treatment of rebels against Saul sent a message to potential rebels in his own kingdom. The message was loud and clear: Don't mess with the Lord's anointed!

As noted in chapter 1, one structural feature of 1–2 Samuel is the use of verse. Near the beginning of the book, the song of Hannah appeared, which celebrated not only the birth of Samuel but the beginning of a revival in Israel. Two poems are included near the end of 2 Samuel (22:1–23:7). Thus, the book is framed by poems. In the middle of the books, in the last verses of 2 Samuel 1, is a third poem. With the song of Hannah, David's lament forms a frame for 1 Samuel, and with the poems at the end of 2 Samuel, it frames the second part of the book of Samuel. Placed at the structural hinge of the book, this poem highlights central themes of the whole. For example, David celebrated Jonathan's loyalty to his father, which reminds us that relations of fathers and sons were crucial to the whole story of 1 Samuel and foreshadowed the difficulties that David had with his sons in 2 Samuel.

The title is "the bow" (v. 18), a word used in verse 22 with reference to Jonathan's bow. Jonathan was linked with "the bow" during his lifetime (1 Sam. 20:18–22), and this title indicates that David lamented Jonathan's death as much as or more than Saul's. It is perhaps significant that verse 22, where Saul and Jonathan are mentioned together for the first time, named the son before the father. The focus on Jonathan is also indicated in the opening line, which states that "glory" had been slain on the high places. The word used for "glory" is not *kabod*, the usual term, but *tsebi*, which can also be translated as "gazelle." 2 Samuel 2:18 uses this word to describe a fleet-footed warrior, and "gazelle" fits 1:23, which describes Jonathan as one swifter than eagles. There is likely a pun in verse 19: The fall of the gazelle Jonathan was the slaying of glory; the glory had departed, because the "gazelle" had been slain.

Jonathan was "the bow," and the identification of a warrior with his weapons is evident elsewhere in the poem, especially in the parallelism of the final verse, which links the "mighty fallen" and "weapons of war perished" (v. 22). Verse 21b is an interesting case of this personification of weaponry: After Gilboa, "the shield of the mighty was defiled, the shield of Saul, not anointed with oil."[4] Ancient warriors rubbed oil on their (normally leather) shields to make them shine and to preserve them. Shields were thus literally "anointed." Since Saul had fallen in battle, his anointed shield lay in the dust, a dramatic image of the fallen "anointed one." The identification of shield and warrior is even more direct, for "shield" is sometimes used in poetic parallelism with "king" or "prince" (Ps. 47:9; 84:9). The Lord's anointed king *is* the shield for his people. Jonathan and Saul not only had weapons but *were* weapons, but now they lie unused and useless on the heights of Gilboa.

Structurally, the poem is marked by an *inclusio* on the line "how have the mighty fallen," found in the second and the next to last lines. Within this *inclusio*, the poem alternates between praise of Jonathan and praise of Saul: Saul alone (v. 21); Jonathan and Saul (v. 22); Saul alone (v. 24); Jonathan (vv. 25–26). In verse 25, the theme phrase, "how have the mighty fallen," is repeated and followed by a line that repeats the first line of the poem. (According to verse 25, Jonathan was slain on high places and confirms that he is the "gazelle" in the corresponding verse 19.) Verses 19–25, in fact, form a clear and complete chiasm:

A   Glory/beauty/gazelle slain; mighty fallen, v. 19
  B   Daughters of Philistia do not rejoice: no offerings to Dagon, v. 20
    C   Fallen shield, v. 21
    C' Bow and sword in life, v. 22–23
  B'   Daughters of Israel, weep: contrast to the Philistine women, v. 24
A'   Mighty fallen; Jonathan slain on heights, v. 25

Yet, the poem continues past verse 25, as if to show that David's grief could not be confined to the limits of poetic structure. It broke out at the mention of Jonathan into a further lament, far more personal and anguished than the rest of the poem. In the

[4] In Hebrew, the word order is chiastic: Defiled is/the shield of the mighty/the shield of Saul/not anointed with oil. Defilement is posed as the opposite of anointing.

final lines, David was no longer speaking in stereotypical terms of the greatness of a king and a warrior; he was crying out at the loss of a friend.

The poem includes a good deal of sacrificial imagery. The gazelle/glory lies slain on the "high places," a word often used for hilltop shrines, and verse 21 curses Mount Gilboa so that it will have no rain or dew, nor "fields of offerings." The bow of Jonathan and the sword of Saul are like predators, devouring blood and fat (v. 22), and the mention of blood and fat also suggests a sacrificial context. As noted in the last chapter, Saul's death not only brought an end to his kingdom, but also made way for a renewed kingdom headed by David. Like the death of the high priest, the death of the king restored the land. The mighty had fallen, but, since they have fallen on high places, a mightier had arisen.

TWELVE VERSUS TWELVE, 2 SAMUEL 2:1–32

Chapter 2 records several episodes from the early part of David's reign. First, David went to Hebron to be anointed king over Judah (vv. 1–4). It is significant that David inquired of the Lord at this point. Saul turned away from inquiring of the Lord, and the Lord eventually stopped communicating with him. The pun on Saul's name is brought up again: David began his reign by "asking" of the Lord (*sha'al*), and he received an answer, proving that he was the true Saul. Verses 1–3 also emphasize the fact that going to Hebron was an "ascension." The verb "go up" is used in each of these verses. Hebron was on high ground so David literally "went up" to the city, but the symbolic dimensions are also important. David had been living outside the land, in Ziklag, and symbolically the land of Israel was the "highest place" of the earth, the land closest to heaven. Moving from exile into the land always involved "going up." The language also emphasized David "ascending" to the throne, to become a high one, as Saul had ascended to Ramah when he was anointed king. Finally, David had been suffering a kind of death, cut off from the land, but he was being raised up and exalted to Hebron.

Hebron was the largest city in the area and was associated with the patriarchs. The only parcel of land that Abraham ever owned was the burial ground at Machpelah near Hebron (Gen. 23:2, 19). David's choice of Hebron thus associated him with the patriarchal tradition of Israel. More precisely, Hebron was the beginning of Abraham's inheritance of the land, one of the places where Abram set up an altar in his liturgical "shadow conquest" of Canaan (Gen. 13:18). It was appropriate for David, who was beginning to conquer and inherit the land, to begin by setting up his throne at Hebron.[5] Hebron was also one of the cities visited by the spies sent by Joshua and was at that time the home of the Anakim (Num. 13:22). Its earlier name, Kiriath-Arba, meant "city of Arba," and Arba was among the most famous of the giants, the Anakim (Josh. 14:15). Hebron was a city of giants, but it became a city of giant-killers, first Caleb, who received Hebron as an inheritance (Josh. 14:6-15), and now David. Hebron was also a city of refuge (Josh. 21:11-13), a sacred city, and perhaps this had something to do with David's choice.

At Hebron, David became a clan chief, the tribal leader over Judah. The text says that the "men of Judah" anointed David, and later, when he was anointed over the whole of Israel, the "elders of Israel" performed the ritual (5:3). Of course, David was the anointed of Yahweh, but Yahweh's choice was mediated through the men of Judah and Israel.[6] David's kingdom was not an oriental despotism but something more like a constitutional monarchy with local and tribal elders retaining and exercising considerable authority. The

[5] Note the connection between David's residence at Hebron and his purchase of the threshing floor of Araunah, which, as we see below, is reminiscent of Abraham's purchase of the cave of Machpelah.

[6] This implies that a ritual is the action of the one who authorizes and commands the ritual, rather than the action of the one who actually performs it. Though David was anointed by the Spirit, each of his public anointings with oil was done by a man, not by God; yet, the anointing was seen as Yahweh's work, for David was "Yahweh's anointed," not "Samuel's anointed" nor "the anointed of the elders of Israel." This Augustinian point is extremely important for a right understanding of baptism: Far from being a human work, baptism is Christ's work because He was the one who commanded it to be done. Mischief follows when this point is missed.

fact that the "men of Judah" anointed their own king suggests that the tribal elders were free to set up their own king/prince, apparently without consultation with other tribes. Though the period of judges had ended, the tribes remained in many ways independent republics.

David was anointed by Samuel as king-designate (1 Sam. 16:13), and he was again anointed as tribal chief. Later, he was anointed as king over all Israel (2 Sam. 5:3). This triple anointing marked out the three stages of David's career: warrior, chief, and high king. David's threefold career had typological overtones: Jesus was anointed with the Spirit at baptism, raised in the Spirit, and then exalted to the throne of the Father in heaven. The sequence also provides a perspective on the progression of the Christian life: in baptism we are anointed with the Spirit as warriors but are not yet prepared to reign; as we are faithful in war, we become rulers on a small scale, tribal chiefs; and as we are faithful in that arena, we are given more responsibility and share in Christ's kingship more fully.[7] The sequence is also evident in the history of the church: The ministry of Jesus corresponds to the early career of David; the apostolic period is the period in "Hebron," when Jesus had been exalted and poured out His Spirit but still had His kingdom centered in Israel; the final stage came after the destruction of Jerusalem, when the church emerged fully from the shadows, and Jesus was proclaimed to the nations as Lord of lords.

Immediately after his anointing, David dealt with the men of Jabesh-gilead. David was following the pattern of Saul's reign, since Saul's first task after becoming king was to rescue Jabesh-gilead from the Ammonites (1 Sam. 11). In the immediate circumstances, the loyalty that the men of Jabesh-gilead showed toward Saul raised delicate political problems for his successor. How would David respond to men who displayed courageous attachment to Saul? He could keep a suspicious eye on them, hoping to discover a false

---

[7] Of course, these distinctions between these stages are not perfectly sharp, and not every Christian's life progresses as smoothly as this scheme suggests. Life is complicated, and this blueprint, like all blueprints, abstracts and ignores many details. Still, it has its use. Or so I think.

move; he could launch a preemptive strike and neutralize Saul's supporters; or he could adopt a cautious waiting policy. David did none of these. Instead of wiping out the city or punishing them, he commended and joined them in admiration for Saul. His speech ended with an effort to convince Jabesh-gilead to transfer loyalty to him (v. 7). Though politically shrewd, David acted on fundamentally theological grounds. He was not commending Jabesh-gilead merely for appearance (vv. 5-6). Rather, they showed *hesed* to Saul their lord, and David prayed that Yahweh would show kindness to them, rewarding their *hesed* with divine *hesed*. Again, love and politics kiss each other.

Meanwhile, Saul's remaining son Ish-bosheth had become king over the other tribes, with Abner playing the role of king-maker. Since Abner was the one with the artillery and infantry, he could make or break Ish-bosheth. At first he made him, but when he withdrew his support later, Ish-bosheth's kingdom quickly collapsed. The fact that Abner used his power to place Saul's son on the throne, rather than taking it for himself, demonstrated Abner's wisdom and humility. Ish-bosheth had little going for him. His name meant "man of shame," and he is elsewhere called "Esh-Baal" ("Fire of Baal" in 1 Chr. 8:33; 9:39). Baal can mean "master" or "husband," and the name could be taken in a positive or neutral sense (see 2 Sam. 5:20). But "Baal" was also the name of a particular Canaanite deity, and the name in 1 Chronicles identifies Ish-bosheth as something like a Canaanite king.[8] As has been emphasized, David

---

[8] There is a chronological issue: Ish-bosheth reigned for only two years (2:10), while David remained at Hebron for seven years and six months (2:11). Where in this seven-year period did Ish-bosheth's reign fall? Some suggest a textual problem, but that is unlikely. Other commentators suggest that David's reign over all Israel actually included part of his time at Hebron, but this is also unlikely. Most probably, Ish-bosheth's reign covered the last two years of David's rule in Hebron. While in Hebron, David ruled only the house of Judah and not all Israel (2:11), and 5:1-9 shows that David moved immediately to capture Jerusalem after being anointed as king over all Israel. In the intervening years, the Philistines had made deep encroachments into the land; having won the battle of Mount Gilboa, they controlled the territory through much of the time that David was in Hebron, and Abner was only able to put Ish-bosheth on the throne after five years. See Bergen, *1, 2 Samuel*, 300-301.

was the true Israel, moving into the land and engaging in war with a "man of Baal." Earlier, Saul had reigned much of his time like a king of the nations. So, David's war to take control of the land repeated Israel's earlier wars against Canaanites.

Looking forward, David's war with the tribes of "Israel" foreshadowed the later division of the kingdom after Solomon. Already in the time of the judges, divisions among the tribes broke out from time to time (Judg. 8:1–3; 12:17), and in David's reign, tension was evident between supporters of David and supporters of Saul and later among David's own sons. The conflict between Joab and Abner was an important part of that tension. Moreover, Abner, more than Ish-bosheth, was the successor to Saul, and his conflict with Joab replayed the story of David and Saul. It took a different turn, however, because Joab was not the man of faith and patience that David was.

The story of this war is told in two distinctive sections: 2:12–3:1 and 3:12–39. Having established Ish-bosheth in the Transjordanian town of Mahanaim, Abner made his way toward Gibeon, where he met Joab and his troops at a pool (2:12–13). Gibeon was the main city of the Gibeonites, who became allies of Israel during the conquest (Josh. 9). In this setting of renewed conquest by David, Abner would play the role of a "Gibeonite" who turned away from his "Canaanite" king to ally with the new Joshua. The statement that Abner "went out" and the fact that he had "servants of Ish-bosheth" with him suggests that he was on a military campaign. Some commentators believe that he was launching a strike against David in an effort to conquer the rest of Israel. If that were true, however, it would be hard to explain why he stopped at Gibeon, which was Benjamite territory. Joab, not Abner, was the one that encroached into the other nations' territory. Abner's attitude toward Joab and his men, moreover, was cordial and fraternal, not what one expects if they were preparing for battle (2:14, 26).

Yet, Abner evidently had some reason to march off with his troops toward Gibeon, and there are several hints in 1–2 Samuel that Gibeon was a centrally important city in Saul's kingdom. At some point, the tabernacle was taken from Nob to Gibeon, perhaps after Saul slaughtered the priests (1 Kgs. 3:4; 2 Chr. 1:3, 13; 16:39; 21:29). Further, Saul attacked Gibeon during his life (2 Sam. 21:1–14), and in 2 Samuel 21:5, the Gibeonites accused Saul of seeking to devour them and to drive them from Israel. This may indicate that Saul was driving them out to make Gibeon his base of operations, his capital city.[9] In Joshua 10:2, Gibeon was described as a "great city, like one of the royal cities," and Saul may well have intended it to be the royal city of the Saulide dynasty.

Whatever the reason for Abner's march, when he met Joab at Gibeon, he suggested a contest (2:14). The word translated as "make sport" or "hold a contest" is normally used for play, amusement, entertainment and sport. It is an alternative form of the verb "laugh," which in the Pentateuch was the basis for the name "Isaac."[10] When the Philistines brought Samson out to amuse them in the temple of Dagon, this verb was used to describe their "sporting" (Judg. 16:25, 27), and the same verb is translated as "laugh" in Psalm 2:4. According to Psalm 104:26, Leviathan "sports" in the deeps. Closer to this context, the verb is used to describe the activity of the women who greeted the warriors returning from war (1 Sam. 18:7), and the "play" of the women consisted of singing and dancing to the accompaniment of tambourines and other instruments (v. 6). Later, this verb is used in 2 Samuel 6:5, 21 where Israel celebrated the coming of the ark to Jerusalem.

However cruel the sport, the word always conveys the idea of "mock" or "pretend" or "amusement." What Abner was proposing, then, was a tournament, a gladiatorial show, not a battle to the death. To be sure, there was a serious intent. At least, the winners would have bragging rights, and most likely the victors would go

[9] Here again there is an inversion of Saul's treatment of the Amalekites. Saul continued carrying out the ban, but against nations with whom Israel was allied.

[10] There are variant spellings of Isaac's name, but in a number of places the spelling comes from the verb under discussion here (cf. Ps. 105:9; Amos 7:9, 16; Jer. 33:26).

away convinced that Yahweh was on their side. The verb suggests that they were "Isaacing," competing to determine who were the true sons of Abraham, a dimension of the contest further symbolized by the fact that each side chose *twelve* warriors.

Abner's intentions were not followed through. Instead of holding a contest and sporting together, the young men seized and killed each other; all twenty-four warriors fell down together (v. 16). Not only did the sport turn bloody, but it left the outcome completely unsettled. If Abner and Joab had taken a moment to contemplate the outcome, they would have realized that Yahweh had acted and had sent a clear message: He was not taking sides in this battle. There are no winners if Israel goes to war with Israel; when twelve fight against twelve, all twenty-four fall! But Abner and Joab did not draw this lesson from the event. Instead, this symbolic civil war turned into a real civil war, and David's efforts to keep Israel together went up in flames.

Once the tournament turned into a battle, the story focused on Abner and Asahel, brothers of Joab and sons of Zeruiah (vv. 18–29). 1 Chronicles 2:16 informs us that Zeruiah was a sister to David, and thus these three are David's nephews. As Abner was fleeing from Asahel, the older warrior gave Asahel two opportunities to turn back. Abner even offered to allow Asahel to attack another of Abner's men without interference (v. 22). Abner did not want to fight Asahel because he knew that Joab stood behind Asahel. No doubt Abner knew something of Joab's choleric temperament, and besides that he was wise to remain on friendly terms with the powerful commander of David's army. Asahel would not listen, and in the end Abner has no choice but to defend himself. Israel had the institution of the "avenger of blood" (Num. 35:9–34), but the avenger was supposed to avenge *murders*; accidental killings and killing in war were not in the avenger's bailiwick. The text makes it clear that Abner did not kill Asahel deliberately or out of malice. Not only did Abner repeatedly warn Asahel to hold off, but Abner did not even turn to face Asahel with the point of his spear. Instead he impaled Asahel in the belly with the butt end of his spear (2:23). Spears in the ancient world were sometimes sharpened at the butt end so that it could be stuck in the ground, and Asahel ran headlong into the end of Abner's spear. Asahel, like Saul, died of a belly wound.

Instead of getting rid of pursuit, Abner found himself pursued by Asahel's two brothers, Joab and Abishai. He gathered his men on a hill in the wilderness of Gibeon, and from this strategic position he addressed Joab, urging him to give up the fight before all of them were killed. Joab agreed to call off his brutes and he returned to Hebron, marching all night and reaching Hebron as day was dawning. Sunrise in Scripture is often the beginning of a new era; but Joab was not one to forgive and forget. He would make sure that this day, which dawned after a day of blood, would be a sign of bloody days yet to come.

ABNER AND AN ANTI-DAVID, 2 SAMUEL 3:1-39

This chapter marks the conclusion of the story of conflict between Joab and Abner that began at the battle at Gibeon. Again the conquest theme is in the background, as is the reference to the Gibeonites. Like the Gibeonites in the conquest, Abner changed sides and came over to David. When Gibeon did this, it was a major boost for Israel. So also here. Abner's defection enabled David to continue the "strategy" he used in response to Saul's attacks, patiently waiting for the Lord to give him the kingdom, not mounting a revolution and not forcefully attacking Saul's house.

Chapter 3 begins with a discussion of David's family, a constant theme throughout this section of 2 Samuel. Yahweh was building David's house, and the growth of his house is often noted after a passage about victory in war. David's house was growing stronger and stronger in the war with the house of Saul (3:1). The sequence from victory to building the house will be picked up again after David defeated the Philistines. This is an exodus motif; the Lord triumphed over Egypt with plagues and brought out great plunder, which was devoted to the building of His house, the tabernacle.

But we encounter an obvious problem here. We learned in 1 Samuel that David had taken three wives: Michal, daughter of Saul, Ahinoam of Jezreel, and Abigail, the widow of Nabal. Here, however, we find that he had six different wives and this did not even include Michal (vv. 2–5). Polygamy was forbidden to Israel's kings, and the history of David's family illustrated the evils of a polygamous royal house (Deut. 17:17). Ominously, Amnon and Absalom are listed here, two sons who would later be in deadly conflict with one another. Importantly, the list of David's sons comes after a summary statement about a long war of succession, and the list showed that David had several potential successors as well, several "firstborns" who would lay claim to his throne. The list is a potent foreshadowing of the danger of another long war of succession following David's reign.[11]

David had an eye for beauty, but his multiplication of wives was not merely the product of vigorous sexuality. The marriages were politically as well as sexually desirable. At least one of David's wives, Abigail, came from Judah, which may well have aided David in consolidating power over his own tribe. Marriages with women from other areas of Israel (Ahinoam from Jezreel, for example) were part of an effort to forge alliances with powerful families throughout the tribes. Ironically, the very institution intended to unify Israel ends up dividing it. There was also a wife from Geshur, a Gentile kingdom in the Transjordan, north of Mahanaim, Ish-bosheth's base of operation; with family alliances in Judah and in the north, David was surrounding his opponent. Though he had not attacked Ish-bosheth directly, his alliances were closing the noose and were foolish provocations to members of Saul's house.

---

[11] The list shows the succession order: Amnon, Chileab, Absalom, Adonijah. Amnon, Absalom, and Adonijah were in line for the throne, but each was eliminated in turn. Chileab is never mentioned as a contender for the throne. As a son of Abigail, he was perhaps intended to be the heir to Nabal's house. David has been following something like a Levirate pattern here. One hint of this is the fact that his name combines the names "Caleb" and "Abigail."

Abner was the power behind the throne of Ish-bosheth, but Ish-bosheth was, like his father, suspicious of his servants. He stupidly accused Abner of taking the king's concubine, Rizpah (3:7). This charge had both sexual and political dimensions. An ancient king's brides and concubines represented the kingdom in several respects. Because they constituted part of a king's household, wives and concubines were part of a king's inheritance, passed into the care if not into the bed of his successor (see 2 Sam. 12:8). Further, the king of Israel was seen as a husband to his people, so the wives of the king symbolized the national "bride." Protecting the bride symbolized the king's ability to protect the kingdom. This was why, for example, Absalom slept with David's concubines when he took over the kingdom (16:22). The message was: If David could not even protect the women of his own house, surely he had no power in the land.[12] Ish-bosheth's accusation against Abner, therefore, implied that Abner had designs on the kingdom.

Abner was indignant (3:8–10). He reminded Ish-bosheth of the *hesed* he had shown to Saul and everyone associated with him. He pointed out that he could have supported David against Ish-bosheth, which would have been an understandable move since David was winning the war. Hovering around this conversation was the truth that both Abner and Ish-bosheth knew: Without Abner, Ish-bosheth was nothing. Instead of seeking his own advantage, Abner had stayed with Ish-bosheth, pursuing what he must have known was a lost cause. Furious at being treated like a dog's head, a worthless thing, he swore that he would help David fulfill the promise that he would rule from "Dan to Beersheba," from north to south.

The Bible never says that Abner took Rizpah, and his protests were honest ones. Ish-bosheth's charge made no sense. If Abner had intended to take Rizpah, why would he give up his plan because of an accusation? So what if ineffectual Ish-bosheth had found out?

---

[12] In 1 Kings, Adonijah requested David's concubine Abishag, and this was seen as an effort to claim the throne (2:13–25). Earlier, Reuben had taken his father's concubine (Gen. 35:22).

Abner had the troops, and he could have taken the throne if he had wanted. On the other hand, if he did not want the throne, he would not have acted so provocatively as to take Saul's concubine. Besides, Abner by this time was no lusty youth; no doubt he remained virile, but, being a generation older than Saul, he must have been well into old age, not normally a time of life when men are ambitious for royalty. Ish-bosheth was a paranoid king like his father, who accused his loyal chief commander of conspiring against him. From Abner's perspective, this episode was the last straw: Ish-bosheth turned out to be another Saul, and Abner had no desire to help another paranoid retain power.

Abner immediately made contact with David.[13] Abner's question, "Whose is the land?" implied the answer: "Mine" (3:12). Elder statesman that he was, Abner had the clout to secure the rest of the land for David's house. He offered a covenant to seal that agreement and to formalize his loyalty toward David. David jumped at the opportunity to accomplish peacefully what he had not been able to accomplish in the "long" civil war. David had only one request, that Michal be returned to him (vv. 14–16). David had every right to make this demand, since Saul took Michal away unlawfully, treating David as a dead man. On the surface it also seemed politically wise, for a reunion with Saul's daughter helped David to reestablish his continuity with the house of Saul. David may also have been thinking ahead to the next generation: A son of Michal and David would unite two royal houses, and further heal the national wounds that had opened up during the civil war. David also hoped to test Abner's ability to make good on his offer, since symbolically, the return of the king's daughter signified the gift of the kingdom.

---

[13] Their encounter is described in a chiastically arranged passage:

    A   Abner offers a covenant with David, v. 12
      B Demand that Michal be returned, vv. 13–16
      B' Abner secures the support of Israel's elders, vv. 17–19
    A'   Feast of covenant, vv. 20–21

This arrangement brings out the connection between the securing of Michal and the securing of the kingdom.

Though these reasons might seem persuasive, the story is told in such a way as to highlight Paltiel's sorrow at losing Michal (3:16). Instead of a triumphant reunion of royal houses, the story is about a lover's loss of his beloved. Moreover, if David hoped Michal's return would unite the houses of Saul and David, he was disappointed, for Michal eventually died childless (6:23). Indeed, this episode foreshadowed a later moment, when David would again take a woman from her husband, and that seizure brought disaster (2 Sam. 11). Far from being shrewd, David's demand for Michal was an error that fueled the pro-Saul agitation against David. Shimei's later charge that David killed Saul was false; but there was some truth in the claim that David had treated Saul's house unfeelingly.[14] Interpreted more cynically, it is possible that the whole episode was a way for David flagrantly to flaunt his superiority over the house of Saul.

Abner secured the king's daughter; and Abner also secured the kingdom, persuading the elders of "Israel" to throw their support to David (vv. 17–19). "Israel" here and elsewhere in 2 Samuel means the tribes other than Judah, the territories ruled by Ishbosheth. Abner even gained the support of the elders of Benjamin by reminding them of a prophecy about David (v. 18). Though this exact promise is not explicitly mentioned in 1 Samuel, it was implicit in David's anointing. According to 1 Samuel 9:16, the anointed one was marked as the deliverer, and thus when David was anointed with oil and the Spirit, he received an implicit promise of victory over his enemies. Having secured Michal and the support of "Israel," Abner and David sealed their covenant with a feast of wine (vv. 20–21). After this, Abner went away "in peace" to make preparations for the covenant-making with the whole people. Abner and David had been on opposite sides of a war, but they made peace by making a covenant. Abner, like Jonathan before him, had kissed the Lord's anointed, another member of Saul's house who acknowledged that David was the legitimate successor.

[14] Thanks to James B. Jordan for steering me right on this point.

Joab had been out raiding and was astonished that David and Abner had made peace (vv. 22–25). On one level, his hostility to Abner was personal, since Joab had determined to take revenge for his brother. Abner was also a great, if aging, military leader, and if he joined David and brought Israel with him, he would surely be rewarded with a high position in the military—not field commander but perhaps chairman of the joint chiefs or secretary of state. In any case, Joab's position would be threatened. Joab was also suspicious of Abner, or at least he pretended to think that Abner was as conniving as he. Abner was a loyal man who had been faithful to the house of Saul until driven out, but Joab could not believe Abner was that good. Abner, he suspected, must have come as a spy to check out David's comings and goings (the phrase often refers to military maneuvers). David saw the visit as an opportunity to make peace with a former enemy and to recover a brother. Like Abishai, his brother, Joab thought of Abner's visit as an opportunity to eliminate an enemy.

The sentence, "David sent him off in peace," occurs three times, but this was not the way that Joab described Abner's departure. Joab said that Abner "went off," and this phrasing is sometimes a euphemism for death in the Bible (Job 27:21; Jer. 22:10).[15] There may also be a sexual connotation to Joab's language. Abner "came in" to David and this is the same idiom that Ish-bosheth used in his accusation against Abner. Moreover, the verb "deceive" or "dupe" is commonly used for sexual seduction (v. 25). Joab, in short, accused Abner in much the same way that Ish-bosheth had: Joab suspected Abner was plotting a political rather than sexual seduction, but the idea was similar. Joab, like Ish-bosheth, believed that Abner had designs on the throne, David's rather than Ish-bosheth's.

Without David's knowledge, Joab called Abner back, pretending that he wanted a private conference. Instead, he struck the unsuspecting Abner in the belly at the middle of the gate (3:27). The word for "belly" is used only a handful of times in the Old

---

[15] Robert Alter, *The David Story: A Translation with Commentary of 1 and 2 Samuel* (New York: Norton, 1999), 212–213.

Testament, but twice in these two chapters. Asahel was killed by Abner with a blow to the belly, and Joab, perhaps thinking it fitting retribution, killed Abner by striking him in the belly. Before this, as we have noted, Saul was struck in the belly.

Joab murdered Abner in the "middle of the gate." A city gate would be too public a place to kill someone, so perhaps the phrase refers to some hidden alcove in the gate of Hebron. Whatever the actual location, the reference to the gate was symbolically fitting. Judgments were passed at the gates of cities, where elders of the city assembled to deliberate and pass judgment (Ruth 4:1–6), and Joab believed he was carrying out righteous vengeance. The irony of this location becomes clear when we recall that the city of Hebron was a city of refuge (Josh. 21:13), reserved for the protection of manslayers. Just as Abner arrived at the gates of a city of refuge, where he should have been able to find safety, he was put to death. According to the law, Joab could *not* be protected in a city of refuge, yet he sauntered into the city as if he were a perfect innocent. The horror of this incident becomes more obvious when we recall that Abner was an elderly man at the time, while Joab was a warrior in the prime of youth.

Joab's actions spoiled any hopes that David had for a peaceful settlement with the house of Saul. With Abner's conversion, David had a breakthrough, a chance to end the war and bring peace. Things seemed to be going very well, until Joab stepped in and set David's efforts back. Worse, it would certainly appear to many that David had ordered Abner's death. Joab, after all, was David's commander, and Abner had been David's enemy. David had to condemn Joab's action, but no matter how severely he condemned it, suspicions would fester for a long time. Joab's murder of Abner was a deal-breaker, and it would be some time before the tribes of Israel finally did come over to David.

David condemned Joab by pronouncing a fivefold curse (vv. 28–29). Several of these have to do with Levitical forms of uncleanness. "One who has a discharge" (*zab*) would not be permitted to enter the tabernacle or come near to God (Lev. 15:1–12), and the leper was in the same situation (Lev. 13–14). "One who holds a distaff" (some translations have "crutch") may refer to a lame man, or, since a distaff was a part of a spinning wheel, a man who held a distaff might be one suited only for women's work, either because he was effeminate or because he was too weak to do man's work. David also brought down of eye-for-eye vengeance against Joab; since Joab had taken up the sword, David hoped that the sword would not depart from Joab's house. Like the priests of Eli's house, David said that Joab's house would be deprived of bread.

A private curse, however, was not sufficient. David had to distance himself publicly from Joab and publicly demonstrate his affection for Abner. David ordered Joab and all the rest of his house to put on sackcloth and lament before Abner's casket, while David brought up the rear of the funeral procession. David wept publicly at the grave (2 Sam. 3:32), fasted until sundown (v. 35), and even composed a lament for the occasion (vv. 33–34). Chapter 3 began with David getting stronger and stronger, but the chapter ends with David weak with sorrow (v. 39). He was not only personally exhausted by the violence of his nephews, but also realized that Joab had weakened the kingdom. Yet, notice also that David is called "king" fives times in the last few verses (vv. 32, 33, 36, 37, 39). Through all the bloodshed, Yahweh was working His will to deliver Israel into the hands of his chosen king. Abner did bring him the kingdom, the second member of the house of Saul who died to bring David to the throne. Only one member of Saul's house remained as an obstacle, and the Lord was about to remove him.

Not for the last time, Joab had spoiled David's work among his brothers, and David's failure to deal with Joab more firmly was a blunder of considerable proportions. David's failure sends an important message to Christian leaders: No matter how faithful a leader is, no matter that he is a "man after God's own heart," his work can be ruined by the follies of his aids and allies. Care in selecting commanders and lieutenants is as crucial as watchfulness in one's own life. Joabs can undermine the achievements of even the most faithful Davids.

ISRAEL DECAPITATED, 2 SAMUEL 4:1–12[16]

There are a number of parallels between the assassination of Ish-bosheth and the death of Saul. Like his father, Ish-bosheth was struck in the belly and beheaded (4:6–7; 1 Sam. 31:4, 9). Further, there are marked parallels between David's reception of the report of Saul's death and his response to Ish-bosheth's. In 2 Samuel 1, the Amalekite said he had killed Saul and plundered his body, offering the plunder as proof. Since he assumed that David wanted Saul dead, he came thinking he brought good news to David, but David executed him. In chapter 4, having killed Ish-bosheth, Baanah and Rechab came to David thinking they brought good news, but David executed the two murderers. In both incidents, "young men" carried out the sentence (cf. 1:15 and 4:12). David even alluded to the execution of the Amalekite when Baanah and Rechab showed up with Ish-bosheth's head; David saw the parallels too. Structurally, chapters 1–4 form a single section marked by this narrative *inclusio*. No wonder Ish-bosheth is identified in 4:1 as the "son of Saul."[17]

---

[16] Youngblood (*1, 2 Samuel*, vol. 3, 843) provides a structural analysis of the passage. Verses 1 and 12 form an *inclusio* since the names Ish-bosheth and Abner appear in both verses, Abner's name appears only in these two verses, and both verses refer to "hands." Hebron itself is mentioned at the beginning and end of the chapter. Within this *inclusio*, the text is divided into three sections of four verses each:

A. Main characters: with background on Rechab, Baanah, Mephibosheth (vv. 1–4)

B. The plot against Ish-bosheth (vv. 5–8)

C. David's response (vv. 9–12)

Grotesquely, the last verse of each section highlights some body part: Mephibosheth's lame feet, Ish-bosheth's head, and the hands, feet, and head of Ish-bosheth and his assassins. The shape of the text highlights this dismemberment.

[17] The assassination was similar to Ehud's assassination of Eglon. The word for "bedroom" (v. 7) is a fairly rare word and is used to describe the place where Ehud killed Eglon (Judg. 3:24). Like Eglon, Ish-bosheth was struck in the belly. Rechab and Baanah doubtless thought they were Ehuds fighting another Eglon; but Ish-bosheth was an Israelite, a legitimate ruler, and a "righteous man" (4:11). The word for "bed" (v. 7) makes a connection in another direction; it is the same word used in 3:31, when David walked behind Abner's "bed" or "coffin." Baanah and Rechab turned Ish-bosheth's bed into a bed of the other sort.

The text also points to similarities between the murders of Ish-bosheth and Abner. Both murders occurred in an inner room or secret place, both involved subterfuge and deceit, and both men died from wounds to the "belly," and in both cases the murders were carried out by brothers—Joab and Abishai (3:30) on the one hand, and Baanah and Rechab on the other (4:2).[18] Thus, the deaths of the members of Saul's house and kingdom interweave with each other, and we cycle through a similar sequence of events three times, first with Saul, then Abner, now Ish-bosheth. In the first and last incidents, David executed the murderer and this forcefully highlights his failure to deal with Joab. Why did Joab not end up like the Amalekite, Baanah, and Rechab? One reason, surely, was that Joab was David's nephew, and David favored him because he was a kinsman. Instead of acting like the Levites in Exodus 32, who did not spare their own family members in their zeal for Yahweh, David showed undue respect for his blood relative. David acted with wisdom toward his "enemy" Abner, but he was less astute in dealing with his "friend" Joab.

Abner's murder leaves David weak, but it also further weakens the house of Saul (4:1), since Ish-bosheth knew that Abner was the only thing standing between him and defeat. Indeed, Joab left everybody weak. In particular, Abner's death leaves Ish-bosheth vulnerable to attacks from men like Baanah and Rechab. These assassins were commanders of "raiding parties" (cf. 1 Sam. 27:8–11, 30:26), and we are given detailed information about their family background (vv. 2–3). They were sons of Rimmon the Beerothite, and "Beeroth" ("wells") was among the cities associated with Gibeon (Josh. 9:17).[19] The Beerothites had "fled to Gittaim,"

---

[18] There are textual problems in verse 6. The Hebrew has a feminine pronoun, though the only antecedents available are Rechab and Baanah. And what does "wheat" have to do with anything? One possibility is that Rechab and Baanah came to the house of Ish-bosheth disguised as "fetchers of wheat." Because they were coming in disguise, they were able to get access to the house. The Septuagint, however, includes a woman gatekeeper at the gate, who has come from gleaning wheat but has fallen asleep.

[19] Joshua 18:25 tells us that Beeroth was one of the cities inherited by the tribe of Benjamin, and 2 Samuel 4:2–3 repeats this information, perhaps to emphasize that disaffection for Ish-bosheth had spread to his own tribe and no doubt had become more intense after Abner's departure.

also in the tribal area of Benjamin, and putting this information together with what we learn in 2 Samuel 21, it seems likely that the Beerothites fled because of Saul's attack on Gibeon. This helps us pinpoint the motives of these two men: Rechab and Baanah were seeking vengeance for Saul's attack on their city and for their forced exile from their homeland.

Verse 4 intervenes in the story of the death of Ish-bosheth, summarizing the story of Mephibosheth.[20] The story is straight-forward, but what is it doing here? For one thing, it demonstrates that the house of Saul was not completely destroyed by the death of Ish-bosheth. Though the family of Saul continued, Mephibosheth's condition made it clear that the family of Saul was not fit to con-tinue on the throne. The surviving member of Saul's house, the only direct heir, was lame and thus an unlikely candidate to be king. In fact, Mephibosheth had no claim on the throne anyway, since his father, Jonathan, had voluntarily renounced his position in favor of David, and Mephibosheth would later demonstrate similar loyalty to his father's friend. He was allied to the true house of Israel, Da-vid's house, and his foot wound marked him as a faithful Israelite, a son of Jacob, who was also wounded in the leg (Gen. 32:22–32).

In contrast to Mephibosheth whose heel was crushed, Ish-bosheth's head was removed. Though David calls Ish-bosheth a righteous man, he opposed David, the Lord's anointed successor to Saul, and so in a sense it was appropriate for him to die by a head wound. Throughout the Bible, there is a connection between the "head" as the top of the body and the "head" as the chief of a society. Ish-bosheth was the "head" of the tribes of Israel, and when the "head" was killed, the political fact was symbolized by the removal of the king's head. This also suggests that the gift of the head to David was symbolically the gift of "headship." David became head of all Israel shortly after receiving the head of his rival, just as he became king in Hebron when he received the crown from

---

[20] This happened when he was five and on the day of Saul's death. By adding the seven years of David's residence in Hebron, we conclude that Mephibosheth was twelve when his uncle was killed.

the head of Saul. These beheadings also pick up on the "headship" theme that began with the "dedicated head" of the Nazirite Samuel in 1 Samuel 1.

David reacted as he did to news of Saul's death. Rechab and Baanah were wicked men who had killed a righteous man and therefore had to be purged from the land. The language is judicial, since David was rendering a verdict. At the end of verse 11, the verb is "burned," and this language is used in the law for capital punishment, in the phrase "purge the wicked man from among you" (Deut. 13:5; 17:7, 12; 19:13, 19). There is no reason to believe that David was insincere in his revulsion to what they had done, but it was also clear that David was concerned about the public relations scandal that could follow. If rumors were already circulating that he had commanded Joab to kill Abner, the assassination of Ish-bosheth would only confirm them. It seemed far too convenient, and David took steps here (very severe steps) to communicate that he had nothing to do with Ish-bosheth's death. Not only did he execute the assassins, but he also displayed their hands and feet at the pool of Hebron as a warning.

There is an interesting omission here, for David said nothing about Ish-bosheth being king or Yahweh's anointed, as he did in 1:14. David did not condemn Rechab and Baanah for regicide, for striking the Lord's anointed, but for murder, for striking down a righteous man.[21] This points to an important distinction between

---

[21] Eugene Peterson offers a useful summary of David's role in all this: "In retrospect, [another element] turns out to be the dominant element, although not nearly so dramatic in the telling: David. David praying. David waiting for the kingdom to be given to him under the sovereignty of God. David refusing to hurry. David trusting in the efficacy of his anointing to finally set him on the throne. David putting up with irritating and disruptive associates. David fierce in his passion for honor and justice. David tender in his laments. . . . David does not lift a hand to take over Saul's throne; and David does not incur what he calls 'bloodguilt.' In contrast to the frenzy of ambition that he sees around him excited by Saul's empty throne, David conducts funerals, composes poetry, marries and has children, and administers justice. In contrast to all the killing going on around him to grab power, David does not kill anyone who could be considered a rival" (*First and Second Samuel*, Westminster Bible Companion [Louisville: John Knox/Westminster, 1999], 155).

Israel and Judah, one that continued throughout the period of the kings: Judah was ruled for almost all its history by anointed descendants of David, while Israel was ruled for the most part by men who were not anointed (though Jehu was). This distinction between a royal "Christ" and a less theologically charged form of monarchy was foreshadowed in the early years of David's reign.

Though David did not want and did not order Ish-bosheth's death, it helped him, as Saul's and Abner's deaths had. After Ish-bosheth's death, David's kingdom was ensured because there were no reasonable alternatives. David came to the throne on the basis of the "sacrifices" of Saul, Abner, and Ish-bosheth, for the king must die if the kingdom is going to be established. The deaths of Benjamite kings secured the throne for the king from Judah.

DAVID THE KING

In 2 Samuel 5–8, the story cycles several times through a "victory-housebuilding" pattern. Three times David fought Israel's enemies, and then the text gives notice about the construction of a house:

	Battle	House
Cycle 1	Jerusalem, 5:6–10	Family/palace, 5:11–16
Cycle 2	Philistines, 5:17–25	Yahweh's house, 6:1–7:29
Cycle 3	Various wars, 8:1–14	Royal household, 8:15–18

These chapters describe the peak of David's reign and show that he was not only a warrior destroying enemies, but a builder forming a new Israel. Since a house was a place of rest, each cycle of the story moves from warfare to Sabbath. Creation is thus in the background, since God also created and then moved into Sabbath. In a sinful world, "creation" always involves conflict and warfare; before Sabbath comes battle. The creation background suggests that David's wars and building formed a new world, and this was literally true. Because of David's work, Jerusalem became the center not just of Israel but of all nations. Because of David's work, Gentiles became worshipers of Yahweh. Because of David's work, Israel was given a place and gained a great name.[1]

---

[1] Chapters 5–8 form a fairly neat chiasm:

A		David becomes king, takes Jerusalem, builds his house, 5:1–16
	B	Victory over Philistines, 5:17–25
		C	Ark taken to Jerusalem, 6:1–23
			D	Davidic covenant, 7:1–17
		C'	David prays before ark, 7:18–29
	B'	Military victories, over Philistines and others, 8:1–14
A'		David's reign and administration, 8:15–18

Chapter 8 also connects to the following section of 2 Samuel, and so it will be treated in the following chapter.

The David-as-Israel typology provides another perspective on these chapters. As noted in the previous chapter, David's wars were a new conquest and David a new Joshua. Chapters 5 and 8 describe further wars, in the course of which Israelite territory grew to unprecedented size. David, in short, conquered portions of the land that Israel had not conquered during the days of Joshua, particularly Jerusalem (5:6–10; see Judg. 1:8, 21, and below). David's conquest thus not only recapitulated but extended Israel's original settlement. Joshua's conquest culminated with the erection of the sanctuary at Shiloh (Josh. 18:1), and David's conquest likewise climaxed with the pitching of a tent for the ark in Zion (2 Sam. 6:17).

Attention turns from David's labors within Israel (the land) to David's relationship with Yahweh and with the Gentiles (garden and world). Though 8:15 tells us that David "reigned over all Israel" and "was doing justice and righteousness for all his people," we never see him doing those things in these chapters. Instead, after a brief description of his anointing as king over Israel, the story focuses on his conquest of Jebus (Jerusalem), his relations with Hiram of Tyre, and his wars against the Philistines and others (5:6–25; 8:1–14). During his wilderness years, David learned to deal wisely with Gentile friends, like Achish, and Gentile enemies, like the Amalekites. As king, David applied the lessons he had learned during those years of trial. He formed an alliance with Hiram of Tyre (5:11), accepted tribute from the Moabites (8:2) and from Toi, king of Hamath (8:9–10), and received the crown of the Ammonite city of Rabbah (12:26–31). On the other hand, he was severe in smiting enemies. Once David had received his third anointing, David became a player on the world stage; Yahweh had "exalted his kingdom" in the eyes of the surrounding nations (5:12).

From this, it is evident that David's three anointings marked out three stages of his career: After his first anointing, he was introduced to Saul's house as a king's servant (garden/father); after his second anointing, he ruled Judah for seven and a half years and worked to reunify Judah and Israel (land/brothers); and after his third anointing he dealt with Gentiles, both allies and enemies (world/Gentiles). Each phase of David's career was an unfolding of an anointing. Analogously, the different aspects and stages of the Christian life can be seen as the blossoming of our union to the Anointed One in our single baptism. Baptism admits us to the sanctuary-garden, joins us to the brotherhood of the church, and marks us as witnesses in the world; baptism governs our relations with our fathers, both biological and spiritual, during our childhood; it shapes our life with our brothers in the church as we grow and with a sister-wife as we come to marriage; and it provides the framework for mature kingly and prophetic ministry in the world.[2]

In the central episodes of these chapters, however, David dealt not with the Gentiles but with Yahweh. The second victory-house-building cycle focuses on Yahweh's victory (5:22–25), the ascension of the ark-throne into Jerusalem (6:1–19), and David's desire to build a house in which the Lord might rest (7:1–2). Though David stood in the place of Saul as a "father" to the nation, he still had to deal with his own Father (7:14) and with Nathan, the prophetic father who delivers God's word to him. And, as he proved himself wise and faithful in his dealings with brothers and with Gentiles, David demonstrated that he was a man after God's own heart by seeking to exalt the Lord's throne and build His house.

KING OVER ALL ISRAEL, 2 SAMUEL 5:1-25

After the death of Ish-bosheth, David became king over all Israel, as the tribes of Israel (that is, the tribes other than Judah) came to David at Hebron and claimed him as a kinsman (5:1–5). The reference to "bone and flesh" often connotes brotherhood (cf. Gen. 29:14; 2 Samuel 19:12; Judg. 9:2), and the tribes recognized, as Abner did earlier, that the men of Judah were brothers with the other tribes, and, as the law required, they chose one of their "brothers"

---

[2] Of course, the masculine tenor of the description that I have offered here is not intended to exclude women. In Christ there is no male or female, and the lives of Christian women are also an unfolding of their "anointing" at baptism.

to rule them (Deut. 17:15). "Bone and flesh" also points to a marital or covenantal relation (Eph. 5:22–33). As the people prepared to enter into a covenant with David, they acknowledged him as a suitable husband for Israel, an image of the divine Husband.

The elders also acknowledged that David had been selected during Saul's reign. Verse 2 begins with a phrase used by Abner when he spoke to the tribes of Israel and to Benjamin (3:17), which literally means "yesterday, even the day before yesterday" and has the sense of "in time past." Specifically, the elders recognized that David was the one who "went out and came in," a phrase frequently used in military contexts (see 3:25). Even though Saul was titular king, David had been the more reliable leader. David had earned his stripes; because he had been a warrior and tribal chief, he was qualified to become king.

Recognizing David's experience was not sufficient, however, and the elders also acknowledged that Yahweh had called David to be "shepherd" and "ruler." At thirty, the same age that Joseph was when he stood before Pharaoh (Gen. 41:46), David was enthroned. Shepherd imagery was associated with kingship throughout the Old Testament and in the ancient Near East, but this is the first time that the title "shepherd" was used explicitly of a ruler in Israel. Shepherding was not unknown to the patriarchs, of course, and Jacob especially was rich in flocks and herds. When David was identified as a shepherd, he was being identified as a new Jacob. There is also a close connection to Numbers 27:17, where Moses selected Joshua to "go out and come in" before Israel so that they would not be like "sheep without a shepherd." This indicates that Joshua was the shepherd of Israel. David the shepherd, then, was a new Joshua, prepared to complete the conquest that Joshua began. Shepherd imagery is filled out in Ezekiel 34, which shows that a good shepherd was one who protected the flock from predators, fed them, and cared for the weak.

In verses 6–16 we see the first instance of the "victory-house-building" pattern. David defeated the Jebusites at Jerusalem, and a reference to two houses of David, his family and his palace, follows.

David's choice of Jerusalem as a capital is unexplained, but a few factors might have entered into his decision. First, Abraham, father of the Israelites, acknowledged Melchizedek, king of Salem/Jerusalem as the religious head of the land by paying tithes (Gen. 14). David, a child of Abraham, treated Melchizedek's city as the chief city of the land. The choice of Jerusalem was, moreover, politically astute. Jerusalem was in Benjamite territory (Josh. 18:28), and for David to designate a Benjamite city as his capital was a gesture calculated to heal the conflicts between the houses of Saul and David. Finally, the fact that David conquered Jerusalem showed that he was a new and better Joshua.[3]

The Jebusites were supremely confident when David began to attack. They had an acropolis so strong that they believed that even the lame and blind could protect it.[4] The portion of the city that David attacked was the "stronghold" and not the entire city (v. 7). Within the outer wall of an ancient city was a second city, the "acropolis," "high city" or "stronghold," the religious center and the last outpost during a siege. If the outer wall was breached by an enemy, the people (at least the important people) could retreat to the acropolis, which was normally higher and more defensible.

Despite the strength of the Jebusite fortress, David was able to capture it. The Hebrew is obscure, but David's men apparently got into the city through the water tunnel (5:8).[5] A long vertical shaft

---

[3] Joshua 15:63 and Judges 1:21 report that Israel did not drive out the Jebusites from Jerusalem, but Judges 1:8 says that the men of Judah did capture Jerusalem. Perhaps the sons of Judah captured a portion of Jerusalem, or perhaps they captured the city but lost it. At any rate, at least the main part of the city was still in Jebusite hands in David's day.

[4] This is probably a pre-fight taunt: Even the weak can protect this fortress, it's so strong. Some commentators suggest that there is somehow a play on the Israel charge that Jebusite gods were impotent: The Jebusites are saying, "Well, you may think so, but even lame and blind gods are strong enough to protect this city." Other scholars have pointed to ancient texts where blind and lame people were used as a curse; there is some evidence that ancient peoples displayed blind and lame people as a way of defying and cursing their enemies.

[5] Many different explanations have been offered, but the most plausible alternative to the interpretation offered here is that David cut off the water supply to the city, crippling it and taking it without a fight.

connects the city of Jerusalem to the springs of Gihon, and perhaps Joab climbed up the shaft to get inside the city walls (see 1 Chr. 11:6). After the victory, David declared his hatred for the blind and the lame. This certainly did not mean that David despised the disabled, for he later welcomed a lame man, Mephibosheth, to his table and made him a virtual prince in his house. When he said that he hated the "blind and lame," David was accepting the Jebusite self-designation: If Jebusites were the blind and lame, then the blind and lame were David's enemies. Survivors of Jebus would not be welcome in David's house. The stronghold was on Mount Zion, one of several mountains in Jerusalem, and this mountain became the center of David's kingdom. He lived in the stronghold on Zion and later brought the ark there (5:11; 6:16). In its original usage, "Zion" was not the name of the temple mount, for the temple was built on Mount Moriah (2 Chr. 3:1).

Once he had conquered, David got to work on various building projects. In 2 Samuel 5:9, he built up all around the stronghold from the "Millo" and inward, and verses 11–12 indicate that David also built himself a house of cedar and stone. Hiram of Tyre assisted with this project, a Gentile pitching in to build the house of the Yahweh's anointed. Later, Hiram would provide materials and expert builders for Solomon's temple. David's friendship with Tyre was the beginning of a long history of interaction between Tyre and Israel, in which Tyre became a paradigmatic converted Gentile city. Like Melchizedek and Jethro before him and Cyrus after him, Hiram was a "Gentile sponsor" of a new covenantal order. In contrast to the Mosaic covenant, where the materials for the tabernacle were plundered from Egypt, Hiram contributed voluntarily to the building of God's kingdom in Israel. Under David's shepherding, Israel was beginning to fulfill the calling she had received at Sinai, to be a priest to the Gentiles (Exod. 19:6). Ultimately, the favor that Hiram showed came from Yahweh; because the Lord was with David, the Gentiles were offering aid (v. 12). David was also building his house in another sense, the people house, which increased by eleven sons and an undisclosed number of daughters.

Again, however, there is an ominous reference to "concubines and wives" (v. 13), indicating that David was continuing his habit of "taking" women.

At the end of chapter 5, the second cycle of the victory-house-building pattern begins with a series of victories over the Philistines (vv. 17–25), apparently the first battles with the Philistines since the death of Saul more than seven years before. As long as David was occupied fighting Ish-bosheth, the Philistines remained securely in control of Israelite territories. But an Israel united under David was a threat and they launched a preemptive strike. The Philistines sought David out and set up their camp in the valley of Rephaim. "Raphah" was a name of a giant (2 Sam. 21:16, 18, 20, 22), and his descendants were called the "Rephaim." Thus David fought the Philistines in the valley of giants, and he again proved himself a skilled giant-killer.[6]

Before the battle began, David "asked" direction from Yahweh (v. 19), and the verb *sha'al* is used, picking up on the "asking" theme from 1 Samuel. The Lord assured David of victory and "broke through" David's enemies. As a result, the place was named "Baal-Perazim," which means "the master of the breakthrough." "Baal" here means "master" or "lord," and Yahweh proved himself the true "Baal," the true master, by breaking through David's enemies like a breakthrough of waters.[7]

As the Philistines fled before the Lord, they left their idols behind (v. 21). The verb "abandoned" or "left behind" is *'azab* and the word for "idol" is *'atsab*. Thus, there is a pun on "abandon-

---

[6] The word also means "shades," referring to the dead. And again, this is appropriate, for the Philistine giants will end up as "shades" (Job 26:5; Ps. 88:10).

[7] Perez was also the son of Judah, and the head of the line that produced David. The image contained in "master of the breakthrough" is not entirely clear. Perhaps the Lord broke through the Philistine lines while David was surrounded, and this allowed David to escape. That would explain why the Philistines were soon back on the battlefield again. David's name and his explanation showed that he acknowledged that the Lord had won this battle for Israel. The Lord broke through David's enemies "before me" (v. 20). The verb "break out" often refers to the breaking out of God's wrath (Exod. 19:22, 24; 1 Chr. 15:13).

ment" and "idol." The Philistines abandoned their idols on the field, but this revealed the nature of idols, namely, that they abandon their worshipers when they come face-to-face with the "master of the breakthrough." Israel last faced the Philistines at Gilboa, where Saul's head and weapons were captured and taken on a tour throughout Philistia "to carry the good news to the house of their idols and to the people" (1 Sam. 31:9). In the valley of Rephaim, the very idols credited with that victory were left behind. This battle not only reversed Gilboa, but also reversed the battle of Aphek: At that earlier battle, the Philistines captured the ark, but now the images of Philistine gods were captured by Israel.

In spite of their loss, the Philistines tried again (5:22–25). There is a cartoonish quality to the second battle, reminiscent of Wile E. Coyote's always-frustrated efforts to capture the Road Runner. Though they describe different battles, verses 18 and 22 are virtually identical, a sign of how hard-hearted the Philistines had become (see 1 Sam. 6:6). Again, David inquired of Yahweh (v. 23), and this time the Lord not only assured David of victory but instructed him to circle around to attack from the rear. David was to wait for Yahweh to go before him. The sound of marching in the tops of the shrubs was the signal for David to attack, because it was the sign that the Lord's army, the hosts of angels, had marched out before the armies of Israel.

It is intriguing to notice the differences between the battles at Jerusalem and the two battles with the Philistines. David did not inquire of the Lord before the battle of Jerusalem, and there was no extraordinary divine intervention. Instead, the victory was David's (and Joab's, according to 1 Chr.), and David's house was built immediately thereafter. When David fought the Philistines, by contrast, the Lord not only directed David to fight but also marched before David, like the Angel of Yahweh during the conquest. Yahweh was the Victor of these battles with the Philistines, and it was therefore appropriate for David to think immediately about building a house for Yahweh: The victor receives the spoils as materials for his house. Victory over the Philistines was the climactic act of this new "conquest." David was a new Joshua, and because the land had been conquered and cleansed it was time to build the Lord's sanctuary (cf. Josh. 18:1).

ENTHRONED IN ZION, 2 SAMUEL 6:1–23[8]

The battle with the Philistines reversed the battle of Aphek, and so it was a propitious moment to reverse the exile of the ark that had begun at Aphek. After a century in the house of Abinadab on the hill, David brought the ark to his stronghold on Zion. As I have remarked elsewhere,[9] there are striking structural links to the earlier story of the capture of the ark. The structure highlights the reversal taking place:

Battle of Aphek
A   Ark taken (house of Eli eliminated), 1 Sam. 4:1–22
  B   Ark in exile in Philistia, 1 Sam. 5:1–6:9
    C Ark returns on cart (Israelite sin regarding ark), 1 Sam. 6:10–21
      D Ark with Abinadab, 1 Sam. 7:1–2

When David restored the ark by taking it into Jerusalem, the same series of events happened in reverse order:

Reverse Battle of Aphek
    C' Ark returns on cart (Israelite sin regarding ark), 2 Sam. 6:1–9
  B'   Ark in the house of Obed-edom, a Gittite, 2 Sam. 6:10–11
A'   Restoration of the ark to a tabernacle (house of Saul eliminated),
        2 Sam. 6:12–19

The first half of the structure describes the death of the Mosaic order and the end of the tabernacle system at Shiloh, while the second half of the structure narrates the "resurrection" of a new order of worship in Jerusalem. And the parallels reinforce the theme that this is the rebirth of what died at the battle of Aphek. This was the coming of a "new creation," since the ark and the central place of worship were

[8] I have discussed chapters 6–7 more briefly in *A House for My Name*, 145–149.
[9] Ibid., 145–146.

in the area of Jerusalem for the first time, an arrangement that would continue throughout the monarchy and in the post-exilic period.[10]

The focus on the enthronement of Yahweh is brought out by the repetition of the word "ark," used fifteen times in this chapter. Of these fifteen occurrences, seven refer to the "ark of God" and seven others use the phrase "ark of the Lord." This double seven points to the Sabbatical theme, since the Lord's enthronement was His entry into Sabbath. The ark was the "throne" of "Yahweh of Hosts" (Sabaoth; 6:2), a divine title that referred to the Lord as a military commander.[11] This was a fitting title for Yahweh, for He had only recently driven the Philistines from Israel. Having gained the victory, Yahweh of Sabaoth becomes Yahweh of the Sabbath.

David gathered "chosen men" to bring the ark to Jerusalem (v. 1), probably warriors of David's army. Possibly, David was anticipating another Philistine attack, and he took precautions to ensure that the ark would not fall into Philistine hands again. The danger was not a chimerical: Yahweh had chased the Philistines back as far as Gezer (5:25), and the ark was located in a town close by. Further, the mention of 30,000 men (6:1) reminds us of 1 Samuel 4:10, where we learn that Israel lost 30,000 foot soldiers at Aphek. The ark is "called by the Name" (6:2), a reminder of Yahweh's promise to choose a place to "set My Name" after He had given rest to Israel (Deut. 12:11). Bringing the ark to the city of David thus established Zion as the central place of worship and announced that the Lord was sharing His Sabbath rest with Israel.

The songs of praise are reminiscent of the victory song at the exodus (Exod. 15:1–21) and of the praise that greeted Saul and David

---

[10] The chapter is organized by a parallel structure (Youngblood, *1, 2 Samuel*, vol. 3, 868):

A   First attempt to bring in the ark (closes with "all house of David," v. 5)

B   Uzzah judged (closes with "all house" of Obed-edom, v. 11)

A'   Second attempt ("blessed," v. 12)

B'   Michal judged ("blessed," v. 20)

[11] This name is also used at the battle of Aphek (1 Sam. 4:4), where the ark was mishandled by Hophni and Phinehas. These are the only two places in the books of Samuel where this designation for the ark is used.

after their victories (1 Sam. 18:6–7). This was Yahweh's victory parade, celebrating Israel's deliverance from Philistine-Egyptians. But this parade was doomed from the beginning. Putting the ark on a cart was already a violation of the law, for Numbers 7:9–10 says that only Kohathites were allowed to carry the ark and that they had to carry it on their shoulders, not on a cart. The last time we saw the ark on a cart, it was the Philistines' doing (1 Sam. 6:7). God did not judge the Philistines because they were not the caretakers of the ark; but when the Israelites put the ark on a cart, they were violating a direct command of Yahweh. The picture of the ark on a cart brings out the parallel with the return of the ark, which also had some disastrous consequences for Israel (1 Sam. 6:19–21). Attentive readers will be anticipating the worst.

If the cart was not bad enough, Uzzah touched the ark. No one was supposed to approach the throne of Yahweh except the High Priest on the day of atonement and the Kohathites who carry the ark, and no one was supposed to see, much less touch it (Num. 4:15). As a result of this incident, the place was named Perez-Uzzah, "the breakthrough against Uzzah" (2 Sam. 6:8). In the previous chapter, Yahweh broke out against the Philistines, but when Uzzah touched the ark He "broke through" against Israelites who were imitating Philistines. Further, this breakthrough against Uzzah was similar to the "breakthrough" against the men of Beth-shemesh when the ark first returned to the land. Like Uzzah, these men touched the ark, committing sacrilege, and the Lord struck 50,070 of them (1 Sam. 6:19–21).

Finally, we learn that this incident happened on a threshing floor (v. 6).[12] Elsewhere, threshing becomes an image of violence

[12] Threshing was part of the process of harvesting grain, designed to separate the chaff from the kernel of grain. With small quantities a flail was beaten against the stalks, but with large amounts, the cut grain was spread on a large flat area called a threshing floor, over which an ox or heifer would be driven. Sometimes carts were used and the wheels would do the threshing, or threshing sledges (wooden constructions that would be pulled by an animal which had stones or iron underneath to thresh the grain) would be employed. After threshing, the grain had to be "winnowed," during which the threshed wheat was tossed into the air to allow the wind to blow away the chaff. See Leland Ryken, et. al., eds.; *Dictionary of Biblical Imagery* (Downers Grove: InterVarsity, 1998), 867.

and violent judgment. A wise king winnows the wicked and drives a threshing wheel over them (Prov. 20:26), and since God is the wisest of kings, He drives the threshing wheel over the wicked to separate the wheat from the chaff (Hab. 3:12). At times, of course, Israel was the nation threshed by the Lord's judgment. The judgments against Israel peeled off the chaff and made it apparent who was wheat and who chaff. So it was symbolically appropriate that God should pass judgment on the threshing floor of Nachon. At the end of 2 Samuel, another threshing floor will be prominent and will also be linked to a sanctuary.

Because of the failure of the first attempt to bring the ark to Jerusalem, David put the ark in the house of Obed-edom. Though some believe that Obed-edom was a Levite, the weight of the evidence is against this. He is called a "Gittite," and everyone else called a "Gittite" in the Old Testament was from the Philistine city of Gath. Several other places have "Gath" in the name, but they are obscure, and one would expect some further explanation if another city were intended. Further, his name meant "servant of Edom," which would be an odd name for an Israelite, to say the least. More generally, David had close ties with the Philistine city of Gath. He had been a vassal to Achish for a time, and six hundred Gittites were in his army (2 Sam. 15:18). Obed-edom, in short, was a Gentile. Instead of bringing plagues, as it did during its sojourn in Philistia, the ark brought blessing to Obed-edom. Noting the Lord's favor to a Gentile, David was "provoked to jealousy," and decided to have another go.[13]

As the ark ascended to Jerusalem the second time, it was again accompanied by music, dancing, and singing. Almost from the moment that Saul was anointed king, music had become a prominent part of the life of Israel (1 Sam. 10:5). After the ark was settled in Jerusalem, David formalized this new reality by forming a Levitical choir and orchestra to perform before the ark (1 Chr. 15:16–24).

---

[13] Note that the ark was with Obed-edom for "three months" (v. 11), which is connected to the three-day motif discussed in an earlier chapter.

The Hebrew word for dancing is *karar*, used only in 2 Samuel 6. The other Old Testament word translated as "dance" means something like "whirl" and is related to a verb used in Jeremiah 23:19 to describe a "whirling tempest" (see 2 Sam. 3:29). Applied to dancing, this latter word apparently described a spinning and turning dance, obviously vigorous. Though a different word is used, David's dance was similar, since he danced with "all his might" and "leaped" (vv. 14, 16). Clearly, David saw his dancing as an act of worship, since it was done "before the Lord" (v. 14), a point that David emphasized to Michal (v. 21).

There are several other examples of "liturgical" dancing in the Old Testament. In Judges 21:16–24, the Benjamites took wives from the women who were dancing during the "feast of the Lord" at Shiloh, where the tabernacle was stationed at the time (vv. 21, 23). The Benjamite men were out near the vineyards waiting for the daughters of Shiloh to "come out" (from the city?), and this suggests that the dancing was not taking place in the tabernacle precincts. Perhaps the feast mentioned here was one of the week-long feasts of Israel, like the feast of Booths, during which there would doubtless be time for dancing in the fields near Shiloh. In any case, this passage indicates that dancing was included in the festivities of the Shiloh tabernacle. A closer parallel to 2 Samuel 6 is found in Exodus 15:20. After the deliverance of Israel at the Red Sea, Miriam led the women with music, song, and dance. The women "went out after her," and this suggests a procession of singing and dancing, like the procession of the ark into Jerusalem. Miriam's dance was clearly an act of praise to Yahweh, performed with song and instrumental music.[14] Apart from these examples, there is little evidence for dancing in worship, and there were no commands or rules concerning dancing at the tabernacle or temple. David did

---

[14] Several Psalms urge dancing. Psalm 87:7 celebrates Zion as the dwelling place of Yahweh and people from every nation being treated as homeborn sons. The Psalm closes with references to singing and "playing" or "dancing" (Heb. *chul*). In Psalms 149 and 150, especially in Psalm 150, the context for the celebration in dance is the sanctuary (vv. 1, 4).

not set up a Levitical dance troupe in the way that he set up the Levitical choir and orchestra. Apparently, dance was not a regular part of worship at the sanctuary but was performed in connection with special celebrations, processions, and feasts.

Distinctions have to be made in trying to apply this to the church today. What is often described as liturgical dance (at least in my church circles) is a performance, with the congregation sitting in pews watching a ballet. This was not the sort of dance described in the Old Testament, where the whole congregation or some significant portion of it participated. David's dance was not entertainment or even "preaching" in dance form, but a response of praise with the body, analogous to the more common practices of bowing, prostrating, and lifting hands. I suspect that it was more like the dancing in modern charismatic churches than a ballet performance. Yet, dancing is nowhere included as a regular and normal part of worship in the Bible. I conclude from the Scriptural evidence that there are moments when dancing is an appropriate expression of joy before the Lord, but that it should not be a performance and it should not be done in every service. If the leaders of China suddenly converted and brought an end to the persecution of Christians, it would be natural for Chinese Christians to break out in dance. And God would smile on their praise.

Once David arrived at Zion, he set up a tent for the ark (v. 17), which was not the same as the tent of meeting Moses set up.[15] The Mosaic tabernacle continued to operate in Gibeon throughout David's reign (1 Chr. 15:16, 16:1–6 and 16:37ff), but a different sort of worship was going on at the tent of David, which housed only the ark. David offered burnt offerings and peace offerings to consecrate the tent, but after that the main sacrifice on Zion was a sacrifice of praise in song and music.

Not everyone was happy with David's performance. Watching through a window, Michal despised David, and when he returned

---

[15] I hope to give detailed attention to the "tabernacle of David" in a future study, to be published by Canon Press.

home she attacked him. Michal criticized David on two counts. She began with "honor" or "glory," a key term associated with the ark. When the ark went into exile, Israel was "Ichabod" because the "glory" had departed (1 Sam. 4:21). With the return of the ark, glory returned. Michal was not impressed with this glory, and her use of the word is bitter and ironic: "Just look at the honor that came back to Israel!" If this is glory, Michal preferred shame, and she would get what she wanted (v. 23). Second, she implied that David was uncovering himself and dancing before the young ladies like a son of Belial.

David responded to the second charge first. He was not dancing before the young ladies, he argued, but before the Lord, rejoicing because the Lord had chosen him above Michal's father and all his house. Sharp words, which surely stung Michal deeply. Second, he redefined honor and shame. He might have embarrassed her today, but he was willing to be even more embarrassing. He was willing to be lightly esteemed and humble in his own eyes, so long as he shamed himself before the Lord. Before the young maidens, those at least who have real discernment, he would be honored for his humility.

Michal sinned, and she was punished for it. The house of Saul was finally cut off from any share in the monarchy of Israel because Michal was childless (6:23). Yet, it is difficult not to feel some sympathy for her. She had been taken from a loving husband and brought into a house full of wives and concubines. Her bitterness was understandable. And, while David was sincere in dancing before the Lord, Michal's charge that he was more interested in the young women was prescient.

SON OF GOD, 2 SAMUEL 7:1-29

2 Samuel 7 is surrounded by passages having to do with David's reign, his wars, and his actions. He fought, he built, he leaped and danced before the Lord. Suddenly, an entire chapter comes up that includes nothing but two short speeches followed by two longer

ones that are almost identical in length.[16] The narrative pace slows to a crawl and instead of action has a banquet of words. These features make the chapter stand out as an oddity.[17] This chapter contains the longest speech from God since Sinai,[18] and this suggests it marks a major transition in the history of Israel. Yahweh speaks again, at length, and clarifies and specifies the terms and future of His covenant. He did not cancel the Mosaic covenant, but built on it to move toward the fulfillment of His work in Christ. Within 1–2 Samuel, this is the first time the Lord has spoken at any length since 1 Samuel 3, the night vision to Samuel. The vision to Samuel threatened that Eli's house would be destroyed. This new speech, also delivered to a prophet at night, promised that a house would be built.

Though the word "covenant" does not appear in the passage, there is ample biblical warrant for saying that this is the announcement of the "Davidic covenant." The passage itself has all the features of a covenant: Yahweh promised that certain things will be "forever" the case, He offered His everlasting *hesed* or "covenant loyalty" to David's son (v. 15), and He threatened to discipline David's sons if they broke the covenant. Moreover, several passages in the Bible describe this incident as a covenant-making event (Ps. 89:19–37; 132:10–12). These covenantal arrangements formed the basis for Israel's life throughout the period of the kingdom, and for her hope during the exile and into the New Testament. The Davidic dynasty lasted four centuries until it was interrupted by the exile. After the exile, no Davidic king ever returned to the throne in Jerusalem, but throughout this interruption of the Davidic line, the prophets assured Israel that God was righteous and would not allow His

---

[16] 197 and 198 words respectively. See Bergen, *1, 2 Samuel*, 336, 342.

[17] The structure is a simple parallelism:

    A   David to Nathan: I want to build a house

      B   Nathan to David: Go, do

    A'   Yahweh to Nathan: David shall not build house

      B' David to Yahweh: thanksgiving

[18] Bergen, *1, 2 Samuel*, 336.

promise to David to fail. A "branch" of David would spring up, and the stump of Jesse would grow back into the royal tree. Yahweh's description of David, "My servant David" (7:5), was in the background of the "servant" passages of Isaiah (chapters 40–54). Ultimately, Jesus was the fulfillment of this covenant: He is the Son of God, the heir to David's throne.

Some time passed between the events of chapter 6 and the covenant in chapter 7. David was living in his house of cedar (7:2; see 5:11), and he had gained rest from his enemies, which suggests that the wars of chapter 8 had already occurred. Now that David and the Lord had gained victory, it was time to think about building Yahweh's house. Again, Deuteronomy 12 is in the background, and Nathan agreed that the moment was ripe to set up a place for the Lord's name.

That very night, the Lord corrected Nathan, informing him that David would not be the king to build Yahweh's house. In 1 Chronicles 28:3, David said he was not permitted to build the house because he was a "man of war" who had "shed blood"; a man of peace would build the house of the Lord. In 2 Samuel 7, however, the focus is on the Lord's promise to build David a house (v. 11) and establish David's kingdom. Before anyone builds a house for David's Lord, the Lord would build a house for David. David planned a place for the Lord, but the Lord instead promised a "place" for Israel (v. 10). In fact, this has always been God's *modus operandi*.[19] He always builds a house for His people, and then calls them to build a house for Him. This is what justification by faith is all about. The Lord also emphasized another reason for this decision: The Lord had been "walking" in the midst of Israel in the tabernacle since the exodus and had never "spoken a word" to the "tribes" of Israel about building a house (vv. 6–7). So long as the Lord had not called for a house, none should be built. It was not for David to decide when the Lord's house would be built; that decision rested with "Master Yahweh."

---

[19] This is a key theme of my *A House for My Name*, 50–52, 58–61, and passim.

A couple of the promises to David were specifications of promises given to Abram. Yahweh promised to give Abram a "great name" (Gen. 12:2), and He reiterated that promise to David (2 Sam. 7:9). God promised a land to Israel (15:7–21), and He promised David a place for Israel to rest (vv. 10–11). Before the Davidic covenant, these promises had been given to the house of Abram in general, but after this they were specifically given to the house of David. Fulfillment of the promises to Abram was henceforth bound up with the royal house of David. David was *the* seed of Abram who would bring blessing to the nations.

The designation of David's son as a "son of God" (v. 14) is another aspect of this focusing of the Abrahamic promises on David's house. Prior to David, adoption language was used primarily for Israel as a whole. At the exodus, Moses came to Pharaoh with the demand, "Israel is My son; let him go" (Exod. 4:22–23). Sonship was exclusively a corporate idea in the early part of Israel's history. With the Davidic covenant, however, the corporate identity of the "son" of God was focused in the single person of the Davidic king. The fortunes of Israel would henceforth turn on the iniquity or righteousness of the "son."[20] This does not mean that the conduct of the Israelites in general was unimportant. If they fell into sin, the nation would be judged, but under the Davidic covenant the conduct of the king was crucial. The blessings and curses of Deuteronomy 28 were contingent upon the obedience or disobedience of the king. The son of David was a new Adam, a representative of the people, and this provided the theological background to the

---

[20] That this is something new for Israel is evident from a comparison of 1 Samuel 12:14 and 2 Samuel 7:14. In the former passage, Samuel promised that the king would follow the Lord so long as the people did; the king's faithfulness depended on the faithfulness of Israel. In the latter passage, the Lord says that Nathan would suffer discipline for his own sins, and this discipline frequently encompassed the whole nation; the nation's future depended on the behavior of the king. Though Saul was head of Israel, he was not head in the same covenantal sense that the Davidic kings were; though Saul was a "son" of Yahweh, he was not officially adopted as David's descendants would be. Of course, practically speaking, both are true: Rulers in some respects mirror the people they rule, but in other respects shape the people they rule.

fact that David's life story previewed the life story of Israel. When Jesus is called "son of God" it means He is the heir of David, and it means that He is the true Israel.

Several examples from the history of Israel's monarchy will help fill out this central point of the Davidic covenant. According to 1 Kings 11:9–13, Yahweh was angry with Solomon because he had gone after other gods, and as a result He warned, "I will surely tear the kingdom from you." The division of the nation clearly affected the whole people, but the cause was *Solomon's* idolatry and disobedience. After the event of Naboth's vineyard, Ahab put on sackcloth and repented despondently. When Yahweh saw Ahab's humility, He decided not to bring "the evil in his days" (1 Kgs. 21:27–29). The whole kingdom was preserved from the disruption of a *coup* by the king's repentance. The Northern Kingdom was overthrown by Assyria because the people had whored after idols (2 Kgs. 17:7–23), but Judah, ruled by a Davidic son of God, suffered exile "because of the sins of Manasseh" (2 Kgs. 24:3). In a number of passages in 1–2 Kings, moreover, the sickness of the king or the king's son serves as a symbol for the sickness of the kingdom (1 Kgs. 14:1–18; 2 Kgs. 1:2; 20:1). This was a major shift in the administration of the covenant and prepared the way for the new covenant.

After hearing the Lord's word through Nathan, David went in "before the Lord" and "sat" (7:18). Elsewhere in this passage, "before the Lord" means before the ark (6:14, 17), and the fact that David "went in" indicates that he went into the tent that he established for the ark. If this was the case, it emphasizes the free access that was available to God's son, David. How could David legitimately "go in" and sit before the ark? An analogy with Moses helps explain this. Prior to the building of the tabernacle, Moses spoke to Yahweh face-to-face in a "tent of meeting" set up outside the Israelite camp (Exod. 33:7–11). Once the tabernacle was erected, the curtains formed a barrier, so that even Moses did not have access (Exod. 40:35). David was like Moses in this respect; he was at the cusp of a new covenant and served as the "prophet" who would deliver the floor plan for a new house. As prophet-king, David had access to the Lord's presence that no one else had, especially after the building of the temple (1 Kgs. 8:10–11).

In any case, David's access to the ark was a sign of the future New Covenant order, when a Son of David went into the heavenly tent before the Lord and brought all his subjects into the tent with Him. Strikingly, David *sat* before the Lord. Priests, as the book of Hebrews tells us, never sat down in the temple because they were always working on labors that could never be completed (Heb. 10:11–12). But David was seated before the Lord's throne, a Melchizedekan king, a king at rest from his enemies. David had just been told that he and his sons were "sons of God," princes of the Great King, and his seated posture symbolized his position as "ruler" over Israel, as "David the king" (v. 18). David had humbled himself before the Lord, dancing like a fool before the ark. But God did not want him to remain in a posture of abject humility. David fell to the ground so that Yahweh could pick him up and set him on a throne.[21]

Word repetitions are used in the passage to highlight several key issues. The word "house" is used seven times, highlighting the Sabbatical theme. Seven times David called Yahweh "Master Yahweh" (*'adonai yahweh*),[22] in recognition of the Lord's sovereignty over him. David was a "prince" of Israel but he was also a subject of the true "Lord" of Israel, Yahweh. The word "forever" is also used several times. God's promises would be in force "forever" and David asked God to confirm His promises "forever" (vv. 13, 25, 29).

David was humbled by the revelation, reminded of the things that God had already done for him and amazed that He intended to do yet more. The Lord took him from the sheep and set him up

[21] This is the only example in the Bible of someone sitting to pray, but it is a specialized example where sitting is not a sign of casualness but of enthronement.

[22] This is often translated as "Lord God," but the word translated as "God" is the name Yahweh.

as king, subduing his enemies. Even more, David looked ahead and was humbled further by the Lord's promises about the future of David's house (v. 19), in comparison to which all that the Lord had already done was "insignificant" in His eyes. Instead of resting content with what He had done so far, the Lord had spoken concerning the "distance." David was amazed not only that God had planned this for his house, but also that He made it known (vv. 19, 22, 27). God had revealed His secret things to David his servant. This revelation served as a basis for David's boldness in prayer (v. 27). David asked God to confirm His promise (v. 25) and prayed that his house would be established (v. 26; cf v. 16) in blessing (v. 29). The fact that his ears had been uncovered, that the Lord had revealed the "distance," had caused him to pray.

The sentence at the end of verse 19 is difficult in a number of respects. It is often translated as a question—"Is this the custom of man?"—but it seems best to translate this as a statement rather than a question. David was not saying (in grateful astonishment), "Is this your customary way of dealing with men?" Rather, he was asserting something about what Yahweh had promised. "Custom" is a translation of *torah*, which normally means "law" or "instruction." Walter Kaiser suggests that the phrase is best translated as "charter for humanity" and that "this" refers to the content of the promises. The Davidic covenant set out the structure for God's future dealings both with Israel and with all men and nations. There is perhaps an allusion to Adam, for the phrase "charter of man" translates *torah ha'adam*. God had been dealing with men through covenants and through Israel, but there was something new: Henceforth, Yahweh would deal with mankind through a king, and specifically through the royal seed of David.

No man could rise higher than this. David was, quite literally, at the top of the world, the Adamic son of God through whom God would work out His plan for humanity. But the higher David rose, the more spectacular was his fall.

FORBIDDEN FRUIT

S aul sinned and lost the kingdom. David sinned and retained his kingdom.

Juxtaposing those two propositions focuses attention on one of the issues that dominates the remainder of 2 Samuel. The first proposition occasions no surprise; what is surprising is the second, and it is all the more surprising when we consider that David's sin was worse than Saul's in virtually every respect. Saul refused to listen to the voice of the prophet (1 Sam. 13; 15), but David broke the clear commandments of the written Torah. Saul never took another man's wife, and his attempts to put Jonathan and David to death were unsuccessful. Further, Saul had not been given the great privileges that David had been given, the privilege of being "son of God." Saul was called directly from the plow to deliver Israel; David had been trained in the wilderness and in Hebron, and had "died and risen" before ascending to the throne.

Modern commentators are wrong to find excuses for Saul; he was plenty good at finding excuses for himself. But the fact that they can offer the pretense of an excuse indicates that Saul's sins can be blurred into ambiguity. No such blurring is possible with David: Adultery is adultery, murder is murder, and David had not a centimeter of wiggle room. David ingeniously committed a sin that combined all of Saul's sins and took them to a higher level; the king trained to serve faithfully in garden, land, and world failed in each one. Seizing Bathsheba was an Adamic sin of seizing forbidden fruit, and a sin of impatience. Taking the wife of his neighbor was an offense against his brother, and murdering Uriah was the sin of Cain. And the whole affair gave "occasion to the enemies of Yahweh to blaspheme" (12:14). Befitting his status as "son of God," David's sin threw Israel into political turmoil far more extreme than anything that happened during the reign of Saul. Saul spent much of his reign struggling with David, but Israel never erupted into full-scale civil war with pitched battles that cost the lives of 20,000 men (see 18:7). David's more serious offenses brought more severe consequences.[1] Yet: Saul sinned and lost his kingdom. David sinned, and sinned more flagrantly, but retained his kingdom.

That is the puzzle that needs to be explained, and the text provides two explanations. First, when Saul was confronted by the prophet, he made excuses and sought to spread the burden of responsibility; when David was confronted with his sin, he immediately confessed and admitted that he and he alone had sinned. Saul's reaction to the prophet was an Adamic reaction, but David's was not. Second, David *did* lose his kingdom during the rebellion of Absalom (see chapter 10 in this book). David regained his kingdom; his kingdom died, but it eventually rose again. And this was because of his free confession and heartfelt repentance (12:13–14; Ps. 51).

In the death and resurrection of David's kingdom, we find a foreshadowing of the later exile and return of Israel. This will be developed further in chapter 10, but a few parallels are summarized in the chart:

David (2 Samuel)	Israel (1 Kings)
promised a son, 7:12	Solomon rules, chs. 1–2
intends to build a house, 7:1–2	builds a house, chs. 6–8
David takes Bathsheba, 11:2–5	Solomon takes many wives, 11:1–4
adversaries (Absalom and Sheba), chs. 13, 20	adversaries, 11:9–40
kingdom divided, chs. 15–19	kingdom divided, 11:26–40; 12:21–33

Throughout the Old Testament, when God established a "son," the son sinned; Adam, the son of God, grasped forbidden fruit; Israel was redeemed from Egypt and entered into covenant at Sinai but set up golden calves; Solomon violated the laws of king-

---

[1] The first two paragraphs of this chapter are indebted to comments from and discussions with James B. Jordan.

ship. What was needed, especially after the establishment of the Davidic covenant, was a son who would not sin, a Son to replace the fallen sons and live in obedience to the Father.

WARS OF DAVID, 2 SAMUEL 8:1–18

Among the promises the Lord gave to David were the promises to "make you a great name," to "appoint a place for My people Israel," and to "give you rest from all your enemies" (vv. 9-11). These very things happened in the events of chapters 8–10.[2] In 8:13, David "made a name" by his conquest of Edom, and throughout the chapter, the Lord extended the boundaries of Israel. By the end of chapter 8, the territory that David directly controlled or that was subject to him had been doubled. Yahweh gave Israel a place, and not just any place: He gave them a roomy place, a place to stretch out in. The chapter is organized geographically in a way that reinforces this point. David's conquests began with the Philistines to the west (v. 1), and then he fought Moab to the east (v. 2). After that, David turned north to fight against Hadadezer of Zobah (vv. 3–12), and his wars ended with battles against the Edomites in the south (v. 14). David extended the kingdom to the four points of the compass, symbolizing the extension of David's kingdom to the "four corners" of the earth.

The boundaries of David's mini-empire coincided with the boundaries that the Lord had promised to Abraham in Genesis 15:18, from the river of Egypt to the Euphrates. Hadadezer's rule

---

[2] Chapters 8-10 form a distinct section of 2 Samuel. The battles recorded at the beginning of chapter 8 are brought up again at the end of chapter 10. Chapter 8:3-12 deals with the defeat of Hadadezer, king of Zobah, and 10:9-19 is an account of another battle with the same king, and these references to battles with Hadadezer form a set of bookends around these chapters. The chapters can be roughly outlined as follows:

    A   Wars of David, 8:1-18 (including the administration of his house)
    B   Kindness to Mephibosheth, 9:1-13
    B   Kindness to Hanun, 10:1-5
    A   War with Arameans and Ammonites, 10:6-19

After chapter 10, the account of David's sin with Bathsheba begins, but this military and political background covered in 8–10 is important to that story.

extended to the Euphrates (v. 3). Scripture tells us that the Philistines were related to the Egyptians (Gen. 10:13–14), and David fought in the south against the Edomites, whose kingdom extended from the Dead Sea and south. David was the "seed of Abraham" who possessed the land.

One of the key words of chapter 8 is "smite." David was "smiting" everyone that came within reach, whether Philistines (v. 1), Moabites (v. 2), Hadadezer of Zobah (v. 3), or Edomites (v. 13). Several of these peoples became tribute-bearers to King David. Moabites were forced to pay tribute (v. 2), and David took the gold shields of Hadadezer (v. 7) and bronze from Hadad's cities (v. 8). When Toi of Hamath heard about David's defeat of Hadadezer, he sent tribute because David had delivered Toi from Hadadezer. First David smote, and then he plundered, and the plunder became holy, consecrated to Yahweh (v. 11). In Chronicles, we learn that David gathered the riches of his conquests to build the temple. As in the exodus, plunder from the enemies of Israel went to build the house of God. It was appropriate that the Lord be enriched by plunder, since, as the text repeatedly states, He "helped David" (vv. 6, 14). Finally, the whole chapter follows a variation of the victory-house-building theme, with battles leading up to a list of David's royal administration and royal household (8:15–18).

Chapter 8 begins with a summary statement about David's wars with the Philistines, which refers back to the battles of chapter 5. As a result of these wars, David took "Metheg Amma" from the Philistines (8:1). This is sometimes thought to be a place name, but there is no other evidence for this. The better interpretation is that it means "bridle of the mother," understanding "bridle" as a symbol of rule and "mother" as a "mother city." Controlling the bridle of the mother meant taking control of the chief city of the Philistines.[3]

---

[3] 1 Chronicles 18:1 says that David took Gath, and this perhaps is the "mother" that 2 Samuel 8 refers to.

The longest section in this chapter has to do with David's victory over Hadadezer of Zobah (vv. 3–12).[4] Hadadezer means "Hadad is a help," and Hadad was an alternate name for the sky or storm god of Canaanites, usually known as "Baal" ("lord" or "master"). Hadadezer was relying on Hadad for help, but Hadadezer was forced to turn to the Arameans of Damascus, and neither they nor Hadad provided much aid (v. 5). Meanwhile, Yahweh was a help to David and "saved" him. Hadadezer's kingdom, Zobah, was a region to the North of Israel populated by Arameans or Syrians, and there were Arameans of Damascus as well as Arameans in Zobah (v. 5). Extending from Zobah to Damascus and as far north as Hamath, Hadadezer's kingdom posed the most serious threat to David's power in the region. Defeating Hadad was thus essential for David to ensure Israel's security. David took the initiative by attacking while Hadad was on his way toward the Euphrates to restore a base of power that had been lost, and he captured a huge number of horsemen, chariots, and infantry. He disabled the horses, keeping one hundred chariots for himself (v. 4) but not breaking the law by increasing his chariot force beyond reasonable limits.

The word for "shields" is rare (v. 7), and some have suggested it means "quivers." In any case, these weapons were ceremonial rather than military, since no one would go out into battle with golden weapons or a golden shield. Some kings of Israel had similar ceremonial golden shields (1 Kgs. 14:26). Bronze taken from these towns was put to use in building the temple and in particular to form the bronze sea, which sat on the back of twelve bulls (1 Chr. 18:8). The sea on the back of the twelve bulls represented, among other things, the sea of nations borne up by the twelve tribes of Israel, and it was appropriate that the sea itself was made of bronze taken from the nations.

Because David was attacking an Aramean king, the Arameans in Damascus counter-attacked. This is a typical pattern in the Bible: Israel often provoked an attack, and then Israel defeated their enemies

[4] Verse 12 repeats verse 3, forming an *inclusio* around this section.

in a defensive battle. In large measure, this was how Joshua's conquest was accomplished, and it is the sequence of events in David's renewed conquest. David won such a decisive victory that he was able to station a garrison or governor in Damascus (v. 6). Arameans became servants to David, and a tributary state, as Yahweh showed Himself superior to Hadad.

David's conquest of Damascus not only kept Hadadezer at bay, but also brought David an ally to the north of Zobah, Hamath, whose capital city was some 120 miles north of Damascus (vv. 9–10). As a result, David had Hadad surrounded, and he also received tribute from Toi, the king of Hamath. Toi had been at war with Hadadezer, and the Hebrew phrase, "a man of wars," suggests that the war was long-standing. Because David defeated Hadad, Toi considered him a savior and gave tribute, sending the tribute by his son. His son's name was "Joram," but in 1 Chronicles 18:10, the son's name was "Hadoram," which means "Hadad is exalted." Hadoram apparently changed his name to "Joram," which means "Yah is exalted." Toi and his kingdom were apparently not only politically "saved" by David, but saved to become Gentile worshipers of Yahweh.[5]

David not only was successful in war, but was a just and fair ruler over Israel (v. 15). He was not so giddy with foreign quarrels that he ignored domestic needs. Among the officials established to oversee his kingdom was Jehoshaphat, a "recorder," a word that comes from the verb *zakar*, to "remember." Jehoshaphat the "recorder" apparently kept David's reign in permanent "memory" by

---

[5] There are several difficulties with 8:13. The text refers to Arameans, but doubtless means Edomites, as some manuscripts indicate. There is also a question about the total number that David killed. The title of Psalm 60 says that Joab slaughtered 12,000 Edomites, while 1 Chronicles 18:12 says that Abishai killed 18,000. Perhaps we are to understand these different numbers as indications of rank. None of the three actually, personally, killed this many. David got credit for the total as the one who commanded the whole army. In Psalm 60, the number perhaps refers to Joab as the commander of a portion of the army that was responsible for 12,000 Edomite deaths, while 1 Chronicles assumes that Abishai was in charge of the campaign, under David. Abishai, therefore, could be given credit for all 18,000 deaths, though his troops apparently only killed 6,000 or less (since Joab's division killed 12,000).

keeping chronicles. David's sons are called "priests." They were certainly not Levitical priests, since they were not in the tribe of Levi. Besides, the text also lists Zadok as priest. Priests were essentially servants in a royal house; David, the anointed "son" of God, had priests who served him, as Yahweh had priests to stand and serve at His throne.

These conquests marked the high point of David's reign, but they were soon to be followed by an astonishing fall into sin. Christian leaders must beware: In defeat, one is tempted to despair, but in victory, one is tempted to become complacent. Watchfulness is as important, more important, in our successes than in our failures.

KINDNESS TO SAUL AND NAHASH, 2 SAMUEL 9-10

In the previous chapter, we noted that 2 Samuel cycles repeatedly through a "victory-housebuilding" pattern. Chapter 8 concluded with a list of David's "household servants," but the concern with the building of David's house continues into chapter 9. After triumphing over his enemies, David welcomed Jonathan's son to his house and his table, building up his house with the discarded remnants of Saul's house.

Chapter 9 records one of the most moving and beautiful stories in the Old Testament, in which David offered the "kindness of God" (v. 3) to Mephibosheth, the son of Jonathan. For many years, Saul was an adversary who pursued David about the land and tried to kill him. Besides, Mephibosheth was the last remaining member of Saul's house, and a potential rival, in spite of his lameness. Yet David brought him to his table to eat as a son and in this we see a picture of the grace of Jesus, the greater David. Though we are members of the house of Adam, a fallen king, He feeds us at His table as king's sons. Though we are enemies, He shows to us the *hesed* of God.

Several details enrich the beauty of the story. The exact meaning of Mephibosheth is uncertain. It could be "one who scatters shame" or "from the mouth of shame," but either way, Mephibosheth, like Ish-bosheth, includes the word "shame." This is what he had suffered, not only as a member of Saul's fallen house, but in his own lameness. When David found him, he was in "Lo-debar" which means "Nothing" or "No-Word" (9:4). This grandson of Israel's first king had lost everything and was living in no man's land. Yet David brought the man of shame from nowhere to the king's palace. David showed this kindness to Mephibosheth because of the covenant he had made with Jonathan. "Lovingkindness" (*hesed*) means faithfulness to covenant obligations that is expressed in acts of generosity and kindness. Lovingkindness may operate in a human-human covenant, as here: David showed his loyalty to Jonathan by showing this kindness to Jonathan's son. But David's loyalty to his covenant with Jonathan was an expression of the "lovingkindness (*hesed*) of God" (v. 3). Just as the Lord had shown Himself faithful to David by doing far more than David asked or imagined, so David was going to do the same for Mephibosheth.

This analogy between David's royal kindness and the kindness of Yahweh may be pressed further by linking Mephibosheth's condition to the ceremonial regulations of the law. According to Leviticus 21:16–24, descendants of Aaron with physical deformities were excluded from service at the altar and in the tabernacle. One of the afflictions that disqualified a man from priestly service was "broken feet" (Lev. 21:19). If Mephibosheth were a descendant of Aaron (which he was not), his lameness would have disqualified him from serving at the altar. Though a disabled priest was not permitted to serve at the altar, however, he was allowed to eat from the priestly portions of the sacrifices (Lev. 21:22). David's table was not, of course, the same as the Lord's table, but David was the human analogue to Yahweh, and David was faithfully applying the law here, by analogy: If a lame man was allowed to feed on Yahweh's bread, he should be permitted to feed on the king's bread. "Lame and blind" Jebusites were cut off from the house of David (5:8), but the lame and blind in Israel were excluded neither from the table of Yahweh nor the table of David.

Verse 12 tells us that Mephibosheth had a son who also came to stay with David.[6] Some have suggested it is a threatening detail, hinting that the house of Saul and tribe of Benjamin might still have a chance to win back the throne. Since Mica is not mentioned again in 2 Samuel, even when David faced Benjamite opposition, this is an unlikely reason. Rather, it shows that David was fully keeping his covenant, not just with Jonathan's son but with his seed, for many generations.

Chapters 9 and 10 are connected by the key word *hesed*. David had shown kindness to Mephibosheth because of the covenant that he had made with Jonathan, and afterward David showed kindness to the son of Nahash, king of the Ammonites, because of the *hesed* that Nahash had shown him. Somewhere along the way, Nahash had shown kindness to David in a way that Saul did not, and Nahash was another Gentile who allied with Yahweh's anointed. The parallel between the two chapters is even more exact than this: Nahash had recently been succeeded by his son, and Mephibosheth was also a descendant of a recently dead king. Though David showed kindness in both chapters, however, the reaction was very different.

It has been suggested that the war recounted in chapter 10 was the same as the war of chapter 8, and indeed there are some similarities in the structure of the passages. In chapter 8, David fought Hadadezer, defeated him, and captured many soldiers. Following that, David plundered the Arameans and stationed garrisons (or governors) in Damascus. In the aftermath, Toi of Hamath became a vassal to David. In chapter 10, David defeated Hadadezer, killing many men, and the kings who served Hadadezer became David's servants. The similarity is deliberate and reinforces the structural

---

[6] This helps us locate the time of this event. Mephibosheth was five years old at the time of the battle of Mount Gilboa when his father and grandfather died (2 Sam. 4:4). When David took the throne over all Israel, he was twelve, since David reigned in Hebron for seven years. If he was now old enough to have a son, he must have been at least twenty and probably several years older. Thus, David must have been near the middle of his forty-year reign when he welcomed Mephibosheth to his table (seven years in Hebron + over a decade in Jerusalem).

unity of this section, but the two accounts are different in a number
of details. In chapter 8, David initiated the war while Hadad was
seeking to establish his power in the eastern part of his kingdom;
in chapter 10, by contrast, Hadadezer responded to David's previous attack, and Hadad mustered his troops to fight David specifically (10:15–16). In chapter 8, David captured 1,700 horsemen and
20,000 foot soldiers, while chapter 10 records that David captured
700 charioteers and 40,000 horsemen. Finally, while Toi became
an ally in chapter 8, there was no mention of other kings coming
over to David's side, as there is in 10:19.

To get the full sequence of events, we have to read chapter
10 in tandem with 11:1 and 12:26–31. After Hanun had insulted
David's official delegation, David attacked Rabbah, the chief city
of the Ammonites. Fearing David's army, the Ammonites hired
Aramean mercenaries, who were little help and eventually retreated
and allied with David instead of with the Ammonites. Defeated,
the Ammonites retreated back into the city (10:14), and Joab laid
siege (11:1). Eventually, Joab and his men broke Rabbah, and at
Joab's urging, David came to finish the job (12:29).[7]

"See" is a key word in chapter 10. The Ammonites "saw" that
David had become their enemy (v. 6), when Joab went out to battle
he "saw" the arrangement of the enemy troops (v. 9), and when the
Ammonites saw Arameans fleeing they retreated (vv. 14–15). The
next stage of the battle begins with the Arameans "seeing" their defeat and gathering to make war again (v. 15). Verse 19 closes out the
theme when the kings associated with Hadadezer "saw" that they
were defeated and turned to David. Finally, the Arameans "feared"
to help Ammon again (v. 19), and, as noted above, the Hebrew verb

----

[7] Chapters 10–12 can thus be read as a single connected narrative with this basic
structure:
    A   War with Ammonites and Arameans, 10:1–11:1
     B   David's sins, 11:2–12:25
    A'   Conquest of Ammonites, 12:26–31
See Philip F. Esler, *Galatians* (New Testament Readings; London: Routledge, 1998),
128–129.

"fear" puns on the verb for "see." The sight of David caused fear and encouraged the Arameans to seek an alliance with Israel.

The Ammonite names are significant. Nahash means "serpent." Saul's victory over (a different?) Nahash was like Adam's first test with the serpent in the garden (1 Sam. 11), but David was aided by a "serpent," making friends with the mammon of unrighteousness, so that when he was cast out of Saul's house he would be received into his dwellings. "Hanun," by contrast, has very positive connotations, being related to a verb that means "to be gracious" (see "Hannah"). Hanun did not live up to his name, for he was anything but gracious. The men of Ammon were like the people that surrounded Saul, suspicious of David's every move and certain that David had sly political motives for everything he did (10:3). They persuaded Hanun that David had sent the men as spies.

The city plays a key role in this chapter as well. When David's men appeared at the city, the sons of Ammon were afraid that they had come to spy (v. 3); they arrayed themselves for battle at the gate of the city (v. 8), and when they were defeated, they retreated into the city (v. 14). It is ironic that though David was acting out of loyalty and kindness, he ultimately *did* overthrow the city and receive the crown (12:30-31). This is one of the ways that God brings good out of evil. The wicked attack the godly, but that is simply God's way of bringing the wicked out on the battlefield, where He can rout them. This is one aspect to the truth that by doing good we heap coals on the heads of our enemies, a truth that David knew long before Paul. When enemies attack the church, or enemies in the church attack the faithful, it may be that God is bringing them out of the dark recesses and into the open so that they can be more easily, and more dramatically, thrashed.

Instead of receiving the condolences and treating David's men with the respect they deserved as a diplomatic delegation, Hanun seized them, cut off half their beards, and cut their clothes to the hip (10:4). He may have intended to mock mourning customs, since cutting or pulling the beard was a mourning ritual, as was tearing clothes.[8] Hanun thought that David's mourning was insincere and therefore turned mourning into a parody of mourning. Cutting the beard was also an assault on masculinity, causing shame. More specifically, Leviticus 19:27 forbade Israelite men from trimming the corners of their beards, and so cutting the beard was an assault on their identity as Israelites. Similarly, each Israelite had a tassel on the corner of his robe as a reminder of the law, and so to cut off the edge of the garment was an assault on the Torah (Num. 15:37–41).[9] This incident also continues the "robe" motif that we have noted earlier. Cutting a garment was an assault on the office, and here the word for "garment" refers to an official uniform (cf. 1 Sam. 17:38), rather than normal clothes.[10] It is as if a foreign ruler ripped an American soldier's uniform or burned the stars and stripes. The men must not only endure personal shame, but also an assault on a symbol of their country.[11]

This was an act of war, and David would not take it lying down. Hearing that David was angry, the Ammonites made the first move by hiring Aramean armies and other mercenaries. Altogether five armies gathered against Israel (v. 6), and this links the battle to the battles that Abram (Gen. 14:1–12) and Joshua fought (Josh. 10:5). Both these earlier battles were defensive conflicts that ended in conquest—like David's war with the Ammonites.

In the course of the battle, the Arameans and Ammonites split up their forces; while the Ammonites set up in battle array around the city of Rabbah, the Arameans and the other armies set up in the fields around the city (v. 8). When the Israelites attacked, they were caught in between, and Joab found himself in the middle of a "two-faced" battle (Hebrew). In response, Joab split up his own

[8] Gordon, *I & II Samuel*, 250.

[9] Bergen, *1, 2 Samuel*, 358.

[10] Alter, *The David Story*, 245. The word is *madim*, and Alter cites 1 Samuel 17:38.

[11] In other passages of the Old Testament, cutting the beard was a sign of submission and conquest (Is. 7:20), and cutting off the garments was also a way of humbling POWs (Is. 20:4). See Youngblood, *1, 2 Samuel*, vol. 3, 922–923.

forces. If Arameans began to triumph over Joab, Abishai was to "save" Joab, but if the Ammonites began to defeat Abishai, Joab came to "save." Joab's little speech used the verb "be strong" four times (vv. 11–12). Arameans and Ammonites may be "too strong," but Joab urged his men to be stronger still. Joab also said that his men were fighting for the "cities of our God" (v. 12). He probably meant that, if the Arameans and Ammonites were to win, they would likely invade Israel. After all, they had already attacked David's emissaries, and it was possible that they would not stop with symbolic assaults on unarmed ambassadors. But Israel was also fighting before a city that would soon become a "city of our God." Joab was hardly an admirable man but he demonstrated genuine faith at Rabbah. He exhorted his men to fight, quickly devising a risky strategy to handle the difficult position he was in, and yet he acknowledged that victory was not in his hands (v. 12).[12] At Rabbah, Joab was more faithful than his master, who remained behind in Jerusalem (11:1).

As it turned out, Joab and Abishai were stronger than the Ammonites and Arameans (vv. 13–14). But the war was not over. Hadadezer was not satisfied with the outcome, his second defeat at David's hands. So he assembled another Aramean force. When David heard that Hadadezer was again mustering troops, he set out in a preemptive move by crossing the Jordan to fight in the Transjordan. There he won a decisive victory, and the kings who had previously served Hadadezer became servants of David. In chapter 8, the battles of David were followed by the taking of plunder. Here the plunder was human plunder. David was the stronger man who plundered the house of the strong Hadadezer, and his god Hadad.

---

[12] A number of things are split in half in the passage. The word "half" is actually used for the beards and the robes of David's officials, and the armies are also split in half. Citing Polzin, Alter suggests that this is beginning a theme that will occupy the later chapters: the divisions and fissures that occur in David's house and family (*The David Story*, 246).

THE FALL OF DAVID, 2 SAMUEL 11–12[13]

Chapters 11–12 tell a single connected story, the story of David, Bathsheba, and Uriah, and these chapters set the course of events for the rest of 2 Samuel. This event can be seen from a number of perspectives. First, it was another fall. The Lord had promised that David's dynasty would continue, that his son would build a temple for the Lord, and that the Seed of David would reign forever. This was the charter of humanity, the *torah ha'adam*, placing David at the center of God's work in world history. Like Adam, David sinned after being given these great privileges; after the "new creation" of the Davidic covenant, there was a "new fall." Like Adam, David sinned in relation to a woman, and as with Adam, the sin was David's, not the woman's. Adam's sin was spiritual adultery, while David's was literal adultery. Like Adam's, David's sin involved tasting forbidden fruit.

Second, as noted at the outset of this chapter, David's sin was comparable to Saul's. David waited patiently to receive the kingdom from the Lord, but after being established as king, he began to seize things, like a king of the nations. In fact, this habit of taking women was, as we have seen, well-developed long before David became king. It was one of his great failures during his training for kingship, and it was nearly fatal. David's sin, like Saul's, was not merely a personal sin, but a threat to the kingdom. If David did not repent of this sin, his robe would be torn from him, as Saul's was.

The public and political significance of David's sin becomes clear when we recall that David's adultery took place during the Ammonite war, a point reinforced by the chiastic shape of the passage:

---

[13] The following section repeats portions of, but also extends, the discussion of David and Bathsheba in my *A House for My Name*, 149–152.

A   Joab is on the field besieging Rabbah, but David has stayed behind in Jerusalem, 1:1 (or, 10:1–11:1)

 B David sleeps with Bathsheba and she becomes pregnant, 11:2–5

  C David arranges for Uriah's death, 11:6–25

   D Bathsheba mourns for Uriah, 11:26–27

    E Nathan confronts David's sin, 12:1–15a

   D' David mourns for his infant son, 12:15b–17

  C' David's son dies, 12:18–23

 B' David sleeps with Bathsheba and she becomes pregnant, 12:24–25

A'   David goes to Rabbah and finishes the siege, then returns to Jerusalem, 12:26–31

Several items in this structure are worth noting. First, the central scene was Nathan's confrontation of David. Up to that point, David had sinned and tried to cover it up, but Nathan uncovered the sin and informed David what punishment he could expect. Nathan's delivery of Yahweh's word was the hinge on which the story turned; Nathan's message, and David's penitent reaction, saved the kingdom.

The threat to the kingdom is emphasized by the references to the siege of Rabbah at the beginning and end of the story. Chapter 11 continues the account of the Ammonite wars that had been described in chapters 8 and 10. The contrast between the A and A' sections of the outline is striking: At the beginning, David was staying home while Joab prosecuted the siege of Rabbah. David did not act like a king at the beginning, since he did not "go out," a phrase used to describe a king's military duties (1 Sam. 8:20; 1 Kgs. 3:7; 2 Chr. 1:10). Instead of "coming in" to protect the brides of Jerusalem, David stayed behind and took one of them. Instead of "going out" to lead his men into battle, he arranged for the death of one of his mighty men. After Nathan corrected him, he "went out" (12:29) to capture Rabbah, receive its crown, and pile up spoils. The passage ends with David "coming in" to Jerusalem, leading the victorious procession back to his throne. By the end of the story, he was fulfilling his proper royal duties.

David did not necessarily have to go out to the field personally. When he avenged himself against Hanun, he sent Joab instead of leading the armies himself, and there was no sin in that (10:7). The problem was not so much David's physical location as his psychological and spiritual engagement in the war. When Uriah came back to Jerusalem, he refused to go to his wife, and we learn that other soldiers of David were also sleeping around the palace courts, apparently as an act of solidarity with the soldiers in the field (11:9). Uriah told David how he should have conducted himself in Jerusalem: "The ark and Israel and Judah are in booths, and my lord Joab and the servants of my lord are camping in the open field. Shall I then go to my house to eat and to drink and to lie with my wife?" (11:11). So long as the army was on the field, *all* of Israel's hosts were under vows of holy war. Had David placed himself under the holiness code required of Israelite warriors, he could have stayed in the capital without sin.[14]

The story begins at "the return of the year" when "messengers" went out. The verse is often translated as "when kings go out," and that is thematically appropriate. (In fact, 1 Chr. 20:1 uses the word "kings" [*melekim*].) In the Hebrew Massoretic Text of 2 Samuel 11:1, however, the word is not "kings" but "messengers," a word that differs from the Hebrew word for "kings" by one consonant. Perhaps there is a pun connecting "kings" with "messengers." In any case, "messenger" is as thematically appropriate as "kings." Throughout the next chapter, messengers carry messages in several directions. Normally, messengers "went out" to conduct war and negotiations and other public business, but here the messengers were used to arrange adultery and then murder (cf. vv. 4, 6, 14, 19, 22, 25). Instead of acting like a king and going out (or at least "going out" in spirit), David contented himself with sending messengers here and there carrying adulterous proposals and death sentences in their hands. The verb "send" is one of the key words of the chapter and brings out the theme of messengers moving back and forth.

The phrase "the return of the year" refers to spring, the normal season for military campaigns in the ancient Near East. Rainy

---

[14] Thanks to James B. Jordan for clarifying this for me.

weather during the winter made it difficult for kings to carry on campaigns (see 1 Kgs. 20:22, 26; 2 Chr. 36:10), since roads were difficult to pass. The reference to spring is also symbolically appropriate. A new year is beginning, and a new year holds promise of renewed blessing and prosperity. Here, the new year is ironic; instead of a new age of prosperity, the "return of the year" brings events that will culminate in civil war. Passover may also be in view, since it was celebrated in the first month. There is a Passover later in the story, a substitutionary death of a son that delivered David.

David was lazing around while the army was on the field. As he arose at evening, he walked on his roof and "saw" the woman who was "good" in appearance; having "seen" something "good," he then "took" her into his house. The sequence is familiar from Genesis 3 and emphasizes David's initiative: Though Bathsheba did commit adultery, David was the one taking forbidden fruit. Bathsheba was a daughter of "Eliam," one of David's "thirty" (2 Sam. 23:34; cf 1 Chr. 3:5) and the son of Ahitophel, one of David's chief advisors. Ahitophel was from Giloh (Josh. 15:51; cf 2 Sam. 15:12), a city of Judah, and thus Bathsheba was from David's own tribe and the granddaughter of one of David's closest advisors (2 Sam. 15:12). In short, she would doubtless be known to David already and was probably a generation younger than the king.[15] Joab's murder of Abner was all the more horrible because it was a young man killing an old man; once we understand Bathsheba's relationship with David, his adultery appears even more disgusting, the work of a dirty old man and leering voyeur, of a sexual predator whose lust was almost incestuous, of a President who demands oral sex from a starstruck intern in the Oval Office.

When he discovered that Bathsheba was pregnant, David called Uriah back from the front. Uriah was a "Hittite," a Gentile,

---

[15] Some translations suggest that Bathsheba was cleansing herself when David first saw her and this has been interpreted to mean that she was cleansing herself from her menstrual impurity. This would prove she was not pregnant before David brought her into his house.

and one of David's "thirty" (2 Sam. 23:39). Clearly, however, Uriah was a converted Hittite who displayed greater devotion to Yahweh than David in this episode. David kept him home for three days. In verses 6-9, David talked with Uriah for the first time. The next morning, David learned that Uriah had not gone into his own home, and on that second day David had another conference that ended with Uriah deciding to stay until the morrow (vv. 10-12), and so verse 13 brings us to the third night. In the morning of the fourth day (v. 14), David sent him back to the front with his own death warrant in his hand. Thus, we have a three-day pattern, but here the three days lead not to "resurrection" but to death.

Some commentators suggest that throughout these three days, Uriah suspected what had been happening at the palace. Uriah must have thought it extraordinarily odd that David summoned him back from the front for three days, with nothing more to talk about than the state of battle, information that could have been relayed to David by any number of messengers. If Uriah knew what had happened, he was playing a clever and dangerous game, not unlike the antic disposition of Shakespeare's Hamlet. Though he remained more oblique than Nathan, Uriah may have deliberately rebuked David's unkingly behavior. More than that, Uriah ended the whole discussion with an oath of David's life: Even if it cost David's life, he would not do what David encouraged him to do (11:11). Was there a veiled threat here?

When David's attempts to manipulate Uriah into breaking his military discipline failed, he decided that the only way to cover up his sin was to get rid of Uriah. What did David think he could accomplish by having Uriah killed? Could he not have weathered the political storm? Could he not have denied everything? In the Old Testament, adultery was a capital crime, and Deuteronomy 17:18–20 makes it clear that kings were under the law as much as the common people. If it could be proven that David had committed adultery, he might have been tried and executed. Surely, though, that was an unlikely outcome for a popular and successful king. Perhaps a better explanation is to notice that David was not acting with sense. After all, he sent Uriah's death warrant with Uriah, which would strike any normal person as more than a little chancy, especially if Uriah had some inkling of David's adultery: Might not Uriah open the letter and find out what he was carrying? Either David had not thought of this possibility (which would mean that he was being foolish) or he had thought of it and dismissed it (which would mean he was being foolish).

Even more, the instructions he gave to Joab show that he was not thinking clearly (11:15). One of his main goals of a coverup is to *limit* the number of people who might become suspicious. David's plan, by contrast, would dramatically increase suspicion, since all the soldiers who withdrew from Uriah would have to be in on the plan, and they would surely be asking themselves why Joab would give them such idiotic and murderous instructions. In a sense, David was trying to limit the damage. He wanted a surgical strike. Joab had wit enough about him to recognize that this "surgical strike" would undermine the overall purpose, which was to get rid of Uriah without making anyone suspect that David was trying to get rid of Uriah. Instead of following David's orders, Joab sent several of his men to the city walls. In the course of the battle, several were killed with Uriah, but this was the price of carrying out the spirit of David's instructions. But it demonstrates one important fact about covering sin: Murderous plans cannot remain under control but extend beyond the intended victim. And David's blundering illustrates another important truth: Logic is not morally neutral; sinners are not only immoral but stupid, and if a leader wants to retain his ingenuity he should look to his integrity.

When Uriah was dead, Joab prepared a messenger to answer questions that David might ask (vv. 20–21). Joab's instructions stand out oddly in the text. The events of Uriah's death are told in a few spare words, but Joab's instructions, which seem unnecessary, take up a number of sentences. This points to the importance of the themes introduced by Joab. An attentive messenger would have found these instructions strange, to say the least. David had just lost a number of soldiers, and Joab warned the messenger that

David might fly into a rage. Then, to *soothe* the king, the messenger was supposed to inform him about another casualty, one of his mighty men. Why should another death *pacify* the king's anger?[16] Like Saul, David had turned his world upside down; instead of mourning the death of a mighty man, he celebrated, and instead of being concerned about the course of the battle, he was concerned only to rid himself of an obstacle.

Joab made an interesting connection with Abimelech (v. 21).[17] Joab's messenger did not have to deal with any of these questions, and the comparison with Abimelech is more meant for the reader of 2 Samuel than for the messenger in the story. According to Judges 9, Abimelech, the son of Gideon, died when his head was crushed by a millstone dropped from the tower of Thebez. Joab compared Uriah to Abimelech, but the real parallel to Abimelech is David. David was the one maintaining his power by killing his brothers (as Abimelech had), and he was the one whose head was in danger of being crushed by a woman. This, at least, was Joab's shrewd assessment of the situation; he knew of David's sexual appetites, and the fact that he alluded to this suggests that the story of David's adultery had already been making the rounds.

The messenger, for his part, gave a distorted report to avoid the rebuke that Joab had prepared him for (vv. 23–24). This throws an ironic light on the opening verse: Messengers were racing hither and yon throughout the story, but the messengers were unreliable and instructions were not carried out. This reinforces the fact that David's adultery had interfered with his ability to rule, and not simply with his personal piety. He acted without sense, and his servants were not obeying orders. Throughout the remainder of 2 Samuel, we have only a few brief glimpses of the great leader that David was prior to his sin.

---

[16] Meir Sternberg, *The Poetics of Biblical Narrative: Ideological Literature and the Drama of Reading* (Bloomington: Indiana University Press, 1987), 215–216. My entire discussion of chapters 11–12 has been deeply shaped by Sternberg's reading of the passage.

[17] The question about Abimelech is the middle of five questions that are arranged chiastically: close-from wall-Abimelech-from wall-close.

David's response to the messenger was chilling (v. 25). On the surface, it was an experienced warrior's weary acknowledgment that "you can't win them all," that "war kills," and that "casualties happen." It was even an encouraging message in its way, as David reassured Joab that he should not take the loss of men too hard. In context, it is another thing entirely. David was manifestly happy that Joab had allowed several men to be killed, so long as Uriah was included; with a shrug at the serendipity of war, he cold-heartedly accepted deaths that he had caused. David was not operating according to the principle that "one man must die for the people," but rather that "many people must die for the one man—the king." A king like the kings of the nations indeed—first taking women and now throwing soldiers away like rubbish.

Nathan was "sent" by Yahweh to David (v. 1), another of the many "messengers" in the story. Yahweh had his own messenger, who came to undo the work of the other messengers. Nathan fulfilled one of the leading functions of the prophets, namely, to rebuke and correct rulers. Samuel had this role in relation to Saul, Elijah in relation to Ahab, Jeremiah in relation to all the kings of the last days of Judah, and so on. Prophets, as the saying goes, spoke truth to power, and one of their key functions was to restrain the king by announcing the word of the Lord.

Nathan came with a case for David to judge, and in some versions, he even introduced the story by saying, "I have a case for you." At the same time, the style of the story was typical of fictional parables. The reference to two unnamed men was a fictional convention and the poor man's attachment to his ewe lamb was wildly exaggerated. The parable was set up to draw attention to the rich man's abuse of position and power. It was a story of exploitation and oppression, not simple theft.

The poor man's attachment to his ewe lamb might have been excessive, but it followed exactly the events that it allegorized. The man ate, drank, and lay with his ewe lamb, and this was what David tried to get Uriah to do and what David actually did with

Uriah's wife. The reference in verse 3 to the ewe lamb in the man's "bosom" anticipates verse 8, where the Lord referred to Saul's wives who had been given into David's "bosom." Verse 3 states that the ewe lamb was like a "daughter" to the poor man, and the word "daughter" is "Bat," the first syllable of "Bathsheba." Nathan came perilously close to giving away the story, but David, uncharacteristically dull (see 2 Sam. 1:1ff.), failed to catch the hint. Nathan's parable used the word "man" four times: rich man, poor man, visiting man, and then David's response used "man" twice again (vv. 5–6). These six uses of "man" set the stage for Nathan's charge, "You are the man," the seventh and climactic use of the word in the passage. The focus of the parable seems to be on David's adultery and not murder. But the ewe lamb was slaughtered (v. 4) and not simply stolen. For the rich man to have his way, it was not enough to steal the lamb. Blood must be shed.

David became angry at the treatment of the poor man, and his anger focused on the word "pity": The rich man thought it a "pity" to take a sheep from his own flock but had no "pity" on his neighbor's lamb (v. 4). That same opposition of pity/no pity characterized David: While he pitied the fictional poor man in the story, he had shown no pity for the real-life Uriah and Bathsheba.[18] David's death sentence was not a legal decision, but it was fitting as a self-condemnation, for he did deserve to die (v. 13). The strict legal decision was in verse 6, a demand for fourfold restitution. According to Exodus 22:1, certain crimes required fourfold restitution rather than the normal "double restitution." This sentence fits neatly into David's own situation, for he paid fourfold for the death of Uriah, losing four sons. All this became clear when Nathan revealed the truth behind his parable: David had passed judgment on "the man" and Nathan turned the tables, "You are the man."

The rebuke is divided into two sections. Verses 7-10 focused attention on the murder of Uriah and the consequences that David

---

[18] Youngblood, *1, 2 Samuel*, 942–943. Youngblood is citing an article by Stuart Lasine.

would suffer as a result, while the second section concentrated on David's adultery and Yahweh's judgment on that. In both cases, Yahweh applied an eye-for-eye justice. David was blamed for Uriah's death, as if he had acted like a Joab and struck him down with his own hand (v. 9). Because he used the sword of the Ammonites to strike down Uriah, the sword would not depart from David's house. Strife dominated David's house and kingdom for the remainder of his reign, and following Solomon's reign, the strife permanently divided the kingdom. Whoever takes up the sword will perish with the sword. Second, David was accused of "taking," which reminds us of Samuel's warning that the kings of the nations take wives and daughters and sons.[19] Here, again, Nathan announced that the punishment would be eye-for-eye. By taking, David had done evil, and the Lord threatened to bring evil and calamity on David (v. 11). More specifically, David took another's wife, so his wives would be taken. The punishment would intensify and not merely repeat David's own sin. David slunk around secretly to steal a wife, but his wives would be stolen and humbled before the eyes of all, in broad daylight. Jesus said that whatever is done in secret will be proclaimed on the housetops. God works to expose the secret sins.[20] David, the "son" of Saul, not only imitated his father's sins but intensified them; when sin got to its "third generation" with David's sons, it had become full-grown.

Nathan's rebuke was reminiscent of Samuel's rebukes to Saul. In 1 Samuel 15:17, the Lord reminded Saul that He had raised him up, anointed him, and sent him on a mission, which he failed to

[19] The reference to the wives of Saul is odd, since it seems to condone David's accumulation of wives. As mentioned above, it was typical practice for a successor to take over the harem of his predecessor, and David received Saul's harem (of which only two women are ever mentioned). This in itself was proper; as Saul's successor, David should care for Saul's household. Taking the women into his "bosom" may mean no more than David cared for them, and there is no evidence that David had sexual relations with Saul's wives. Certainly, he had no children by any wives of Saul. Finally, God did not promise that He would have multiplied wives, but only promised to add "this and that."

[20] The film *Magnolia* treats this theme in a very interesting, though extremely vulgar, fashion. The sins of the fathers are passed on to the sons, but the sons take their fathers' sins to "another level."

complete. Nathan reminded David of the Lord's mercies to him: Yahweh raised up David, delivered him, and gave him all that he could possibly want. Yet he was not satisfied, but instead started taking from the poor man who lived next door. Saul despised the prophet's word and David had "despised the Word of the Lord," the Torah (v. 9), which was the equivalent of "despising God" Himself (v. 10).[21]

David was delivered, but punishment must be carried out, and it was carried out on David's son. David had acted like a Pharaoh, seizing a bride, and like Pharaoh, he lost his son as a result. Yet, the death of David's son was not only a punishment but a substitutionary death. When the child died, taking David's deserved death, David arose, washed, anointed himself, changed clothes, worshiped and ate. David rose from the dust of death to the table, a resurrection for David that depended on the death of David's son. David then went to Bathsheba and they conceived a second son. Solomon is clearly the replacement for the dead son, the son "passed over" by the angel of death. Even the name *shelomo* may have the sense of "replacement" (also taken as "his peace"). This helps to extend the typology of the passage: Jesus died and rose again to take David's throne; Solomon did not die and rise again, but one son of David died and was replaced by another. The replacement theme that we saw frequently in 1 Samuel makes a reappearance.

Yahweh gave Solomon a second name, Jedidiah, which means "favored of Yah" or "beloved of Yah" (v. 25). This name is not used elsewhere, but several factors suggest the Yahweh was designating Solomon as heir. It was common for ancient kings to receive a throne name. In Solomon's case, the second name came from Yahweh and designated him as the "favored" one. If Solomon was

---

[21] "Enemies" (v. 14) may not have been in the original. In the Hebrew, the text states that David has shown "contempt for the enemies of Yahweh," but that hardly seems worthy of condemnation. The NASB translation is an effort to rescue a sensible meaning, but does not reflect the Hebrew: "given occasion to the enemies of Yahweh to blaspheme." Perhaps "enemies" has been added and the original sense is "show contempt for Yahweh," the same sin that led to Eli's sons' demise.

in fact marked out as David's heir from birth, this helps to explain
Bathsheba's and Nathan's efforts to place Solomon on the throne
(1 Kgs. 1:11–31). This suggestion also intensifies a contrast between
Solomon and Absalom that is an underlying motif in the remainder of 2 Samuel. Both Solomon's name and Absalom's contain the
word *shalom*, peace, and the verbal echo in their names sets up a
contrast between the two characters. Absalom hardly lived up to
his name; he was the false son. Solomon was the true son, the true
man of peace.

Chapter 12 ends where chapter 11 began, with the siege of
Rabbah. Joab was about to capture the city and asked David to
come out to take credit for the conquest. In verse 27, Joab composed a poetic announcement of his capture, and the parallelism
suggests that the "city of waters" was a portion of Rabbah or an
alternative designation for Rabbah itself. Whichever was the case,
a "city of waters" suggests an Edenic city. Through his repentance
and because of the death of his son, David gained the "city of waters." As part of this restoration of his kingdom, David took the gold
crown of the Ammonites, which weighed 65–75 pounds (v. 30). It
was placed on David's head, but it is unlikely that he wore it around
the palace on his days off. It was the crown of "their king," but the
word could be translated as "Milcom," the name of an Ammonite
god. Possibly the crown had once adorned the head of a statue of
the Ammonite god. David defeated not only the king of the city
of waters, but by Yahweh's strength, he overcame the gods of the
Ammonites. He became king of kings, taking on many crowns.

Verse 31 is difficult, for many translations suggest that David dismembered the Ammonites and burned them in crematoria.
There are instructions in Scripture to carry out the ban on the
Canaanites, slaughtering everything that breathes, but there are no
instructions to put conquered people under "saws" or into "brick-
kilns." Alternatively, the verse may be translated to indicate that
the Ammonites were put to work with saws and axes and to make
bricks (one consonant change is necessary for "pass through" to

turn to "serve"). Thus, the Ammonites were put to forced labor. This was consistent with David's practices in other wars; he had brought a number of other cities and kings under his dominion and made them vassal states. It also fits the pattern of victory-building that has been noted above.

Because of his sin, David's kingdom was tottering. But he repented, and he had been delivered because of the substitutionary "death and resurrection" of his son. And the victory at Rabbah gave hope: David was back as a warrior, for he had captured the city of waters and taken the crown; and he was back as a builder, putting the Ammonites to labor.[22]

---

[22] This clause has been translated as "And he made them transgress against (i.e., desecrate) the Molechs" (see P. Kyle McCarter, *II Samuel*, Anchor Bible #9 [New York: Doubleday, 1984], 311; McCarter rejects this translation).

CHAPTER**TEN**

2 SAMUEL 13–20[1]

DAVID'S KINGDOM, DEAD AND REBORN

Nathan's prophecy that the sword would never depart from David's house began to work itself out in strife between David's sons and in the rebellion of Absalom, and it began to work itself out in such a way that the sins of David were repeated and exaggerated by his sons. Overall, the storyline of chapters 13–20 is like the story of David and Bathsheba. A sexual sin (David and Bathsheba; Amnon with Tamar) was followed by a murder (David killed Uriah; Absalom killed Amnon), and afterwards someone came to David telling a parable that tricked him into passing judgment against himself (Nathan and the wise woman of Tekoa).

In keeping with this emphasis, the storyline of Absalom's life should be familiar: A king's son, he fled from the land to escape the wrath of the king, sojourned among Gentiles (Arameans in Geshur), and then returned to Jerusalem (2 Sam. 13:23–14:33). Once back in Jerusalem, he conspired against David and was proclaimed king in Hebron (15:1–12). Absalom's life history was clearly a repetition of David's own history. Like his son, David fled from the wrath of a king, spent time in exile among Gentiles, came back into the land and was proclaimed king—in Hebron. Of course, Absalom

---

[1] This section of 2 Samuel covers chapters 13–20 and can be outlined as follows:
  13:1–22: Amnon and Tamar: household divided
    13:23–14:33: Absalom kills Amnon and flees and returns (Joab)
      15:1–12: Absalom's conspiracy
        15:13–16:14: David's flight from Jerusalem
          16:15–17:14: Hushai and Ahitophel's advice
            17:15–29: Messengers arrive, and David to Mahanaim
              18:1–18: battle and death of Absalom (Joab)
              18:19–33: David receives news in Mahanaim; messengers
            19:1–8: Joab advises David
          19:8b–39: David's return
        19:40–20:3: Split of Israel and Judah; Sheba's revolt
      20:4–22: Sheba defeated; Amasa killed; wise woman involved (Joab)
    20:23–26: David's household restored, after a fashion

249

was a photo negative of David, a counterfeit image of his father.[2] David fled from Saul because of Saul's irrational hostility to him, not because of any evil on his part, but Absalom fled because he had committed fratricide. Further, David did not try to seize the kingdom, while Absalom conspired against his father. Absalom, we might say, was the man that Saul thought David was. How appropriate: David acted like Saul, and as a result found himself opposed by a "David."

Though the antics of Absalom are central in these chapters, this section also highlights several things about David. As emphasized in the last chapter, David's sin with Bathsheba was an abuse of his authority as king, and the events of these chapters confirm that his adultery, private though it may have been, had enormous public consequences. Because of his sin, David lost the kingdom for a time; Absalom moved in and took over David's concubines, as David had taken Saul's. In the end, David's kingdom was revived, but not without considerable loss of life, authority, prestige, and vitality. David also suffered grievous personal consequences from his sin. On several occasions, David was manipulated into the middle of conflicts among his sons and even unconsciously enabled his sons to act against him. After chapter 12, we never see him fighting again. When Absalom threatened and took over the kingdom, David let Joab take care of the battle, while David waited in Mahanaim, and when Sheba, a Benjamite, revolted, Joab again handled the battle. To be sure, David was getting old, but old age was no impediment to a Moses or a Caleb (Deut. 34:7; Josh. 14:10–12). Though David was forgiven and though he regained the kingdom, he never recovered his vigor. He lost initiative and spent the rest of his reign feebly reacting to events rather than taking things in hand. David became a pitiable figure, an empty robe, an

---

[2] Solomon, by contrast, was the true image of his father: He was anointed king by a prophet (1 Kgs. 1:34), "loved Yahweh" (3:3), had good relations with Hiram of Tyre (5:1–12), built the house that David hoped to build (chs. 6–8), and brought the ark there (8:1–11). Absalom tore down everything his father built; Solomon erected a more glorious kingdom on David's foundations. Of course, he also repeated David's sin in taking many wives (11:1–8).

old man shivering in his bed (1 Kgs. 1:1–4). Christian leaders take
warning: Your private sins will not remain private; even if they are
never discovered, they will sap your fervor and energy and endan-
ger your ministry.

Echoes of a number of earlier biblical events may be heard in
these chapters. In the last chapter, we noted that David's sin combined all the sins of Saul, which in turn repeated the sins in Genesis
1–6. We may use the same scheme to understand the sequence of
events that followed David's sin. Taking Bathsheba was an Adamic
sin, a sin of seizing forbidden fruit, and David was driven out of the
garden-city as a result. The curse on David's house worked itself out
in a Cain-and-Abel rivalry between Absalom and Amnon, which
leads to Absalom's exile from the land. These two sins together
interrupted David's kingdom, and this stands in the place of the
"flood" judgment in Genesis 6–9. In a somewhat modified sense,
Absalom sinned in all three zones:

Creation	Absalom's Sin
Garden/father	Conspiracy/David's concubines
Land/brother	Murder of Amnon
World/nation	Steals hearts of Israel

David presided over a divided house much as Jacob did, and
like Jacob, David lost control of his sons. In Genesis, Jacob's older
sons were one-by-one eliminated from being heirs: Reuben lost
his position by a sin against his father, taking his concubine (Gen.
35:22; 49:4), and Simeon and Levi were cursed because they slew
the circumcised "brothers" in the city of Shechem (Gen. 34:1–31;
49:5–7). As a result, the fourth son, Judah, became preeminent
among his brothers. In David's family, Amnon was killed, Absalom
died during the civil war, and later Adonijah was put to death after
an attempt to take the kingdom from Solomon (1 Kgs. 2:13–25).
When the dust cleared, Solomon, the fourth son and true "Judah,"
remained on the throne. It is another variation on the "replacement" theme from 1 Samuel, though in this case the "replacement"
son is also a biological son.

Girard's notion of "mimetic rivalry," discussed in an earlier chapter, also illumines the action. Several of David's sons were envious of Solomon and sought to displace him and seize the crown. In this they were acting like Saul, who considered David a rival. By contrast, we never see Solomon scraping and clawing for power; he is rather aloof from the action until the crown falls into his lap. The violent rivalries that marked the latter years of David's reign, however, were largely David's responsibility. His weakness, stemming from his sin, opened the field for rivals to fight it out; without restraint from the father, the sons struggled to succeed him.

David was not only following the footsteps of Jacob, but was also continuing to enact the history of the nation of Israel. The events of these chapters provide a preview of Israel's history from the time of Solomon to the time of the return from exile:

David (2 Samuel)	Israel
David's adultery, 11:1–5	Solomon's foreign wives, 1 Kgs. 11:1–8
prophecy: sword in house, 12:9	prophecy: kingdom torn, 1 Kgs. 11:26–40
Absalom's exile and return, 13:1–14:33	Jeroboam's exile and return, 1 Kgs. 11:40–12:2
kingdom divided as Israel/Judah, 15:6; 18:7	kingdom divided as Israel/Judah, 1 Kgs. 12:16–20
David exiled from land, 15:13–17:26	Israel/Judah exiled from land, 2 Kgs. 17; 25
David returns to land, 19:9–20:3	Israel returns to land, 2 Chr. 36:22–23; Ezra 1

No wonder the prophets continually spoke of the return from exile as if it involved a revival of David's kingdom (e.g., Is. 9:7; 11:1; 11:10; Jer. 30:9; 33:14–18).

AMNON, TAMAR, AND ABSALOM, 2 SAMUEL 13:1–22[3]

This episode includes a number of allusions to earlier events of the Old Testament, especially to several events in Genesis. Another Tamar is a prominent character in Genesis 38; two of Judah's sons

---

[3] 2 Samuel 13:1–22 forms a distinct section of the story. The phrase "now it was after this" at the beginning of chapter 13 marks the beginning of a new section. Further, verse 22 forms an *inclusio* with verse 1, since the three main parties are mentioned in both

married Tamar and each died. In 2 Samuel 13 we again have a woman named Tamar and several dying brothers. Moreover, Genesis lays out a careful contrast between Judah and Joseph. Judah slept with Tamar when she was dressed as a prostitute and fathered his own grandsons (Gen. 38:12–30), but in the very next chapter Joseph resisted the aggressive seductions of Potiphar's wife (39:7–18). Allusions to the story of Joseph and Potiphar's wife are also found in 2 Samuel 13. Amnon said "come lie with me" (2 Sam. 13:11), speaking the same words that Potiphar's wife spoke to Joseph (Gen. 39:12). When Amnon seized Tamar, she said "No" four times and called Amnon's actions a "disgraceful thing" (2 Sam. 13:12–13), echoing Joseph's objection that sex with Potiphar's wife would be a "great sin" (Gen. 39:9). Tamar wore a "long-sleeved garment" (2 Sam. 13:18), the same phrase used to describe the robe that Jacob gave to Joseph (Gen. 37:3). These allusions comment in various ways on the sin of David. In Genesis 38, Judah slept with the disguised Tamar, and though David did not sleep with his daughter,

---

verses: Absalom, Tamar, and Amnon. Though parallel, verses 1 and 22 are also sharply opposed; the story begins with Amnon's love for Tamar, but ends with Absalom's hatred for Amnon. This transition from love to hate takes place in the middle of the story, when Amnon begins to hate Tamar after he has raped her (vv. 14–15). The whole section is chiastically organized:

A   Amnon's love for Tamar, 13:1–2
  B   Amnon and Jonadab, 13:3–5
    C   Amnon and David, 13:6–7
      D Tamar and Amnon, 13:8–19
    C' Absalom and Tamar, 13:20
  B'   David's anger, 13:21
A'   Absalom's hatred for Amnon, 13:22
The central section forms a chiasm as well:
A   Tamar arrives and fixes cakes, 13:8–9a
  B   Amnon sends everyone out, 13:9b
    C   Amnon's proposal, 13:10–14a (protest; ends with "he would not listen")
      D Rape, 13:14b–15a
    C' Amnon rejects her, 13:15b–16 (protest; ends with "he would not listen")
  B'   Amnon calls attendant back in, 13:17
A'   Tamar leaves mourning, 13:18–19
See the somewhat different conclusions of Youngblood, *1, 2 Samuel*, vol. 3, 954–946.

he was like another Judah, whose sons were dying. And the contrast between Judah and Joseph is at work here, for David was another Judah, and not another Joseph.

The very phrase "disgraceful thing" (2 Sam. 13:12) was used in Genesis 34:7, the story of the seduction of Dinah, and this forms a particularly intriguing allusion. Amnon was like Shechem, who did a "disgraceful thing" by seducing the daughter of Jacob. In response, Levi and Simeon encouraged all the men of Shechem to be circumcised and then slaughtered them. The similarity between the two situations highlights a radical difference between Shechem and Amnon: Shechem loved Dinah and was willing to become a member of Jacob's tribe to marry her (Gen. 34:3, 18–24); after Amnon had taken Tamar, he hated and rejected her (2 Sam. 13:15). Absalom played the role of Levi and Simeon, taking vengeance for his sister's rape, while David was another Jacob, standing helplessly by while his sons created havoc wherever they went. The phrase "disgraceful thing" reappears in Judges 20:6, 10 to condemn the rape and murder of the Levite's concubine by the sodomite men of Gibeah. That "disgraceful act" led to a civil war between Benjamin and the other tribes, and the rape of Tamar had a similar outcome. Within the books of Samuel, Eli's sons were condemned for sleeping with the dedicated virgins that served in the tabernacle (1 Sam. 2:22). Apparently the princesses of David's house were in a similar protected position, for Tamar wore a robe that symbolized her virginity (2 Sam. 13:18). Like Eli, David failed to restrain the Hophnis and Phineahases in his own house, and their princely abominations brought desolation not unlike the desolation caused by the priests.

Both Absalom and Amnon are designated as "sons of David" (2 Sam. 13:1).[4] The fact that two "sons of David" were at odds

---

[4] Notice the order of names in verse 1. Tamar is mentioned in the middle of the two men, and she is going to be at the center of their relations with each other. The opening verse is like a movie poster with the woman standing between her two lovers. Notice the same device in verse 20: brother, brother, sister, brother, brother.

showed that the "sword" that Nathan threatened had come to divide David's house. Amnon was the eldest son of David and possibly the heir apparent, since Ahinoam was one of David's early wives (2 Sam. 3:2). By his sin, Amnon ruined his chances to inherit the kingdom, much as David endangered his kingdom by his adultery. As mentioned before, the fissures in David's family were rooted in his polygamy for, though brothers, Amnon and Absalom had different mothers and probably grew up virtually unknown to one another. There is another, darker, reason why both Amnon and Absalom are called "sons of David." Both, after all, behaved as David did, repeating David's own sins with interest. David "took" Bathsheba but did not rape her; what Amnon did to Tamar brought to light the hidden violence in David's adultery. David plotted to kill Uriah, but worked hard to cover up his crime; Absalom gave the order to kill Amnon in the open. Like father, like sons.

Amnon's love for Tamar was like that of a courtly lover who had made himself ill over his beloved. While Amnon was pining away, he got advice from a cousin, Jonadab, the son of one of David's brothers, who apparently was hanging around the palace. The text calls him a "shrewd" man (v. 3), using a word that often refers to genuine godly wisdom. Here, it has the connotation of counterfeit wisdom; Jonadab was shrewd in the way that the serpent was shrewd in the garden, and like the serpent he encouraged Amnon to seize forbidden fruit. Jonadab's shrewdness was evident particularly in the way he maneuvered David into the middle of things (v. 5). He knew that if David asked Tamar to visit Amnon, she would not be suspicious of the request. Jonadab's plan was more fitting than he imagined, for David was in fact right in the middle of things, the one who set this whole disastrous series of events in motion when he called Bathsheba to visit his bed.

Jonadab advised Amnon to pretend sickness and ask for Tamar to visit and bake some cakes, and the word for bed is the same used for David's bed in 11:2. Amnon planned to rise from bed to "take" his sister. Like father, like son once again.

The text emphasizes food (vv. 8–9a), and no doubt some connection between sex and food is intended, a connection brought out by the fact that the cakes were "heart cakes." Like a king of the nations, Amnon took Tamar as a "baker." There is also an emphasis on his superior strength. "Seize" is the verbal form of "force" (v. 11) and is the same word root as "stronger" in verse 14. Crudely, verse 14 records that Amnon "laid her," rather than the more common idiom, "lay with her," which makes it clear that this was not consensual. Again, a parallel with David is being drawn: Though David did not force Bathsheba, Amnon's use of his superior strength provides an unexpurgated view of what David actually did. Just like Amnon, David had used his superior "strength" to take a woman. In the more shameless actions of his sons, Yahweh was bringing to light the truth of David's sin.

When Amnon seized her, Tamar protested that David would allow them to marry if Amnon asked (v. 13). According to Leviticus 18:9, an Israelite man was not allowed to marry his "sister," whether a father's daughter or a mother's daughter, and whether or not the sister lived in the same house. Leviticus 18:11 reiterates this: "You are not to uncover the nakedness of a father's wife's daughter." Tamar was a "father's wife's daughter" to Amnon, and thus marriage between the two was forbidden.[5] No doubt Tamar knew this, but was grasping at straws and hoping that she could put Amnon off long enough to get to flee.

After his sexual passions had been satisfied, Amnon sent Tamar away, despising her. This compounded his sin, since the law required a payment to compensate for her loss of virginity (Exod. 22:16–17; Deut. 22:28–29).[6] Amnon intended to have nothing

---

[5] Though a forbidden degree of consanguinity, brother-sister marriage apparently was not punished by any civil sanction. Leviticus 20 gives the punishments for incest and indicates that cross-generational incest was punishable by death, but does not specify a punishment for a man who takes his sister; it is a disgrace and they shall be cut off, but this does not mean that they will be put to death (v. 17). The fact that "they" are cut off may suggest that they are being treated as a couple.

[6] As pointed out by Bergen, *1, 2 Samuel*, 383.

more to do with her and even called her "this thing" as he drove her away (v. 17). Tamar was disgraced and mourned as if mourning for a death, with ashes on her head. She rent her garment; what had been a sign of her virginity became a token of virginity torn.

Verse 21 is crucial. David was angry, but said nothing and did nothing. Perhaps David discerned the parallel with his own sin and was reluctant to punish another for something he himself had done. Perhaps he had turned Stoic and was simply accepting that the sword would devour no matter what he did. In any case, David was acting like an Eli, and his failure to act left an opening for Absalom to take things into his own hands. Similar episodes occurred again and again during this period of David's reign: Weakened by his sin, David failed to rule firmly and thus gave passive encouragement to brazenly violent men to gain power and shape events. Christian leaders would do well to take this soberly to heart.

ABSALOM'S EXILE, 2 SAMUEL 13:23–14:33[7]

This section covers a period of seven years; the stages of which are explicitly noted in the text.[8] Furthermore, there are seven scenes in the story:

1. David and Absalom, 13:23–27
2. Absalom kills Amnon, 13:28–29
3. A report reaches David, 13:30–33
4. Absalom flees, 13:34–39
5. Joab gets Absalom back, 14:1–24
6. Absalom's handsomeness and hair, 14:25–27
7. David and Absalom, 14:28–33

---

[7] Chapter 13:23–14:33 is one connected story. The first section begins with "after two full years" (13:23), and the same phrase is found in 14:28, and this repetition forms an *inclusio* around the whole section. Further, the opening and closing scenes both describe meetings of David and Absalom.

[8] From the time that Amnon raped Tamar to the time that Absalom killed Amnon was two years (13:23), and after killing Amnon, Absalom fled to Geshur, where he remained three years (13:38). At that point, Joab brought Absalom back, but for another two years he did not see his father (14:28). Thus, from the first scene with David and Absalom to the second is seven years, a "week" of years.

Sevenfold patterns in Scripture usually reflect the sequence of creation and suggest that a new world is under construction. If a reference to creation is intended here, it must be intended ironically, for the story is one of decreation. The section ends with Absalom achieving a kind of Sabbath by his return to the land, but the results for Israel as a whole were anything but restful.

Absalom's patience in dealing with Amnon is noteworthy (13:20–23). Instead of attacking Amnon immediately, when he would have been on his guard, he waited two years until Amnon would be unsuspecting. Absalom was also shrewd to invite David to the feast at Baal-hazor. Had Absalom come right out asking to take Amnon with him, David might have been suspicious; he was suspicious anyway (13:26). Once the king refused (as, perhaps, Absalom hoped and expected he would) Amnon was a reasonable replacement (vv. 24–27). Absalom, moreover, like Amnon, worked David into the middle of his plot. David had played pander for a "tryst" between his son and daughter, and now he was aiding and abetting Absalom's plot to murder Amnon. The feast also provided a cover for Absalom, especially since the other sons of the king were all invited. It all looked perfectly harmless, and we might almost imagine David thinking with satisfaction about how peaceful everything was at home. It is ironic that Absalom's vengeance for Amnon's rape of Tamar involved food; Amnon's use of food as a ruse came back on his own head.

The last sheep-shearing festival we saw in 1–2 Samuel involved Nabal, whose heart, like Amnon's, died while merry with wine (2 Sam. 13:28; 1 Sam. 25:36). Amnon had also played the fool, as Tamar said twice, when she warned him against doing a "disgraceful thing" (*nebalah*) and charged that he was acting like one of the nebalim (13:12–13). Amnon lived like a Nabal, and he died like a Nabal. The connection between Nabal and Amnon also highlights the difference between Absalom and his father: When David encountered the fool, he was ready to take vengeance, but was restrained. Absalom showed no such restraint, and no Abigail was forthcoming to restrain. Unrestrained by his father or anyone else, Absalom stretched out his hand against his Nabalite brother, and in the same way he would raise his hand against the "Nabal" who ruled the kingdom. When the feast turned to slaughter, the report went out that Absalom had killed all the king's sons (13:30–33). Jonadab was there again, with "good news" for David: "Only Amnon is dead." Like the "good news" of Uriah's death, Jonadab's announcement that Amnon had been killed was oddly comforting to the king.[9]

After Absalom had been in Geshur for three years, Joab enlisted the help of a wise woman of Tekoa, who tricked David into pardoning Absalom, much as Nathan's parable had caught the conscience of the king.[10] Why did Joab want Absalom back? He did not have any particular affection for him; Absalom later burned Joab's field (14:28–33), and Joab eventually killed Absalom (18:14–15). Certainly, Joab was not loyal to Absalom, for even when Absalom took the throne, Joab remained with David. Joab's motivation is not stated, but several possibilities can be inferred. First, these events took place late in David's reign (see below); Joab discerned that the king was weak and that the succession might be troublesome. Amnon, the eldest prince, was dead, and Absalom, who was apparently next in line, was in exile. Joab wanted Absalom back to ensure that the kingdom would not fall apart after David's death. Joab's Realpolitik backfired badly: Returning Absalom divided and almost destroyed the kingdom.

[9] There is some uncertainty about verse 39. Most translations says something about David's renewed affections for Absalom, but this is hard to square with the subsequent story, for even after Absalom returned, David refused to see him for two years. The phrase "go out to" is sometimes used to mean "march out against," and therefore some commentators suggest that it should be translated, "David's desire to march out against Absalom was spent." That is, he had initially intended to punish Absalom, but after some time his resolution failed.

[10] "Wise woman" probably did not mean merely a "smart woman," but refers to some kind of quasi-official position. She may be like a sibyl, a woman who is consulted for advice and counsel. If this is the case, it would sharpen the parallel with the prophet Nathan.

Second, Joab may have been supporting Absalom to prevent Solomon from becoming king. Below, I provide a chronology for the latter part of David's reign, which shows that Absalom's conspiracy took place in David's final year. Moreover, I suggested in an earlier chapter that Solomon was designated crown prince at his birth and given a crown name by Yahweh Himself. Consistently with this thesis, 1 Chronicles 23:1 reports that "when David became old and sated with days, he made his son Solomon king over Israel." Though it cannot be conclusively demonstrated, it is likely that David had already designated Solomon as king when Joab helped Absalom to return. Joab, it appears, hoped that Absalom would be restored to David's good graces and to what Joab believed was his rightful position as king-designate. Bringing back Absalom was Joab's way of undermining Solomon.

Narratively, this account of Joab's motives sheds light on a number of subsequent events. Almost certainly, David had already designated Solomon as king when Absalom mounted his conspiracy. Like Macbeth, Absalom tried to seize the kingdom because he had been passed over in the succession; we can imagine Absalom saying the lines Macbeth uttered when Duncan designated Malcom as heir: It was "a step on which I must fall down, or else o'erleap, for in my way it lies" (Macbeth 1.4.48–50). Joab's later actions are also clarified if we understand that they were motivated by a persistent opposition to Solomon. As we shall see later in this chapter, during the secession led by Sheba (2 Sam. 20), Joab jockeyed himself into a position to be king-maker, a position he tried to exploit a short time later by supporting Adonijah's succession campaign (1 Kgs. 1:5–10), which looked suspiciously like Absalom's. Thematically, if Absalom's putsch was part of an anti-Solomon move, the contrast of Absalom and Solomon is further sharpened.

The wise woman hired by Joab played the role of a bereaved widow, claiming that her two sons had had a quarrel in which one killed the other (14:4–7). In accord with the law, the guilty son was being pursued by the avenger of blood. Though this was a legitimate procedure, the death of her second son would obviously deprive the widow of her last male protection and would bring an end to her husband's name. Reassuringly, David promised not to allow her son to die (v. 8). The parallels with Cain and Abel are obvious: Two sons struggle "in the field," one strikes down the other, and there is a threat to the surviving son from the rest of the clan. Bergen makes the interesting suggestion that the woman actually intended for David to notice the parallels and render a verdict based on the story of Cain and Abel.[11] In Genesis 4:13–15, Yahweh protected Cain and threatened to take vengeance against anyone who sought to kill Cain. By hinting at this precedent from the Torah, the wise woman was encouraging David to follow Yahweh's lead in protecting "Cain."

Once David had rendered the decision, she revealed that her story was an allegory of Absalom's history (vv. 12–17). Israel was the widow in the story; her two leading sons were Amnon and Absalom; Amnon was dead, and if Absalom was killed or permanently banished, widow Israel would be left with no one to carry on the family heritage.[12] Without Absalom, Israel would be like water poured out that cannot be regathered (v. 14). The woman spoke in a sharply accusing tone, arguing that David's treatment of Absalom contradicted the verdict he had just rendered in her own fictional case. David was willing to show mercy to the widow's murderous son, but no compassion to his own murderous son. As with Nathan, David was convinced and convicted by the parable, and he called Joab to tell him to bring the prodigal home.

The most famous thing about Absalom was his hair, but we have been reading about Absalom for a chapter and a half without knowing this (vv. 25–27). Why is it brought up here? The reason

---

[11] Bergen, *1, 2 Samuel,* 389–390.

[12] This throws the comment about a "coal" into an ironic light (v. 7). If the woman lost her son, there would be no possibility of stoking up the fire of the family again. Allegorically, Absalom was the remaining coal, and he did stoke up a fire by the end of the chapter.

probably has to do with parallels between Absalom and the two kings already presented in 1–2 Samuel. Saul was introduced as "choice and handsome" while on his way to be anointed by Samuel (1 Sam. 9:2), and David was described in a similar fashion shortly before he was announced as king-designate (1 Sam. 16:12–13). Now, Absalom's physical appearance is described just before he makes his bid for the throne. Verse 27 continues the cross-comparisons: Absalom's house, like David's, was being built up. The comparison with Saul was particularly close: Both are described as the most handsome Israelites of their time (1 Sam. 9:2; 2 Sam. 14:25), and both were distinguished by their heads—Saul by his towering head, Absalom by his head of hair. In the subsequent story, these similarities are filled out, for Absalom's treatment of David was very like Saul's.

The emphasis on Absalom's hair is significant in several respects. Hair is a crown and glory, and Absalom's evident pride in his hair shows him to be a man full of his own glory. There is perhaps also a connection with Esau, which, given the analogies between David and Jacob, makes sense in the context. In the broader sweep of 1–2 Samuel, Absalom stood in contrast with the Nazirite Samuel. Absalom apparently took a vow each year and cut his hair at the end of the year, following the procedure of a Nazirite holy warrior. Violent Absalom, however, was an anti-Nazirite, vain about the beauty and weight of his glorious crown of hair, more ready to fight his own battles than the Lord's.[13] The Nazirite Samuel set up the kingdom of David; the anti-Nazirite Absalom tore it apart.

Absalom's perversion of the notion of holy war is evident in the final episode of chapter 14. Two years after his return, Absalom was frustrated that he had not been reintroduced at court. To get Joab's attention, he burned his barley field (v. 30). Absalom was willing to destroy his neighbor's property to get his way, and this action foreshadowed the "fire" that he was about to kindle in Israel.

---

[13] Thanks to James B. Jordan for drawing attention to this parallel.

STEALING THE HEARTS OF ISRAEL, 2 SAMUEL 15:1–12[14]

The chronology of this period is made difficult by the "forty years" mentioned in verse 7. This cannot refer to a forty-year period between Absalom's return to the land and the beginning of his conspiracy. David only reigned for forty years, and Absalom's murder of Amnon certainly did not take place at the beginning of David's reign. Another possibility is that the number refers to Absalom's age, but this option does not appear to work either. According to 2 Samuel 3:2, Absalom was born in Hebron at the beginning of David's reign, so if Absalom was forty, he must have been born in David's first year at Hebron and the events of chapters 15–19 must have taken place in the last year of David's reign. A final possibility is that the text is corrupt, and some manuscripts have "four" instead of "forty."

My preferred solution is that "forty" is the original reading and that it refers to the fortieth year of David's reign, which must also be the fortieth year of Absalom's life. This enables us to work backward to determine the chronology of the events of the last few chapters. As noted above, Amnon raped Tamar seven years before Absalom's return to the land, and Absalom's conspiracy must have taken a year or two to organize. If we assume that Absalom took two years to organize his coup, that means he returned in David's thirty-eighth year, and Amnon must have raped Tamar in the thirty-first year of David's reign. David's sin with Bathsheba and Uriah would have taken place some time before that, perhaps a year or two. We also know that David reigned in Hebron for seven and a half years before moving to Jerusalem. Thus, the overall chronology of David's reign is something like this:

---

[14] 15:1–12 is divided into two parts. The chapter begins with "now it came about after this," and this elaborate introductory phrase marks the beginning of a new phase of the story. Verse 7 repeats the phrase, "now it came about at the end of forty years." The first six verses tell of Absalom's preparations for seizing the kingdom, and in verses 7–12 he carried out the plot.

Event	Year of Reign	David's Age
Hebron	Years 1–7	30–37
Jerusalem (before sin)	Years 8–19	38–49
David's sin with Bathsheba	Year 19	49[15]
Mephibosheth brought to David	Year 20	50
Amnon rapes Tamar	Year 31	61
Absalom kills Amnon	Year 33	63
Absalom in exile	Years 33–35	63–65
Absalom returns to Jerusalem	Year 36	66
Absalom reconciled to David	Year 38	68
Absalom's conspiracy	Year 40	70
Sheba's conspiracy	Year 40	70
(Joab's putsch, see below)		
Adonijah's conspiracy (1 Kings)	Year 40	70

If this is correct, the last year of David's reign was an eventful one, to say the least. Again, the chaos of David's final year was not happenstance but a direct result of David's sin, since the king's weakness left the door wide open to a series of adversaries. Reference to a fortieth year also has symbolic connotations. Forty years is a period of testing and trial, and it also highlights the fact that David fled back into the wilderness, where Israel had wandered for forty years.

Absalom carefully prepared his coup. First, he acquired a chariot and horses, along with fifty men as runners (15:1; cf. 1 Kgs. 1:5). Ancient Near Eastern kings often moved about with a retinue of

---

[15] This is only an estimation, but it represents the latest realistic date for David's adultery. To show why, we must work back from the reign of Rehoboam, the first king of the Southern kingdom of Judah. According to 1 Kings 14:21, Rehoboam was forty-one years old when he became king after the death of Solomon. Since Solomon reigned forty years (1 Kgs. 11:42), Rehoboam was born in the year before Solomon succeeded David. Thus, in David's thirty-ninth year, Solomon had a son, and thus must have been born at least twenty years before, around David's nineteenth year. And, since Solomon was born after David's adultery, that incident must have taken place some time before. In fact, it is certainly possible that David's adultery took place much earlier; we are not told how old Solomon was when he became king, but if he were thirty, then he was born in David's tenth year, and David's adultery must have taken place within a few years after his move to Jerusalem. All this raises the interesting point that the judgment on David's sin—the turmoil in his house—did not begin to fall until more than a decade (and possibly, nearly two decades) after his original sin. God's judgments may seem slow, but they are sure (see 2 Pet. 3:9).

warriors, and Absalom's first step was to surround himself with the trappings of royalty. If he looked like a king, people would start thinking of him as a king. Like David, Absalom became king by collecting regalia. Gathering horses and chariots was also a significant move. Neither David nor Saul ever had horses or chariots, which were associated with Israel's Gentile enemies.[16] Further, the Torah contained specific warnings against acquiring horses and chariots (Deut. 17:16; cf. 1 Sam. 8:11). Absalom took on the trappings of a king like the kings of the nations. As in the days of Saul, David was again faced with an Israelite king acting like a Gentile. Absalom also manipulated symbols by the way he greeted people coming to the capital city for judgment. Instead of treating them as subjects, he embraced them as brothers; when they bowed, he raised them up to kiss them. Absalom presented himself as a man of the people, a democrat who treated everyone with respect.[17]

According to verses 2–4, Absalom made a practice of stationing himself outside the gate of Jerusalem on the road leading to the city. By rising early, Absalom was able to intercept people coming to the capital to put their cases before David. Absalom claimed to support their claims and lamented that no one in the palace was willing to listen to them (v. 3). By all evidence, this was a lie, or at least a distortion of David's practice. In an earlier chapter, the wise woman of Tekoa came directly to the king to present her case. If this was indicative of David's practice, it showed he was willing to hear the complaints of his people and capable of judging with mercy and justice. By flattering the people and deceiving them about the workings of David's court, however, Absalom stole the hearts of all Israel, who once loved David (v. 6).

---

[16] Bergen, *1, 2 Samuel*, 396.

[17] There is an important political point here. Absalom began his conspiracy by manipulating the symbols and images of kingship. Few moderns are very alert to these things, but they are still very important. Bill Clinton was a master at creating an image of his administration: cool, energetic, young, creative, and he did this by surrounding himself with actors and sports personalities. Do not believe Rush Limbaugh when he says that "substance" rather than "symbol" is the important thing about politics.

Absalom also gained power by exploiting divisions within Israel that David had worked so hard to overcome. One of the crucial aspects of Absalom's plan is the way he dealt with men from the "tribes of Israel," that is, from outside Judah (v. 2). We have already noted a number of hints that Judah and the other tribes were at odds, and Absalom used that mutual hostility to his advantage. Apparently, if a man was from the tribe of Judah, Absalom would let him through to see the king. But when Absalom found a supplicant from another tribe, he warned them that they would not get a hearing from David. In this way, Absalom controlled access to the king and made it appear that David was willing to hear cases only from members of his own tribe—precisely what Absalom was claiming. Absalom plotted so that his charge came true.

In his actual conspiracy (vv. 7–12), Absalom again put David in the middle. He got permission to go to his birthplace in Hebron, claiming that he had to fulfill a vow, another link with the Nazirite. Hebron was apparently functioning as a shrine or cult center, for "serving the Lord" implies worship (v. 8). Absalom's hypocrisy was Pharisaical: While maintaining a show of piety, he was actually plotting revolution, if not parricide. As noted above, Absalom's life tracked the life of David, and Absalom might have self-consciously built on this parallel. He wanted to become king in Hebron, as his father did, and then move into Jerusalem. It must have seemed wonderfully suitable that his path to royalty followed the steps of what he believed was his father's seizure of power from the house of Saul. David again was wholly unaware of Absalom's plan and completely insensitive to the tensions that Absalom was exploiting so skillfully. David even wished him "peace" as he left.

Once in Hebron, Absalom sent spies throughout the land to stir up support for him (v. 10). This served a practical necessity, since the spies could agitate for Absalom and organize demonstrations, which would appear to be a spontaneous overflow of support for Absalom. Spies also remind us of the conquest of the land; both Moses and Joshua sent spies into the land as a preliminary to conquering, and Absalom prepared for his conquest in a similar way. Absalom also took two hundred men of Jerusalem to Hebron (v. 11). Though the text does not state it explicitly, it is most likely that they were prominent citizens, since not everyone would be invited to a feast with a prince. Inviting these men helped to cover Absalom's aims, just as inviting all the king's sons to his sheep-shearing festival covered his plot against Amnon. More than this, Absalom deprived David of some of the leading citizens of the capital city. David found himself in a crisis but did not have the men around him that he needed to handle it. The intentions of the two hundred were unknown to David and his circle; the text tells us that they were not allies of Absalom (v. 11), but David had no way of knowing that. When word spread that Absalom had been proclaimed king, the news that two hundred prominent citizens of Jerusalem were with him in Hebron would give the impression that Absalom had widespread support.

Absalom did gain the support of Ahitophel the Gilonite (v. 12), one of David's most trusted counselors, whose advice was accepted like the word of God (16:23). Ahitophel was father of Bathsheba's father (2 Sam. 23:34), and perhaps his decision to support Absalom was based on his knowledge or suspicion that David had played an evil game with his granddaughter and grandson-in-law.

BACK TO THE FUTURE, 2 SAMUEL 15:13–16:14
Several centuries had passed since Israel first entered the land. Many enemies had invaded and enslaved Israel during the period of the judges and in the early monarchy, but Israel had remained settled in Canaan. But when David fled Jerusalem, "Israel" went into exile. As noted at the outset of this chapter, David's life as the representative Israelite foreshadowed the future history of Israel. Faced with a powerful conspiracy and with Absalom moving toward Jerusalem from Hebron, David fled east. His entourage moved past the city gates, past the "last house" (v. 17), which was perhaps the last house of the settlement outside the gates, then across the wadi Kidron

(v. 23) and up the slope of the Mount of Olives (v. 30). Once past the summit, he continued moving east over the Jordan toward Mahanaim (17:21–24). Eastward movement in the Old Testament is always movement away from the presence of God. Adam and Eve were driven out of the garden to the East, and later Israel was driven from their Edenic land into exile in Babylon.

David's quick decision to leave the city rather than to stay and fight was probably guided by several factors (v. 14). He may have believed that the two hundred men of the city who were with Absalom were cooperating willingly. He hoped to get out of Absalom's way before Absalom arrived, avoiding a direct confrontation, as he consistently did in his dealings with Saul. He may also have thought it best for Absalom to move into Jerusalem peacefully, rather than forcing the city to endure a siege. David was in danger of losing his position, but he willingly sacrificed himself to save the city. David was acting like a king, in a way that he had not since his sin: Plotting against Uriah, he was willing that many should die for one; threatened by Absalom, he was willing to be the one who should die to preserve the city.

David brought his whole household, but left ten concubines to keep the house (v. 16). If David fought Absalom, the women would be a burden rather than a help. The text says that the concubines were left to "guard" the house. Though they would not literally stand guard, they were symbolically the guardians of the royal house, and leaving them behind made them a symbolic target for Absalom. By taking these women, Absalom was laying claim to the kingdom and shaming the "guardians" of the king's house.

David's flight from Jerusalem was a pageant of his life in reverse order. The passage is divided into five scenes of meeting:

1. Members of his royal household, 15:13–23
2. Zadok with the ark, 15:24–29
3. Hushai, 15:30–37
4. Ziba, steward of Mephibosheth, 16:1–4
5. Shimei, a member of Saul's house, 16:5–14

The first few encounters were with people who served King David in Jerusalem, and as he moved (back!) to the wilderness, he encountered members of the house of Saul. The stages of his flight reversed David's rise to power; the kingdom of David was unraveling, disintegrating, a decreation in the fortieth year.

Several key words are used throughout the passage. "Go out" (vv. 16, 17; *yatsa'*) has obvious literal relevance to the story, but it also resonates with the story of the exodus (Exod. 12:41; 13:8; 23:15; 34:18). Though David's flight was in one sense a preview of the Babylonian exile, from another perspective, it is an exodus from "Egypt," with Absalom as a Pharaoh figure persecuting the true Israel and pursuing him across the river into the wilderness. This exodus theme is reinforced by the repeated use of "pass over," a word used in connection with the angel of death moving through the land of Egypt (vv. 18, 23; Exod. 12:12; 12:23). Another key word in this section is "head." David's head was covered as he walked (v. 30), and when he came to the "head" of the Mount of Olives (v. 30), he met Hushai who has dust on his head (v. 32)—all this in a story about the "head" of Jerusalem being forced to flee before a prince whose distinguishing characteristic is his "head" of hair.

While David paused at the last house, the Cherethites, Pelethites, and Gittites marched by, David's personal bodyguard (v. 18). The Cherethites were mentioned in 1 Samuel 30:14 as a people living in the "Negev," the area to the south of Judah, and they are often mentioned in connection with the Philistines (Ezek. 25:16; Zeph. 2:5). The same goes for the Pelethites, which may be a corruption of "Philistines," and the Gittites were Philistines from Gath. Foreigners were commonly used as bodyguards in the ancient world, since foreigners were less likely to get involved in domestic political squabbles but remain loyal to the king. As he did during his days of flight from Saul, David again found a welcome among Gentiles. Though David's own son conspired against him and won the hearts of Israel, these Gentiles remained loyal to David and thus were part of the "true Israel." Similarly, Jesus was opposed by "his own" but accepted by Gentiles, demonstrating that "not all Israel are of Israel."

David spoke to Ittai, leader of the Gittites (vv. 19–22), urging him to return to the city. This was perhaps a test of his loyalty. "Yesterday" (v. 20) was an exaggeration, but David was reminding Ittai that he could return to the city without anyone thinking him a traitor. Even though he was not an Israelite, he wanted to remain with his lord, whether in life or in death. This expression of discipleship, similar to the declaration of Ruth to Naomi, was stated in an oath form (v. 21: "as Yahweh lives"). Ittai's faithfulness was underlined by a persistent word play on his name. His name is similar to the Hebrew phrase "with me," and this highlights the fact that he remained "with him," with David.

After they had crossed the brook Kidron, which runs through the valley of Kidron between Jerusalem and the Mount of Olives, Zadok the priest came with the ark, with Abiathar and other Levites. Perhaps the priests believed that the ark would bring favor and protection to David, or perhaps they associated the ark with David's house and kingdom. David, however, sent them back to the city. The ark had been set up in its place, and that was the place where God had chosen to dwell. Whatever happened to David, the Lord's throne would not be removed. The ark was taken out of the land once before in the book of Samuel (1 Sam. 4–6). This time, the ark remained, while David, the anointed king, went into exile. This encounter sets up a connection between David's exile and the exile of the ark: David was the bearer of the Lord's presence, the "throne" of the Lord, the true "Israel" who suffered exile.

David ascended up the Mount of Olives and came to the summit (head) of the mountain "where God was worshiped" (v. 32). As David reached the peak, which evidently housed a shrine, he was informed that Ahitophel had thrown in his lot with Absalom, a significant blow to David given Ahitophel's reputation for wise counsel (16:23). At the place "where God was worshiped," David prayed that the Lord would confuse the counsel of Ahitophel.

Immediately Hushai appeared, an answer to David's prayer.[18] Recognizing that Hushai could serve David more effectively by staying in Jerusalem, David sent him back, suggested a deception to get close to Absalom, and linked him up with the spy network of the priests. Hushai would be the crucial weapon against Absalom's conspiracy. Persecuted by members of his own house, David prayed that Yahweh would confound his adversaries, a common prayer in the Bible, and one that should be more common in the church.

The last two encounters were with members of the house of Saul. First, David met Ziba, the servant of Mephibosheth, who made a show of loyalty to David by bringing food and drink and donkeys (16:1–4). Ziba's motives are unclear, but he was apparently playing a double game. On the one hand, Ziba helped David and thereby ingratiated himself to him. Ziba also told David that Mephibosheth was using the opportunity of Absalom's conspiracy to reassert the claims of the house of Saul. Believing that Mephibosheth had betrayed him, David granted all the lands and property of Mephibosheth to Ziba.[19] Yet, Ziba made no offer to accompany David into exile. He had secured favor with David, but he went back to the city to wait things out, to see how Absalom's reign developed. If he needed to escape from Absalom, he knew where he could go.

The second member of Saul's house was openly hostile. Shimei was a descendant of "Gera," one of the sons of Benjamin (Gen. 46:21). He came out cursing David for shedding the blood of the house of Saul and throwing stones at him in mock execution. In Shimei's view, David had usurped the kingdom by eliminating the previous king and his house, not only Saul, but Ish-bosheth and Abner as well. Abishai, true to form, suggested beheading Shimei,

---

[18] Hushai is called "David's friend," a quasi-official or official title for a close royal advisor. Note in 1 Chronicles 27:32ff, where a list of David's advisors includes Hushai as "king's friend."

[19] Ziba's story was not very plausible. It was highly unlikely that Absalom would give up his power to a lame member of the tribe of Benjamin, and indeed much more likely that descendants of Saul would be watched carefully or even eliminated.

but David submitted to the cursing, as he had submitted to the enmity of Saul. He waited for the Lord then, and again waited for the Lord to vindicate him. Two members of Saul's house appeared, one friendly and the other hostile. This repeated David's earlier wilderness experience: Jonathan provided for him, while Saul attacked him. David was back where he had started, in the wilderness, being cursed by a Benjamite.

David's journey "outside the camp" corresponded in a number of particulars to Jesus' via dolorosa:[20]

David (2 Samuel)	Jesus
Kidron to Mount of Olives, 15:23, 30	Kidron to Mount of Olives, Jn. 18:1
Ark returned,15:24–29	Leaves temple, Mt. 24:1–3
Ittai, a Gentile, is "with him", 15:19–22	Joseph of Arimathea with him, Mt. 27:57
Betrayal by Ahitophel, 15:31	Betrayal by Judas, Mt. 26:47–50
Ahitophel hangs himself, 17:23	Judas hangs himself, Mt. 27:5
Meph. appears to fall away, 16:1–4	Disciples do fall away, Mt. 26:56
Shimei, house of Saul, taunts, 16:5–8	Jews taunt, Mt. 27:39–43

A great deal could be made of these parallels, but let me highlight one theological implication of this typology: David, as has been emphasized, was departing from the land as the "true Israel," foreshadowing of Israel's later exile, and the fact that he also foreshadowed the movement of Jesus indicates that Jesus' suffering and death was also an "exile." Unlike David, however, who suffered exile for his own sins, Jesus, as true Israel and righteous son of David, suffered exile in place of His people, and His exile secured a return for Israel.

As in his previous exile in the wilderness, David used ruses and deception to protect himself and undermine his opponents. He instructed Hushai to deceive Absalom in order to subvert the advice of Ahitophel (15:34), and Hushai played the role to the hilt. Absalom was surprised to find Hushai in the city, since he was

[20] Thanks to James B. Jordan for sketching out these parallels, which he drew from Arthur Pink's *Life of David*.

David's "friend" (16:17). Hushai, for his part, greeted Absalom as
if he were a loyal subject of the new king. Readers know that he
was playing a role and therefore we can see that everything he said
had a double sense. When Hushai proclaimed, "Long live the king"
(16:16), Absalom obviously understood it as a declaration of loyalty
to him, but Hushai meant it for David. Absalom was suspicious,
but Hushai claimed that he would follow whomever Yahweh, the
people, and the men of Israel had chosen (16:18). Again he meant
that he would follow David, since Yahweh had not chosen Absalom
to be king. Even verse 19 has an underside. On the surface, Hushai
promised to serve the son as loyally as he served the father. But how
had he served David? With utter faithfulness to the one whom the
Lord chose. He intended to serve Absalom in the same way—with
utter loyalty to David.

Hushai's act was so persuasive that Absalom not only allowed
him to stay, but sought advice from him. Absalom first consulted
with Ahitophel, who advised him on two matters. First, he advised
Absalom to sleep with the royal concubines who had been left behind in the city. As mentioned above, concubines represented the
kingdom, and seizing the king's harem was equivalent to seizing
the kingdom. Symbolically, the king was married to the "bride,"
Israel, and his bride(s) represented the nation. More pragmatically,
if the king could not protect his brides, then he was incapable of
protecting the nation. When Absalom slept with his father's concubines, he was sending a message that he was now in charge of
the royal house. Ahitophel also saw that this action would make
Absalom odious to his father (v. 21). In the early stages of the rebellion, many in Israel were still on the fence, waiting to see if perhaps
Absalom and David would come to an agreement. When Absalom
seized David's concubines, it became clear that there was no retreat
and no possibility of reconciliation. By this provocation, Absalom
forced the people to make a choice.

Taking Ahitophel's advice, Absalom had sex with the concubines "before all Israel" (v. 22), but this was not literally a public

sex show. He pitched a tent and brought the concubines in, but everyone knew what was going on inside. The location Absalom chose was appropriate, for the tent was on the same roof where David first looked lustfully at Bathsheba. Ahitophel's advice was like an oracle of God, not because the advice was necessarily virtuous, but because it was shrewd. It was like an oracle of God also in the sense that it fulfilled Nathan's oracle against David (see 12:11).[21] What David did in secret was openly exposed.

Second, Ahitophel gave Absalom military advice (17:1–3), making several key points. David had six hundred Cherethites, Pelethites, and Gittites. Perhaps some others would join him, but the 12,000 that Ahitophel asked for was a far larger force than David could gather on short notice. "Twelve" represents Israel and suggests that Ahitophel discerned that the contest was about which was the true Israel, Absalom's kingdom or David's.[22] Once the 12,000 were assembled, Ahitophel wanted to launch a strike immediately. David was on the run, he had women and children with him (15:22), and he would be tired from a march. If Ahitophel could strike David before he had a chance to get himself organized, he would have the advantage of surprise and might be able to spread panic among David's troops. Ahitophel also hoped to limit the damage of the rebellion. If David's troops fled from their king, Ahitophel would be able to isolate David and strike him alone. Once David was out of the way, it would be a simple matter for Ahitophel to "bring back all the people to you" (17:3). The return of the whole people would be accomplished with minimal bloodshed and in minimal time, and then Absalom could fulfill his name ("father of peace"; v. 3). Strikingly, Ahitophel was suggesting that Absalom do to David what David had intended to do to Uriah—isolate and kill. Politically and militarily, Ahitophel's was

---

[21] Behind this is a reference to Reuben's sin with his father's concubines; Absalom, the current "firstborn" of the kingdom, took his father's concubines and would lose his position. David, of course, continued to play the role of Jacob.

[22] Baldwin, *1 & 2 Samuel*, 265.

shrewd advice (v. 14). It would be far better to end the civil war in a day and with a single battle than to risk letting it drag on and on, which would only embitter people against Absalom.

By contrast with Ahitophel's straightforward and realistic speech, Hushai's advice was delivered in an ornate and allusive rhetoric. Hushai shocked everyone with an initial statement that Ahitophel's advice was "not good," the first words of the speech in Hebrew (17:7). Then he filled his speech with allusions to David's life, vivid descriptions, and striking metaphors. David was "like a bear robbed of his cubs," he was "hiding in one of the pits," and would emerge like a wraith to fall on Absalom's troops (vv. 8–9). If David struck Absalom's army, even the man "whose heart is like the heart of a lion" would quail (v. 10). Hushai evoked the legend of David, reminding Absalom of David's wilderness years by saying that his men were "mighty men" and "bitter of soul." References to bears and lions stirred up images of David's youth, when, as a shepherd, he delivered his sheep from predators.

Practically, Hushai made several points. First, he claimed that David, being a seasoned warrior, would be expecting a quick attack and would be hidden away, far from the rest of his army (v. 8–9). Ahitophel's attack would be useless—or worse, since Absalom risked losing the initial battle, an eventuality that might undermine the entire coup (vv. 9–10). Positively, Hushai argued that Absalom should wait until he had an overwhelming force and make sure that he had no chance of losing. The 12,000 Ahitophel asked for were nothing; what Absalom needed was an army like the sand of the sea (v. 11), an all-Israelite army (cf. Gen. 13:16). And Absalom, not Ahitophel, should lead the army, for why should grandfatherly old Ahitophel receive the glory of victory? Hushai described Absalom leading the troops in phrases similar to those used of the angel of the Lord in the exodus, which suggests that Absalom would be like the angel of Yahweh leading the hosts of Israel.[23] Nor should

---

[23] Robert Gordon, *I & II Samuel*, 281.

Absalom be satisfied with killing David; Ahitophel wanted a surgical strike, but Hushai advised Absalom to initiate a slaughter (v. 12) and to carry out the ban against David's men and against any city that had the temerity to give him aid. Hushai knew that he was dealing with a murderer, a man who burned fields when his phone calls were not returned, a man who loved blood. He knew that the spectacle of a bloodbath, led by Absalom himself, would appeal to Absalom, the counterfeit holy warrior.

Thus, Hushai played to Absalom's fears and vanity, undermined Absalom's confidence in Ahitophel's advice and wisdom, and, above all, gave David time to regroup and choose where he would fight. The only task remaining was to get word to David. The priests, Jonathan and Ahimaaz, were both staying at "En-rogel," the "spring of Rogel," and a maidservant brought information from the city to them (17:17). The network, however, broke down when an informant let Absalom know where the two priests were hiding. They fled to Bahurim, the same place where David encountered Shimei, but the reception was very different this time. Instead of a Shimei, they discovered another Rahab who hid the two spies and lied to their pursuers. Deceived by a woman, Absalom was playing the role of the king of Jericho, while David's exit from the land included an episode like Joshua's entrance to the land. Not only David's life, but the history of Israel, was moving in reverse.

Ahitophel's advice was rejected, but suicide seems an extreme overreaction (17:23). Ahitophel lost face and realized that he was not going to be the leading advisor, but, more importantly, he doubtless realized that Hushai's advice would be disastrous for Absalom. If, as now seemed likely, David returned to the throne, Ahitophel's life would be worth nothing anyway. Bergen points out that this section of 2 Samuel includes a running critique of human wisdom. "Shrewd" Jonadab earlier had given advice to Amnon that ended with Amnon murdered, and Ahitophel gave shrewd advice, only to see it undermined. Wisdom is a royal virtue in the Bible, but

Absalom proved that he was notably short of this quality. Absalom, in short, was no Solomon.[24]

Chapter 17 ends with David arriving in Mahanaim (vv. 24, 27–29). Jacob stopped at Mahanaim on his return from Haran (Gen. 32:1–2), and David's exile there associated him with the patriarch. More Gentiles came out to aid him, including the recently conquered prince of Rabbah, Shobi, who had replaced his brother Hanun as head of the city (doubtless with David's help!). As in David's first wilderness period, Yahweh provided David with food, which, significantly, came from Gentiles. David was received into Gentile hospitality, as Israel later would be in Babylon (2 Kgs. 25:17–30), and as the Gentiles would later receive the "exiled" Jesus.

ABSALOM, ABSALOM, 2 SAMUEL 18–19:8[25]

Curiously, Ahitophel's strategy was followed in the battle between David and Absalom, but it was carried out by David's armies rather than Absalom's. Ahitophel wanted to cause panic in David's army, but Absalom's army was the one that fled (18:17). Ahitophel wanted to isolate David alone, but Absalom was the one isolated (18:9–15). Ahitophel thought that finishing off David would finish the war, but as it turned out, the death that brought peace was the death of Absalom, the "father of peace" (18:16–18).

In preparation for battle, David organized his troops in groups of hundreds and thousands and set commanders over them (vv. 1–5). The numbers indicate that he had gathered many more

---

[24] Bergen, *1, 2 Samuel*, 416.

[25] This is the central passage in this section of 2 Samuel and is organized chiastically:

    A   Absalom takes advice from Hushai, 16:20–17:14
      B   Jonathan and Ahimaaz bring the information to David, 17:15–29
        C   The battle, 18:1–19
      B'   Ahimaaz and a Cushite bring David a report, 18:20–33
    A'   David takes counsel from Joab, 19:1–8

Chapter 18 itself contains three episodes: David's plans for the battle, the battle itself, and the report of the battle returning to David.

warriors than the six hundred in his bodyguard, and this in turn suggests that some time had passed since David fled Jerusalem. Hushai's plot was successful, for he had bought enough time for David to prepare. The division of the army into hundreds and thousands was similar to the organization of Israel in the wilderness (Exod. 18:17–23) and is another indication that David and his allies formed a "new Israel." David then divided the army in thirds for a multi-pronged attack, similar to earlier battles in which an army was divided into three (Gen. 14:15; Judg. 7:20). David intended to lead his men into battle, but they realized that Absalom's army might be seeking to capture or kill David specifically. If David was captured, his men would have nothing left to fight for and would have to accept Absalom as king. The statement about 10,000 (v. 3) is often translated to suggest that David was worth so many of his troops, but it could mean that there were actually 10,000 additional troops available, and therefore David must be left behind to plan and carry out future battles, should they be necessary. Absalom's troops showed no similar concerns for their leader. Hushai, deliberately giving bad advice, told Absalom he should lead the troops, putting him in harm's way. David's men, who genuinely loved their leader, advised him to stay behind.

David gave explicit and public instructions to deal gently with Absalom, orders that anticipate the events of the battle itself (v. 5). These instructions were consistent with David's treatment of all his enemies; he had treated Saul well, and just recently he had restrained Abishai from cutting down Shimei. He knew what Joab was capable of, and he wanted all his men to know that he treated enemies with kindness and compassion. David's behavior again provided an Old Testament illustration of Jesus' teaching about loving enemies.

The account of the battle is brief, but several details are important. The battle was fought between the "men of Israel" on the one hand, and the "servants of David" on the other (18:7), yet another indication of the rift that existed within Israel prior to the division of the kingdom. Throughout the passage, moreover, David is called "king," emphasizing that he was the rightful ruler, even if he was in exile (vv. 2, 4, 5). The battle claimed a huge number of men from Israel, 20,000, and verse 8 shows that many men of Israel died because they panicked. The battle was not confined to one area, but spread throughout the country; in this respect, the battle followed the strategy that Hushai had advised, except that David's men chased down Absalom's rather than the reverse. According to verse 8, the forest fought on David's side, devouring more than the sword devoured. Forcing the battle into a forested area was probably part of David's strategy to neutralize Absalom's superiority in numbers, but this was not merely strategy at work. As in Joshua's conquest, the Lord fought for "Israel" by sending natural disasters of various sorts. The forest "devoured," and the word is "eat." In exile, David received abundant food, but when Absalom crossed the Jordan, his troops were eaten.

Absalom was among those consumed by the forest (v. 9). Though the text does not say that Absalom was caught by the hair, a connection is implied.[26] His hair was his glory and crown, but this glory led to his downfall. The emphasis on his head being caught brings out an analogy with others who died by head wounds. Absalom was a Satanic king and an anti-Nazirite, whose pseudo-dedicated head trapped him in the end. He was a Saulide king, for Saul's head was removed. Further, Absalom was hanging between heaven and earth, and this indicates that he was comparable to Ahitophel, who died by "strangling." Hanging in a tree, he was rejected by both heaven and earth. The royal mule, meanwhile, ran out from under him, a sign that he was losing control of the reins of the kingdom. According to Deuteronomy 21:23, one "hung on a tree" is the "curse of God," and Paul quoted this passage in Deuteronomy to explain the significance of the cross (Gal. 3:13). Like Saul, Absalom's death was a type of the cross, pointing to the death of a king/prince that would bring peace to the land and en-

---

[26] In 14:26, the phrase "hair of his head" is "head" in Hebrew, though it is obviously referring to his hair.

able Israel to return from exile. David's kingdom was resurrected by the death of another "Saul."

One of David's men saw Absalom hanging but did nothing more than report to Joab (v. 10). Along with everyone else in David's army, he had heard David's instructions about Absalom and obeyed his commander. He realized that if he had taken things into his own hands, Joab would have not have supported him (v. 13). Joab, however, had no scruples about ignoring David. Even before he discovered Absalom in the tree, Joab had offered a reward for the death of Absalom (v. 11). As he did many times in this last year of David's life, Joab acted against David's explicit instructions, though he doubtless believed he was doing what was necessary to save David from his own errors. Finding Absalom, Joab ran him through the heart and then gathered his armor bearers around to finish the kill. By enlisting his men to help, Joab spread responsibility for Absalom's death. "Who killed Absalom?" David would ask. And Joab would respond, "Gee, it's hard to say. There were so many people around." Earlier, Joab saw Absalom's return as politically necessary to secure the succession. Absalom had become expendable, and in Joab's mind, the security of David's throne depended on getting rid of him.

Absalom's burial was significant in a number of respects (18:18). Hushai warned Absalom that David would be hiding in a "pit," and after the battle Absalom was thrown into a pit (the word is the same in Hebrew). Before the battle, David's priestly spies hid in wells under the earth, but they were brought up again. David's men went into pits but rose up to fight another day; Absalom went into a pit and never came out. Further, Absalom was laid to rest outside the land, while David's exile was temporary. Absalom was placed beneath a pile of stones; he had committed capital crimes, and his body was "stoned."[27]

---

[27] Bergen, *1, 2 Samuel*, 422, citing Deuteronomy 21:21. The text tells us that Absalom had already put up a monument because he had no sons, but this seems to contradict 2 Samuel 14:27, which says that he had three sons. Apparently, they died before Absalom did, and this again shows a similarity to David, who also lost a series of sons.

Joab knew that the outcome of the battle would not be good news for David and that David did not take kindly to bad news (see 2 Sam. 1:11–16). So Joab sent a Cushite messenger to report to David at Mahanaim (2 Sam. 18:19–23). Absalom was another persecuting king, another Saul, and the announcement of his death to David came, like the announcement of Saul's death, through a foreigner. Yet, Ahimaaz insisted on going, and Joab finally relented and let him. Beginning in verse 24, the writer adopts David's point of view. He was sitting "between the two gates," perhaps between the gate of the inner wall and the gate of the outer wall. This reminds us of the place where Absalom started his conspiracy and is also reminiscent of Eli waiting for news of the battle and of the ark. As he watched, David saw a single runner heading toward the city. A single runner was a good sign because it meant he was not part of a retreating army (18:26). David got the report of victory first, but his only concern was for the life of one man (vv. 29, 32). The last time we saw David awaiting news of a battle, he was eager to hear about a man's death. Here, he was eager to hear that a man had been spared.

The story of the battle and its immediate aftermath continues to 19:8.[28] David was distraught over Absalom's death and word of David's grief spread throughout the army, turning the victory into a defeat (19:2). The day was a day of salvation from Absalom, but the men "steal away" to the city, as men who fled in defeat. David covered his face in mourning (v. 4) and this brought disgrace to the faces of his men. Like Eli, David learned that a son had died in battle, and he fell to the dust in a ritual death.

[28] This section, 18:33–19:8, is about David's response to the news of Absalom's death, and thus it is connected to chapter 18 by its content. Further, there is a clear link between 18:33 and 19:4, with the repetition of Absalom's name, the emphasis on "my son" (five times in 18:33; three times in 19:4), and David's mourning and crying in a loud voice common to the two verses. 19:5–8a records Joab's response to David's mourning and David's response to Joab. These verses form a second paragraph, and this divides 18:33–19:8 into two sections, the first having to do with David's mourning and the second with Joab's rebuke. Yet, the two sections are linked, partly by the incidents, and also by verbal repetitions. "Cover" is used in verses 3 and 5, and the section is brought together by *inclusio* with "gate" in 18:33 and 19:8a.

Unlike Eli, he rose from death. But he did not rise from death without the help of Joab. Joab noted the demoralization of David's troops and his rebuke was sharp and direct (19:5–7). He treated David as an equal or even as an inferior, a sign of his growing confidence that he could run the country better than his master. By mourning for his son who had rebelled against him, David was sending a message to his troops: He loved Absalom more than he loved them. Israel had been saved, but David was mourning the death of a single man. Again, this ironically echoed Uriah's death, when David showed no concern for the deaths of several of his men, so long as Uriah was dead. Joab advised David that he needed to act and reinforced the urgency of his advice by repeating the word "today" (vv. 5, 6). Verse 7 may even be read as a threat: Joab swore that if David did not speak to his men to restore their loyalty, David could end up abandoned and isolated. Joab may well have meant, "If you don't shape up, David, I'm going to take over." In chapter 20, Joab made good on the threat.

Taking Joab's advice, David went out to the gate of Mahanaim, and the men appeared before him. Sitting in the gate symbolized that David had returned to his royal office, enthroned in a place of judgment, and in the remainder of chapter 19, David exercised this judicial function in several cases. Chapter 19 demonstrated that David was back again; Joab had saved the kingdom from a period of headless anarchy. Though he had lost his son in battle, he had not fallen from his "chair" or broken his neck.

SECOND ENTHRONEMENT, 2 SAMUEL 19:8–43

David's return to Jerusalem was marked by continuing strife and conflict within Israel. One of the key issues, which appears at the beginning and end of chapter 19 (vv. 8b–15; 40–43) is, Who should bring David back to the land? The whole section is framed by notices about the divisions between Israel and Judah, and their divisions focus on their claims to the king. Within this frame, the passage reports on three encounters that David had as he returned to the capital: Shimei, Mephibosheth, and Barzillai. These correspond to three of David's encounters on his way out of Jerusalem, though in reverse order:

Chapters 15–16:   Hushai
                  Ziba (Mephibosheth's steward)
                  Shimei
Chapter 19:   Shimei
                  Mephibosheth
               Barzillai

The links are obvious except perhaps that between Hushai and Barzillai. These two are similar in several ways: Both were older men of property and wealth who remained utterly loyal to David; neither accompanied David; each was said to be a "burden" to David (15:33; 19:35).

Given this structure, we can draw some conclusions about the point of the individual encounters. The large-scale political point of the chapter was David's return to the throne, but there are practical political problems with the return. Would David be able to regain Israel's confidence and love, the hearts that Absalom had stolen away? How would he deal with traitors? Would David return and restore his allies to positions of leadership? Would he unleash harsh reprisals against his adversaries? Would David act wisely, as he did when he first became king, to heal the divisions of the nation? The individual encounters illustrated how David dealt with these problems and reveal that David's actions were something of a mixed bag. As always, David dealt well with enemies, but was less careful and shrewd in dealing with his allies. Because of that, in spite of his best efforts to reunite the kingdom, animosity among the tribes continued, and chapter 20 records yet another insurrection.

As David began to return, factions in Israel surfaced. The men of Israel had returned home (v. 8b), and they were wondering where or even who the king was. Absalom, whom they had followed, was dead, yet King David had not returned to his land (18:6–7), and they were discussing whether they should take the initiative to bring him back. There were good arguments for going out to greet David: If they were fearful of reprisals, receiving him back into the

land would demonstrate their renewed loyalty and serve as a new
pledge of allegiance. Even if they did not fear that David would
take vengeance, participating in his return to the capital would be
a good way to ingratiate themselves to him. Far better to participate
in the celebration of his victory than to sulk in defeat. On the other
hand, many families in Israel had lost family members and friends
among the 20,000 who died in battle. To celebrate the return of
the one who led the armies that slaughtered your cousins was dis-
tasteful at best. Unable to resolve these different considerations, the
tribes of Israel remained where they were.

Meanwhile, David appealed to the tribe of Judah to come and
escort him across the fords of the Jordan to Jerusalem (19:11–12).
Reminding the men of Judah that he was "bone and flesh" with
them, he claimed that they should be the first to welcome him back.
David's appeal to Judah ended up being interpreted as a provocative
move (19:41–42) and was a mistake on David's part. Part of the
pretext for Absalom's rebellion was that David showed favoritism
to Judah, and now as he returned to the kingdom, it looked as if
he were still showing favoritism to Judah.[29] David's message to the
men of Judah provoked a response, and they came to Gilgal to meet
him. Gilgal was the first place that Israel camped when they entered the land under Joshua, and the allusion suggests that David's
return was a new, post-exilic conquest, like the "conquest" in the
time of Ezra and Nehemiah. Others were unhappy that the men of
Judah were getting dibs on the king, so they hurried past Gilgal all
the way down to the ford of the Jordan. At the same time, David
installed Amasa as the new chief of his army (v. 13). Perhaps by
this time David had heard about Joab's treachery against Absalom,
but David also wanted to show that he was not bearing grudges
against Absalom's allies. Amasa had led the rebel troops of Absalom
(17:25), and by receiving him back into the army and giving him
command, David offered a grand gesture of reconciliation.

---

[29] Baldwin agrees (*1 & 2 Samuel*, 275).

There is a general and a more specific lesson in this series of events. The general lesson is that one's work can be undermined by friends as well as by enemies. And the specific lesson is that Christian leaders must pay careful attention not only to the rightness of their actions, but to the symbolics of their actions. It is not enough to ask, Would I sin if I did this? Leaders especially must also ask, Is it the right time to do this? What message will I send if I do this? What message do I want to send, and what is the best way to send it? What is the rhetoric of my action?[30]

As David proceeded toward Gilgal, he not only encountered some of the people he met on the way out of the land, but also had to make several judicial decisions. He was back "seated in the gate" and had to pass judgment. Significantly, Shimei was among the men of Israel who met David at the fords of the Jordan. He was a very different Shimei, repentant and obsequious, confessing his sin, and saying that he was the first of all the tribe of "Joseph" to greet David (19:19–20). Abishai, ever in character, wanted to kill him, but David rebuked Abishai as a "satan," and also implicitly Joab (he used the plural in condemning the "sons of Zeruiah"). This was not a day for executions; a day of victory was a day for mercy. To be sure, Abishai had grounds for demanding punishment, since cursing a leader was prohibited by the law (Exod. 22:28), but David showed magnanimity. David's policy also underlines that this was a second coronation, since it was common in the ancient Near East for a king to dole out gifts and clemency upon his accession to the throne. The king was in the gate, and his verdict stood.

Ziba and Mephibosheth had come to the fords as well. Mephibosheth explained that Ziba slipped away without him and used the situation to his advantage (vv. 24–30). Oddly, David, again

---

[30] One of qualities that made Pope John Paul II far and away the greatest Christian leader of the twentieth century has been his apparently infallible (no pun intended, really!) sense of symbolism. George Weigel's biography of the Pope is full of examples and repays careful reading, even—I am tempted to say, especially—for Protestants. Weigel, *Witness to Hope: The Biography of Pope John Paul II* (New York: Cliff Street Books, 1999).

acting as judge, decided to split the inheritance of Saul between the two of them. Why? If Ziba lied about Mephibosheth, why should he receive any? If Mephibosheth really was a traitor, why should he receive any? Perhaps David determined he would never be able to sort out the truth and just split the property to bring an end to it. That interpretation is unlikely; David could surely have determined that Ziba's story was nonsense, and Mephibosheth had clearly been mourning since David left (v. 24). The better explanation is that David was testing Mephibosheth's loyalty, and his offer to divide the land was analogous to Solomon's proposal to divide the infant (1 Kgs. 3:16–28). David wanted to find out whether Mephibosheth was interested only in his property, or whether he was genuinely loyal to David. If this was a test, Mephibosheth passed with an A+, demonstrating that he was a true son of Jonathan.

David's final encounter was with Barzillai the Gileadite. Barzillai brought food to David in Mahanaim (17:27–29), and David wanted to return the favor by inviting Barzillai to share his food in Jerusalem (19:33). Barzillai refused because of his age, but he sent Chimham, presumably Barzillai's son, with David to Jerusalem. David dealt wisely with an enemy (Shimei) and a supposed enemy (Mephibosheth). But he did not forget to reward those who remained loyal to him.

As David came to Gilgal, the tensions between the tribes were coming to a boil. The men of Israel were angry that the men of Judah had brought David across the Jordan before the rest of Israel could get there. Only "half" of Israel was in the escort (v. 40), and the men of Israel complained that they should have been better represented, since they have a greater share of David (v. 43). The men of Judah answered that they were the escorts because David was a close relative (v. 42), hardly the best thing to point out under the circumstances since it fed suspicions that the men of Judah were favored by the king. What should have been a reunion of the tribes at Gilgal, therefore, fell apart in adolescent squabbling.

Nathan had prophesied that there would be a sword in David's house. But that sword was not confined to the palace or David's immediate family. The sword had cut the whole of Israel in two.

SHEBA'S REVOLT, 2 SAMUEL 20:1-22

Chapters 19 and 20 are very closely connected.[31] One link is location. At the end of chapter 19, Israel and Judah were gathered at Gilgal (19:40), and chapter 20 begins with a reference to the "man of Belial," Sheba of Benjamin, who "happened to be there" (v. 1). "There" means Gilgal, and so Sheba's revolt began during the meeting described in chapter 19. The other link between the chapters is the theme of division between Israel and Judah. As noted above, the Gilgal "covenant renewal" ended in quarreling, and Sheba's revolt was premised on this division: "We have no portion in David," he announced to the northern tribes (20:1). Both these chapters, further, describe David's return to the throne. The previous section began with David sitting in the gate at Mahanaim, a sign of David's return to normalcy and to the kingdom. In keeping with the idea that this is the resurrection of the Davidic kingdom, his restoration to the throne was remarkably similar to his initial rise to power at the beginning of 2 Samuel.

Sheba's revolt reversed the claims of the men of Israel. In 19:43, they claimed ten parts of David, to the one part for Judah. But Sheba concluded from the attitude of the men of Judah that the northern tribes had no part in David (v. 1). This anticipated the

[31] Though chapter 20 is related to chapter 19, it does form a separate section. There is *inclusio* with "trumpet" and "tents" in verses 1 and 22. In the first instance, Sheba called for Israel to return to its tents, that is, to go home and have nothing more to do with David. At the end of the chapter, after Sheba had been killed and his movement ended, Joab blew his trumpet and everyone returned to their tents. Joab reversed Sheba's revolt, but the structure also brings out a parallel between Joab's actions and Sheba's. Within this *inclusio*, we have a generally chiastic structure:
  A   Revolt of Sheba: trumpet and tents, 20:1–2
   B   David organizes troops to deal with rebellion, 20:3–7
    C   Joab and Amasa, 20:8–13
   B'   Joab deals with rebellion, 20:14–22a
  A'   Joab sends troops home: trumpet and tents, 20:22b

claim later made by the northern tribes in 1 Kings 12:16, where "no part in David" became a rallying cry of Jeroboam's secession. Sheba's revolt was not an effort to remove David from the throne but a secession movement, with the northern tribes breaking away to become a separate country. Sheba's father, "Bichri," may have been the "Becorath" of 1 Samuel 9:1, one of Saul's ancestors. Whether closely related to Saul or not, Sheba was a Benjamite, and so the struggle in 2 Samuel 20 was like the struggle between the house of Saul and the house of David in 2 Samuel 2–4. A Benjamite again led one faction, the men of Israel, and David led the men of Judah.

For two chapters, the story has been building to David's restoration to the capital, but instead of recording a re-coronation ceremony, the only reference to his return is this pitiful notice about the concubines (v. 3). At the very least, David's return to Jerusalem was anticlimactic. Perhaps David put them under guard to ensure that they would not be violated again, since another civil war was erupting. More positively, putting the concubines in a safe place sent the message that David was back in charge as the "husband" and "guardian" of the land. Perhaps the best way to understand verse 3 is as a combination of these motifs. David protected his concubines, which was a good and royal thing for him to do. But they had become widows, and that is a sign that Israel itself had been widowed. The fact that there were ten concubines might also point to a connection with the "ten tribes" of Israel. When David put his concubines in protective custody, he was symbolizing that the "ten tribes" were being restored to David's household.

Imperiled by Sheba, David called on his new commander, Amasa, to raise the army, but Amasa delayed. David realized that he needed to strike quickly before the revolt was established.[32] David had removed Joab from his position (19:13), and when Amasa failed to carry out orders, David put Abishai in charge. But it was

---

[32] Notice the parallel with the advice of Ahitophel. Note also that David was worried that Sheba would be able to make his way to a fortified city, which was what he did.

Joab who led the army against Sheba, and the men were even called "Joab's men" (v. 7). Joab had gotten completely out of David's control. He had killed Absalom against orders, and now he took control of the Cherethites and Pelethites, David's personal bodyguard. This becomes even more striking when we look at verse 6. Abishai was ordered to collect "your lord's servants and pursue him," but then in the very next verse, these same men are called "Joab's men." Who was Abishai's lord? David or Joab?

What Joab did during the rebellion of Sheba amounts to a coup. Sheba's rebellion was never so dangerous as Absalom's rebellion, and the text draws a parallel not so much between Absalom and Sheba as between Absalom and Joab. To defeat Sheba, Joab had to establish undisputed control of the whole army, which was impossible as long as Amasa stood in his way. Joab's creed was simple: When someone stands in your way, kill him (vv. 8–12). Notice that Joab murdered Amasa in Gibeon, the same city where the tournament between Joab and Abner broke out in civil war (2 Sam. 2:12–32). The text notes also that Joab killed Amasa at a "great stone," which hints at a sacrificial dimension to Joab's action and also reminds us of Abimelech, who slaughtered his brothers on a stone before laying claim to the kingdom (Judg. 9:5). The allusion suggests that Joab was following the path of Abimelech. He was not merely eliminating a rival commander but making a bid, if not for the crown, at least for the power to give the crown to whom he pleased. Later in the same year, Joab's success in the rebellion of Sheba encouraged him to flout David's will again and attempt to put Adonijah on the throne (1 Kgs. 1:5–10).

Joab's method for killing Amasa was similar to the method used by his men at the earlier battle at Gibeon (v. 10; 2 Sam. 2:16). Josephus understood this passage to mean that Joab deliberately let the sword drop from its scabbard, bent to pick it up, and thrust it into Amasa's belly as he stood up.[33] He covered over his intention by

---

[33] Note that Amasa is struck in the belly, as were Asahel, Abner, and Ish-bosheth.

kissing Amasa and calling him brother, a method similar to the one he used to dispose of Abner (2 Sam. 3:27). Seeing Amasa wallowing in blood in the middle of the road, the confused soldiers stopped their pursuit, but one of Joab's men threw Amasa into the field and urged "whoever favors Joab and whoever is for David" to follow Joab. It was surely not an accident that Joab's name was first.

Sheba, meanwhile, had escaped to the walled city of Abel Beth-maacah, and Joab besieged the city. Abel was a city far to the north, nearly as far as Dan, at the northern limit of Israel. As verse 14 says, Sheba had gone all through the tribes of Israel but had won the support of only a few cities and the Berites. Apparently nobody was following Sheba. He was not the real threat in this episode; Joab was. Not for the first time in 1–2 Samuel, a "wise woman" saved the day, interceding with a warrior, like Abigail, to prevent further violence and bloodshed. Unlike the wisdom of Jonadab, which led to rape and murder, and unlike the wisdom of Ahitophel which ended in suicide, the woman's wisdom was a saving wisdom.

According to the wise woman, she and her town were not rebels but among the "peaceable and faithful" in Israel. Since the city is a mother, destroying the city would be a kind of matricide (20:19). To save the mother city, one man must die, and he died by a head wound. The whole scene is reminiscent of Abimelech's siege of Shechem in Judges 9. In Judges, Abimelech, the pretender to the throne, was outside the walls and had his head crushed. Here, the rebel was inside the walls and had his head cut off. But the allusion gives a curious perspective on this episode: Joab, not Sheba, was the one standing in Abimelech's place, at the wall speaking to a woman. But his head was not crushed. If Joab was an Abimelech, he was a successful one, one that would raise up his uncrushed head and seek to become head over Israel.

In a supremely understated way, the text confirms that Joab essentially took over the kingdom at this point. Normally, lists of officials are placed near the beginning of the record of a king's reign

(1 Sam. 8:15–18), and its presence here indicates that David's reign had begun all over again, risen from the dead. One striking thing is missing from this list, however. The earlier list was prefaced with "David reigned over all Israel," and the same was true of the list of Solomon's officials in 1 Kings 4:1–19. In 2 Samuel 20 there is no reference to David ruling, and the list of officials begins with Joab; his name stands in the text where we expect to find David's name (v. 23). Textually, Joab has replaced David, and this is a subtle indication that the same thing had happened in Israel itself.

THE TRUE KING

The final chapters of 1–2 Samuel are often seen as an "appendix" disconnected from the book as a whole. Though the narratives in chapters 21 and 24 are out of chronological order, however, these chapters provide a suitable conclusion to the book. The immediately preceding chapters have recounted the rebellions of Absalom and Sheba, the "coup" of Joab, and the divisions within Israel that occurred in connection with those rebellions. At a number of points, chapters 21–24 offer a commentary on these events, commentary that, in context, sometimes takes an ironic twist.[1] In the poetic meditation on kingship in 23:1–7, for example, the ideal king is portrayed as one who takes up his spear against the "thorns" (vv. 6–7). Absalom and Sheba were precisely such brambles, but David was very ineffectual in dealing with them. Even more blatantly, David failed to deal with Joab, who was a thorny problem for David from the first years of his reign. The analogies drawn between Joab and Abimelech in chapter 20 reinforce this point: Abimelech was the bramble king *par excellence* (Judg. 9:7–21), and Joab was following his example. If an ideal king "thrusts away" the thorns, then we must conclude that David fell some ways shy of being an ideal king. To illustrate further: 23:8–39 recounts the heroic exploits of a number of David's mighty men and concludes with a list of the "thirty." But the passage that celebrates David's army ends with the name "Uriah the Hittite" (23:39), and everything turns sour.

These chapters not only cap off the immediately preceding chapters but also close out themes brought up in the early parts of 1 Samuel. As noted in an earlier chapter, 22:1–23:7 forms a poetic

---

[1] Thanks to James B. Jordan for pointing out some of the connections between chapters 21–24 and earlier portions of 2 Samuel.

inclusio with 1 Samuel 2:1–10 and 2 Samuel 1:18–27. Further, David's dealings with the house of Saul were concluded in chapter 21. Most crucially, chapter 24 tells the story of David's purchase of the location for the temple, which brings to a close the story of the destruction of Shiloh and the wanderings of the ark from 1 Samuel 4–6. Though the Lord's house is not yet built, David had set up the sanctuary for the ark in Jerusalem, and the book of Samuel ends with the promise of a more glorious house. The purchase of the threshing floor of Araunah, as we shall see below, also meant that the land promised to Abraham's seed had finally come into their (or his) hands.

Structurally, chapters 21-24 are arranged in an obvious chiasm:

> A   Deliverance from famine, 21:1–14
> B   Giant-killers, 21:15–22[2]
>   C David's Psalm, 22:1–51
>   C' David's last words, 23:1–7
> B'   The three and the thirty, 23:8–39
> A'   Deliverance from a pestilence, 24:1–25

As this outline makes clear, the central sections are words of praise to God for His many deliverances, together with a brief poem concerning the nature of true kingship, and these poetic sections highlight the themes of the narratives that surround them. At the beginning and end are stories of deliverance from the Lord's wrath, and the "B" sections highlight the deliverances accomplished by David's warriors, who were inspired by David's own example of courage. Though some details of these chapters offer a darker portrait of David, in general the chapters are a celebration of the ideal king, the king on which David's reign was modeled.

DELIVERANCE FROM FAMINE, 2 SAMUEL 21:1–14

Among other things, this narrative contrasts David and Saul in terms of their faithfulness in keeping covenants. The Gibeonites

---

[2] The two "B" sections will be discussed together, after the two "C" sections.

became servants to Israel in the time of Joshua. They tricked Joshua
into cutting a covenant with them, and Joshua warned that breach-
ing this covenant would bring Yahweh's wrath on Israel (Josh.
9:20). When Israel attacked the Gibeonites, they were violating
the holy name of Yahweh, in which they took their covenant oath,
and they were laying hands on a people under Yahweh's special
protection. Saul, in short, committed sacrilege when he attacked
the Gibeonites, and sacrilege always arouses Yahweh's wrath. Saul
thus broke a covenant that had been established centuries before
by Joshua, but David avenged the Gibeonites and simultaneously
kept the covenant he made with Jonathan. Keeping both covenants
required wisdom, but David showed both faithfulness and wisdom
here.

The story of Saul's attack on the Gibeonites is not told in
1 Samuel, but in an earlier chapter I suggested that Saul was attempting to conquer the city in order to make it the capital city of
the Saulide dynasty. This would be consistent with verse 2, which
says that Saul acted "in his zeal for the sons of Israel and Judah."
Possibly, Saul killed the Gibeonites, who served the altar of Yahweh, when he slaughtered the priests at Nob.

The time period when David avenged the Gibeonites is not
explicit. It is certain that this episode did not occur after the events
of chapter 20, but it did happen some time after David had brought
Mephibosheth into his house (cf. v. 7), around the middle of David's reign. Whenever this event happened in David's reign, it
clearly took place after Saul's reign was over, yet the famine that
plagued Israel was a result of Saul's sin. That wrong needed to be
made right before the Lord would be moved with entreaty for the
land. Sons suffer the consequences of the sins of their fathers, and
the sons *must* make amends and rectify wrongs.[3] Ignoring the evils

---

[3] This passage thus belies the convenient conservative idea that contemporary Americans bear no responsibility for our ancestors' treatment of blacks or American Indians. If
the fathers did evil, the sons are responsible to make restitution and will labor under the
curse of God until they do.

of a previous generation is not an option; we must either repent of them or suffer the consequences.

A difficult ethical question comes up in this incident. On the one hand, the blood of murder defiled the land and needed to be expiated (Deut. 19:11-13). Like Abel's blood, the blood of an innocent victim cried out from the land and could only be quieted by the blood of the murderer. In this case, however, the perpetrator was dead, and it seems that David did *not* have the option of punishing Saul's descendants for Saul's sins. Sons bear the weight of the father's sins in the sense that sons bear the consequences, but the law specifically forbade punishing a son for his father's crime (Deut. 24:16). Yet David put seven members of Saul's house to death for Saul's wrong. Evidently, David did the right thing, since the Lord turned from his anger, but how was David's action just?

One way to resolve this dilemma is to suggest that the members of Saul's house that were punished actually participated in the slaughter of the Gibeonites. Though theoretically plausible, the fact that some of them were Saul's grandsons makes it unlikely that they were old enough. A better explanation is that David was applying an eye-for-eye justice. Saul was carrying out a kind of holy war against the Gibeonites, putting the whole city to death (v. 1) and seeking to "exterminate" them (v. 5). Since Saul illegitimately carried out holy war against the Gibeonites, David justly carries out holy war (symbolically) against the "house of blood."[4]

Older commentators often suggested David must have had some special direction from Yahweh to pass such a sentence. David did consult Yahweh to discover the cause of the famine, but he did not consult Him in rendering his sentence (21:1, 6). David's verdict was so unusual that if Yahweh had given special direction, we would expect the text to tell us. Apparently, David was applying some principle of justice that might be applied to other situations. Pol Pot, for example, attempted a kind of *herem* war of extermina-

---

[4] This conclusion is defended by James B. Jordan in taped lectures.

tion against the Cambodian people, and the example of this passage suggests that it would be just, since Pol Pot himself is dead, to
punish surviving members of his family for the crime.

Another unusual aspect of this passage is that the language of
"atonement" is applied to capital punishment. The execution of the
members of Saul's house seems a kind of human sacrifice, since it
was offered "before Yahweh" and turned away His wrath (vv. 9, 14).
In 24:25, a normal animal sacrifice had the same effect. This passage thus highlights a truth that is evident from a close study of the
Levitical system: Human sacrifice was the cornerstone Israelite sacrifice. From Genesis 1 it was clear that only a human sacrifice will
atone for sins. A man sinned, and a man had to die for sin. The Old
Testament sacrifices were symbols of the worshiper's self-sacrifice,
since the worshiper identified with the animal as his representative
and then slaughtered it (cf. Lev. 1:4). Animal sacrifices were symbolic of the human sacrifice of Jesus. In the context of 2 Samuel,
this story provides a comment on the death of Absalom. Like the
death of Saul's descendants, Absalom's death was "before Yahweh"
and restored His favor to the land. As has been emphasized several
times, the death of kings Saul and Absalom were the basis for the
establishment and renewal of David's kingdom. Typologically, this
pointed to Jesus, the king who offered Himself up in death so that
He could inherit the throne.

David allowed the Gibeonites to choose the method of compensation, and this puts the lie to the theory of many modern scholars that David was using the situation as a pretext to attack Saul's
house.[5] The Gibeonite demand, however, put David in a conflict
of covenant obligations. David had covenanted to protect the sons
of Jonathan, but Joshua had covenanted to protect the Gibeonites.
How can both covenants be upheld in this situation? David avoided
the horns of this dilemma by choosing descendants from Saul who

[5] There is a pun in the Hebrew on the word "seven" and "oath," since both words
have the same consonants. The "seven" are demanded as payment for violation of an
oath.

were not part of Jonathan's line: two sons of Rizpah, Saul's concubine, and fives sons of Merab, the daughter of Saul.[6]

The victims were "hanged" (v. 9). This may refer to crucifixion, but from other records, it seems that crucifixion was invented
by the Persians. Probably the victims were first killed and then
their bodies were exposed (since the Hebrew word translated as
"hanged" literally means "exposed"). The reference to the barley
harvest placed this in springtime, and the reference is significant
because the land had been suffering under a famine. The death of
these members of Saul's house cleansed the land and made it fruitful again. Rain was also a cleansing agent, baptizing the land.

It was just for the Gibeonites to demand Saul's descendants as
compensation, but they went beyond this and acted cruelly toward
the bodies (v. 9). An ancient man or woman wanted to be buried
in the land of his fathers, and being left to the birds and beasts
was a sign of utter desolation. Rizpah, a Hebrew Antigone, did not
permit the bodies to be destroyed. She pitched a tent of sackcloth
to show that these dead members of the house of Saul would not go
unmourned and unremembered, and she prevented the birds and
beasts from devouring the bodies. David found Rizpah's action
commendable and realized that he had failed to honor Saul and
Jonathan as they should be honored. They too were "hanged" after
their deaths, in the Philistine city of Beth-shan. Even though their
bones were now buried (after being burned), David recognized that
he should honor them by returning them to the land. All the members of Saul's house were brought to the burial site of Kish, and the
"sacrifice" was effective only when the bones were laid to rest. Then
the Lord began to hear the entreaties of His people.

---

[6] The Massoretic Text says "Michal," but this is a textual error. Michal, so far as we
know elsewhere, was not married to an "Adriel," and she did not have any children (2 Sam.
6:23). Furthermore, 1 Samuel 18:19 records that Merab was given to Adriel.

SONG OF DELIVERANCE, 2 SAMUEL 22:1–51

The Psalm that takes up chapter 22 is basically the same as Psalm 18, with some minor differences that need not concern us. It is not certain when this Psalm was composed, but since it celebrates David's deliverance from Saul (v. 1), it is perhaps an early Psalm. In the previous chapter, we noted the parallels between Saul and Absalom, and so, in context, David's Psalm of praise for deliverance from Saul applies also to his deliverance from the new Saul, Absalom.

In the structure of 1–2 Samuel, this Psalm matches the song of Hannah that began the book of Samuel. The two Psalms share a number of images: "horn" (1 Sam. 2:1, 10; 2 Sam. 22:3); the Lord as a "rock" (1 Sam. 2:2; 2 Sam. 22:2–3, 32, 47); the general theme of the Lord's intervention to save His people (1 Sam. 2:4; 2 Sam. 22 passim); and the "anointed" of the Lord (1 Sam. 2:10; 2 Sam. 22:51). Given these parallels, it is possible to read the two Psalms as promise and fulfillment; Hannah looked forward to the coming of the Lord's anointed who would deliver Israel from Philistines and wicked priests, while David's Psalm looks back in gladness at this fulfilled hope.

The Psalm has a generally chiastic structure:

A   Praise of Yahweh, vv. 2–3
  B   The Lord delivers David, vv. 4–20
    C David's "cleanness" and the Lord's faithfulness, vv. 21–28
  B'   Yahweh delivers strength to David to crush his enemies, vv. 29–46
A'   Praise of Yahweh, vv. 47–51

Several features of this structure are noteworthy. First, each section of the Psalm begins with a direct reference to Yahweh (vv. 2, 4, 22, 29, 47). Though "Yahweh" is used at several other points in the Psalm, this outline highlights these direct addresses or references to Yahweh. Second, the correspondences between the different sections are illuminating. Sections A and A' frame the poem, so that the Psalm begins and ends with a litany of names and metaphors for God's character, a framing device particularly emphasized by the "rock" image which is repeated in verses 2–3 and again in 47. Verse 3 says that Yahweh delivers David from "violence," and verse 49 speaks of deliverance from the "violent man."

In the overall structure, sections B and B' are linked by the emphasis on David's deliverance from his enemies, but a progression takes place from B to B'. In section B,[7] the Lord lifts David from among his enemies, but in B' it looks as if David is delivering himself: Without Yahweh's direct intervention, David's enemies are consumed (v. 38), devoured and shattered (v. 39), fall under his feet (v. 39), flee (v. 41), are destroyed (v. 41), pulverized, crushed, and stamped (v. 43), and suffer other assorted mishaps. Frequently, corresponding sections of a chiastic text do not merely state the same thing twice; rather, the second of the pair builds on and expands the first. Here, the B sections could be summarized this way: "Yahweh delivers from enemies, and, what's more, He enables me to trample them into the mire of the streets."[8] At the center of the chiasm is David's claim to cleanness and uprightness, a claim that raises important theological issues, which we will deal with below.

We turn to a more detailed examination of the poem. In verses 1–3, David employs nine metaphors to describe God's character, and these are arranged into three sets of three:[9]

---

[7] Section B is itself organized chiastically and includes some internal chiastic patterns:

    A   Call to the Lord, vv. 4–7 (*inclusio* on call, Yahweh in vv. 4, 7; images of waves/torrents, cords/snares)
      B   Earthquake, v. 8
        C   Lord's anger: Smoke, fire, coals, v. 9
          D Lord's arrival (heaven-dark-cherub-wind-dark-sky), vv. 10–12
        C'   Brightness and coals, v. 13
      B'   Lord's voice and the parting of the sea, vv. 14–16
    A'   Delivered from enemies, vv. 17–20 (waters; Yahweh; enemies)

[8] John Breck calls this the "what's more" factor. See *The Shape of Biblical Language* (Crestwood: St. Vladimir's Seminary Press, 1994), passim.

[9] Youngblood, *1, 2 Samuel*, vol. 3, 1066.

Yah is
Rock, fortress, deliverer
God
Rock of refuge, shield, horn of salvation

———

Stronghold, refuge, savior

The images expand and become clarified as the lines progress. The first two triads begin with "rock," but the "rock" becomes a "rock of refuge" in the second triad and a mountain stronghold in the third. The parallel thus indicates the specific significance of the "rock" image, namely, that Yahweh is a rock that provides protection and shelter. The second term in each triad speaks of defense from enemies (fortress, shield, refuge), and the last term in each triad emphasizes that Yahweh is a Deliverer. The horn image is used here and may refer to an animal that uses his horns to fight off enemies. "Horn" also sometimes refers to mountain peaks (e.g., Is. 5:1), analogous to the "horns" on the altar. Within the Psalm, a reference to the "horned peaks" would be relevant, since the Psalm has already emphasized that the Lord is a refuge and protecting rock.

David calls on the Lord in expectation of deliverance and salvation from his enemies (vv. 4–7), and the imagery in verses 5–6 is of particular interest. David cries out because he is encompassed by waves and torrents. Water imagery is a common way to describe enemies. Israel is often pictured as the land sitting in the midst of the sea, while the nations are the sea beating against the land to overwhelm it.[10] At the same time, David's enemies are also described as "Sheol," the place of the dead (v. 6). This is no doubt literally true, since David's life is threatened by Saul, Absalom, and his other enemies. But the reference to "Sheol" also fits with the imagery of the sea, which is sometimes compared to the realm of the dead (see Jon. 2). In the Bible, the universe is depicted as a three-story house, with the sea corresponding to hell and death. In

---

[10] See the examples in my *A House for My Name*, 43–48.

particular, David intended to bring out a pun on Saul's name—*sha'ul* was the one who drove David to the brink of *she'ol*.[11]

At the conclusion of the B section, David returns to the imagery of waters and an explicit reference to enemies (vv. 16–18). David's deliverance occurs when the Lord opens the channels of the sea, an image that recalls the Lord's rebuke of the Red Sea and Israel's deliverance from Pharaoh. David has been surrounded by a sea of enemies, by the oppressive "Pharaohs" Saul and Absalom, but he calls on the God of the exodus to split the sea again and make a path of safety to a broad place. The salvation of the anointed king is compared to the salvation of the nation as a whole. Verse 16 is also reminiscent of Day 3 of creation week, when the waters parted to form the dry land (Gen. 1:9–13). David's deliverance is not only an exodus, but a new creation.

Verses 8–16 describe the Lord's response to the call of helpless David. The Lord appears in cloud, fire, and smoke, bringing thunder, earthquake and lightning, phenomena often associated with the glory-theophany of the Lord. Again there is an exodus connection, for the Lord was with Israel in the cloud as they passed through the sea. Verse 11 says that the Lord "rode on a cherub," which refers to the cherubim that formed the Lord's glory-chariot. Yahweh appears in a cloud, which functions like a movable throne or chariot (see Ezek. 1). The Lord comes not only as the glorious one, but as a great warrior: His thundering is a war cry, and He shoots lightning-arrows at the enemies of David (v. 15).

The central section of the Psalm is problematic (vv. 21–28). David praises Yahweh for His deliverance but also insists that this deliverance was consistent with David's own righteousness. David's rescue is "according to my righteousness" and "according to the cleanness of my hands" (vv. 21, 25). He claims that he has "kept the ways of the Lord" and not "acted wickedly against my God" (v. 22) and also asserts that this fits with Yahweh's characteristic

---

[11] Thanks to James B. Jordan for pointing this out, though I am embarrassed to admit I did not see it myself!

way of dealing with men: He is faithful and upright with the faithful and upright, but he is astute with the perverse.

Two obvious problems come up here. First, how can David say this when he had committed adultery and arranged for Uriah's murder? It is possible that the Psalm was written before his sin with Bathsheba, but that does not relieve the problem, since in the text of 1–2 Samuel the Psalm comes after the sin, and the writer must have anticipated that readers of chapter 22 would have read chapters 11–12. Second, how are David's words consistent with the doctrine of justification by faith? Did David believe in a form of "works righteousness" where God owes David salvation because of David's own righteousness? Or should we conform David's language to what we expect from Paul and interpret "righteousness" as "imputed righteousness"?

The last issue may be addressed first. It is impossibly artificial to import the category of imputation or the doctrine of justification in its Reformation form into this Psalm. Even if we interpret the Psalm typologically and say (with Augustine) that these are the words of Jesus, we are still left with the question, What did David himself mean by the statement? And when we raise that question, it is quite clear that David was not talking about imputed righteousness, but about the righteousness of his life, his actions and ways. The difficulty becomes more acute when we realize that this is not an isolated example. The Psalms are full of this kind of thing. At times, the Psalms plead with God concerning a particular accusation: "If I have done *this*, if there is iniquity in my hands, then may I be judged" (e.g., Ps. 7:3–6). At other times, as here in 2 Samuel 22, the claim is broader and includes the claim that David is blameless and righteous in general.

This question can be resolved when we recognize the covenantal context of David's prayer. David's prayer presumes a prior relationship with the Lord, a relationship in which the Lord has promised deliverance and salvation and demanded faithfulness from David. Yahweh entered this covenant relationship purely because of His grace and love, and anything that David enjoys or achieves within the covenant is a gift of his covenant Lord. David knows that it is Yahweh who "makes me great" (v. 36). Yet God has made commitments to those who are in covenant with Him, and these commitments constitute the covenant. In particular, He has committed to rescue His people when they are under threat. David's claim is thus simply that the Lord has kept his promise, the promise to rescue those who live in conformity with the covenant. David is not saying he has a claim on God because of his independent moral achievements; he is assuming that he has a claim on God because God gave him a claim.

The covenant context also helps us understand how David could make these assertions after he had committed serious sins. David was not claiming sinless perfection, for when we look at his Psalms as a whole, it is obvious that he realized he was a sinner (Ps. 51). Within the covenant, however, there were designated pathways for sinners to be reconciled to God. An Israelite who sinned had to confess, repent and offer sacrifice, trusting Yahweh to keep His promise and forgive, and in this way sinners do keep the covenant and lead "blameless" lives (see Lk. 1:6; Phil. 3:6). Though David was not sinless, in those cases where he sinned, he repented when confronted and offered sacrifice when it was necessary (2 Sam. 21, 24). In this way, he proved himself not merely a pious man, but an ideal king.

David's claim that God rescued him "according to my righteousness" is rooted in an understanding of God's character. Yahweh is loyal to those who are loyal to Him, complete with the complete, pure with the pure, but to the perverted He is "twisted" (vv. 26–27). An eye-for-eye principle is at work here; God responds to people the way they respond to Him. He wears a different mask depending on the way we live before Him. This is an intriguing theological insight and helps explain the experience of many unbelievers. There is only one God, but the experience that a perverse and wicked man has of this one God is different from the experi-

ence of a believer. Paganism frequently presents God or the gods
as hostile to man, as a power that toys with them, sets traps for
them, and draws them malevolently to their death (cf. Oedipus;
Captain Ahab). According to David, such experiences are genuine
encounters with the living God, but they are encounters with the
"twistedness" of God. Clearly, God is no indulgent grandpappy in
the sky, smiling placidly at the foibles of men. Yahweh is patient
and merciful and good to all His creation; but Yahweh is also a
trickster God, more cunning than Dionysus.

The next section returns to the theme of deliverance, but, as
noted above, the deliverance is described in a very different way in
B' than it was in B. Instead of coming in cloud and fire and smoke,
Yahweh delivers David by empowering him for battle, so that he
can run at a troop and leap over a wall; Yahweh trains his hands for
war and enlarges his steps so that his feet do not slip (vv. 35–40).
David represents his victories as a victory at law (v. 44). The word
for "contention" means a legal contention. David's enemies bring
a "case" against Him, and David appeals to Yahweh, the Judge of
heaven and earth, to decide in his favor. David's deliverance from
his enemies is his justification, concrete evidence of the Lord's verdict in favor of His king, His declaration of righteousness. As we
have seen throughout this book, this was the bedrock to David's
treatment of Saul and other enemies; knowing that Yahweh will
vindicate the righteous, David could rest and wait on the Lord.
Justification by faith was the foundation of David's politics.

Because of David's prowess and victory, other nations submit to David without a fight (vv. 45–46). This reminds us of the
conquest, when Rahab and the Gibeonites made alliances with
Joshua because they heard of the great victories of Yahweh. David
described his initial deliverance from his enemies as a new exodus
and now describes his victories as a new conquest. The progression
in the poem follows the progression of Israel's history, and David is
again represented, indeed he represents himself, as the new Israel.

THE SUN KING, 2 SAMUEL 23:1–7

The poem in 23:1–7 is the other part of the central section of this "appendix," and it raises another main theme of the section. Instead of concentrating on Yahweh's deliverance of His anointed, it speaks of the importance and blessing of a faithful king. It thus answers the hope that Hannah's song expressed and shows that the "revolution of the elites" that she hoped for had occurred. This poem especially summarizes the thrust of the practical focus that I have taken throughout this book, for it describes the blessings that come upon a people when their leaders "rule over men righteously" and "in the fear of God" (23:3). This poem especially shows that the promise of faithful leadership is good news for the people of God; that it is gospel.

Though introduced as "the last words of David," these were not the very last words that David uttered. He gave a deathbed speech to Solomon, urging him to take care of unfinished business (1 Kgs. 2:1–9). 2 Samuel 23:1–7 represents David's last official and public utterance, a "last will and testament." Though, as we have seen above, the description of the ideal king provides some ironic commentary on David's own reign, our attention here will be on David's description of the ruler and his effects on a people.

David begins with several descriptions of himself in the third person. He is the "son of Jesse," a significant description in several respects. Jesse was a man of wealth in the tribe of Judah, but he did not play a highly significant role in Israel's history (other than being David's father). Further, he was a man of Bethlehem, and Bethlehem was not only a small town but had a history of corruption. To say that he was a "son of Jesse," then, emphasized that Yahweh raised him from relative obscurity, from a despised place, even as his Greater Son came from despised Galilee. On the other hand, Jesse was a member of the royal tribe of Judah (Gen. 49:8–12) and a descendant of Boaz. The fact that David comes from Judah shows that his kingship fulfilled a prophecy from many centuries before.

Though he had begun in a comparatively lowly position, David had been raised up on high. Verse 2 refers to his exaltation as king, and it anticipates the imagery of the king as a "sun" (vv. 3–4). The Hebrew word for "declares" at the end of this line means "oracle" and indicates that David is functioning in prophetic capacity, speaking in the power of the Spirit (v. 2). David refers to himself as the anointed one, the "Christ." This refers to his ritual anointing with oil, but verse 2 speaks of the Spirit, who has also anointed David. David also mentions his relation to the Psalms. Many translations render this line as the "sweet Psalmist of Israel," but the Hebrew is more ambiguous. It literally says, "the sweet one of the chants of Israel," and this could mean either that David was the one who wrote the chants of Israel or that David was the *subject* of the chants of Israel. We have already learned one such chant in 1 Samuel 18:8: "Saul has killed his thousands, but David has killed his ten thousands." And we know that David also wrote Psalms. Both senses of the phrase are true, and it is no doubt deliberately, and pregnantly, ambiguous.

A king who rules in righteousness is defined as a king who rules in the fear of God (v. 3), and Yahweh compares such a ruler to the light of the morning sun. The association of the sun with rulers is rooted in Genesis 1:16, where God created the sun and moon to rule the day and night. Heavenly bodies, since they are raised up high, represent the king who is raised up above his people. That is the generic significance of the imagery, but the Lord speaks specifically here about light of the "morning" sun and the sun that shines "without clouds" on the "tender grass." The image is extended to show the specific ways in which the righteous king is like the sun.

Several points emerge from this. First, the king brings light out of darkness; he brings morning. This is an image that David used in the previous chapter, where he spoke of the Lord as the lamp that illumined his darkness (23:29). What the Lord was to David, so David, the anointed of the Lord, was to Israel. He had been raised to bring light after the darkness of Saul's reign and the darkness of Absalom's civil war, during which Israel stumbled around aimlessly, lost in a dark wood. With the sun now risen, Israel could see where she was going. Second, the sun also brings fertility from the earth, causing vegetation to shoot up.[12] Sunshine and rain make the land flourish like a fruitful garden (see Ps. 72:1–7). The word for "earth" could be translated as "land," which would imply that David had the fruitfulness of the promised land particularly in view. Under the light and warmth of a righteous king, the land becomes truly a land of milk and honey. As noted a number of times above, this was specifically true under the terms of the Davidic covenant, since the fruitfulness of Israel depended on the light that came from the Davidic king (2 Sam. 7).

Of course, grass represents the people of Israel. Men spring from the earth as grass does, and they are compared to grass in several places of Scripture. Usually this comparison emphasizes the brevity of life; our lives are like grass that flourishes in the morning and dies in the afternoon (e.g., Ps. 103:15–16). Here, by contrast, the flourishing grass is a sign of the fertility of the nation, and the king is the one who makes the nation flourish.[13]

David's response to the Lord's oracle about the king comes in two sections. First, David referred to the everlasting covenant that the Lord had made with him. The first line of verse 5 is difficult, but probably should be translated as "Is not my house so

[12] The word for "grass" is used in Genesis 1:12 to describe the "vegetation" that sprang up on the third day of creation. In Genesis 1, the vegetation included plants yielding seed and trees yielding fruit. Thus the "grass" in 23:4 refers to plants in general, not simply to grass in our sense.

[13] Americans, especially many conservative Christians, have a strong tendency to think of political rulers as something of a necessary evil. This has become even more pronounced in the past decade with the scandalous Clinton presidency, and more generally during the twentieth century when the federal government has expanded at a tremendous rate into many areas of our lives. But the attitude seems to go back to the founding. Americans want to be left alone, and we believe that the role of the political ruler is to stand back and let us be. The Bible does not teach that the ruler is a "necessary evil." Instead, the righteous ruler here is described as the sun that brings fertility and prosperity, and elsewhere rulers are spoken of as "shepherds" to the people of Israel, fathers, nursing fathers. In this passage in particular, righteous rulers are described as one of the conditions for the flourishing of a people, and we need to conform our political instincts to this biblical picture. Rulers can be a plague, but they are not inherently so.

with God?" This question expects a positive answer: Yes, the house of David is thus with God. Just as the righteous ruler is a sun that ensures the flourishing of the land, so also the Lord is the sun that causes the flourishing of David's house. Specifically, the Lord made a covenant with David, ordered and secure, an "everlasting covenant," that ensured that David would have all his "salvation and desire." Obviously, this is a reference back to the covenant made in 2 Samuel 7, when Yahweh promised to establish David's house forever.

David's other response has to do with those in Israel that are not "grass" but weeds. David's poem contrasts two types of plants, a contrast that goes back to Genesis 1–3. Grass, which includes grains and other productive plants, flourishes under the sun king, but there are also unproductive thorns that only harm those who try to pull them up. A righteous king has to make war against the weeds and against the thorns (v. 7), taking up iron and spear to battle them. The king is a gardener who has to weed out the wicked and cast them into the fire (Is. 27:2–6). Making sure that the grass is not choked out by thorns is one of the key ways that the king enables the grass to flourish.

The king described applies to some degree to David, but the idea of the king as the rising sun is ultimately applied to the Messiah. 2 Samuel 23:1–7 is a full-length portrait of Jesus. He is the one who rules righteously and in the fear of the Lord, who brings the light of the new creation in His coming, who causes the land to flourish like a garden, and who takes up armor and spear against the thorns. But, as the next section makes clear, a righteous king also inspires imitation in his subordinates, and Jesus does the same, so that leaders of the church should aspire to approximate Him. All pastors and elders would do well to place 2 Samuel 23:1–7 on the doorposts of their houses, on their wrists, on the frontals of their foreheads.

GIANT KILLERS, THE THREE AND THE THIRTY, 2 SAMUEL 21:15–22; 23:8–39

2 Samuel 21:15-22 forms a separate section, though it is connected to the narrative in 21:1–14 by the idea of deliverance. This section details the exploits of four of David's warriors, all of whom fought descendants of the "Rapha," which means "giant" or even "Titan." From his youth, David fought giants, and the fact that his men were also giant-killers is a testimony to the power of his example. A faithful and courageous king inspires similar conduct in his follow-ers, and this applies not only to Jesus but to faithful leaders of the church. Again, in context, the vignettes in this section refer most immediately to the rebellions of Absalom and Sheba. These two had lifted up their heads against David, acting like giants in the land; but David and his men were experienced giant-killers.

Verse 19 reports that Elhanan killed Goliath the Gittite, and as it stands, there is a contradiction with 1 Samuel 17. Several possible interpretations have been offered. Some have argued that Elhanan is another name of David and Jaare-oregim another name for Jesse. Others have even speculated that "David" was a throne name, but there is no evidence for this elsewhere. In all likelihood, a copying mistake has crept into the text, and the parallel in 1 Chronicles 20:5 preserves. The latter passage claims that Elhanan killed Lahmi, the brother of Goliath, rather than Goliath himself.

Other mighty men are listed in 23:8–29.[14] This section is set in the context of the "last words of David," and the poem leads into the following section in a couple of ways. In 23:8–39 we see that the ideal king is surrounded by warriors who fight following their king's example. In one sense, the function of these men was like the function of Eve to Adam, helpers suitable to the king. David was a new Adam, a ruler and a representative of his people, and he

---

[14] This section of chapter 23 has several main sections:

A. Description of the exploits of the "three," vv. 8–12

B. Three men from the thirty: Abishai and Benaiah are two of them, vv. 13–23

C. A list of the "thirty," vv. 24–39

had close aids who assisted him in tending the garden-land of Israel
and in battling weeds.

The reference to the "house" of David in the poem is also significant (23:5). 2 Samuel, as we have seen, has made frequent use
of a victory-housebuilding pattern. In 23:8–39, a house of David is
listed again, but here the house is not his family or administration
but the house of mighty men who fought with him. Verses 8–12
speak of "the three," which were David's most famous and powerful
warriors. In terms of architectural imagery, the three form, with the
king, the four cornerstones of the house of Israel. In having "the
three," David pointed ahead to Jesus and his "three mighty men,"
Peter, James and John, who formed the cornerstones of the New
Testament house, along with the other apostles who are pictured
as foundation stones of the New Jerusalem in the book of Revelation.[15]

The three are Josheb-basshebeth, Eleazar, and Shammah,
names that we have not encountered in 1–2 Samuel. For each of
the three, we have a vignette of their exploits, recounting how
they brought victory or "salvation."[16] Verse 8 tells about Josheb-
basshebeth, who was apparently also called "Adino the Eznite."
He killed eight hundred men "at one time," that is, in the course
of one battle.[17] Eleazar's exploit came during a battle with the Philistines, when the rest of the army had abandoned the field (v. 9).

---

[15] That this is part of the imagination of Israel is evident from the way that the
word *pinnah* is used. It normally means "cornerstone" or "corner," but in Judges 20:2 and
1 Samuel 14:28, the word is used to refer to chiefs of the people. Even when the word is
translated as "corner" it is sometimes referring to people as the cornerstones of some social
"building" (Is. 19:13; 28:16).

[16] Through Eleazar Yahweh brought about a "great victory" (v. 10), but the Hebrew word is related to *yeshua*, "savior" (cf. v. 12). One important dimension of salvation
throughout the Scriptures is this idea of victory. To be saved is to be delivered; where
there is salvation, there is victory over enemies. Jesus' very name might be taken not only
as "savior" but as "victor."

[17] There is a textual problem here. 1 Chronicles 11:11 says that he killed three hundred. Perhaps the two passages refer to two different battles, or perhaps he personally killed
three hundred but was responsible for eight hundred deaths. Finally, it may be that the text
has been garbled, and one or the other contains an original reading.

He is called an "Ahohite," and there is an "Ahoah" mentioned in 1 Chronicles 8:4 among the descendants of Benjamin. Possibly Eleazar descended from this Benjamite, and if this is the case it is significant that one of David's "three" was a Benjamite warrior. David was plundering the tribe of Saul and fixing Benjamite "stones" into the foundation of his kingdom (see vv. 27, 29).

The third of the three, Shammah, fought in the midst of a plot of lentils on another occasion when the army fled (vv. 11–12). Lentils are mentioned only a few times in the Old Testament. Esau asked Jacob for the red lentil stew that Jacob had made and gave up his birthright for a bowl (Gen. 25:34). In other passages, lentils are a food of exile. When David fled from Absalom, Barzillai brought out food, including lentils (2 Sam. 17:28), and the only other time they are mentioned is in Ezekiel 4:9, as one of the ingredients in the bread that Ezekiel baked and ate. Ezekiel's bread, baked over a fire made from human dung, was a sign that Israel would eat "their bread unclean among the nations where I shall banish them." There was a hierarchy of vegetable food, as there was of meat. Lentils were not Israel's main food, certainly not the most desired food, and certainly not sanctuary food. Canaan was not a land of lentils, but a land of milk and honey. Shammah probably fought a raiding party that was stealing food, as Israel's enemies often did in the time of the judges. But Shammah did not let the Philistines take the plot, and his heroics were all the more dramatic because lentils were less than a delicacy. Shammah defended the food source of Israel and the land (symbolized by a single plot) even when all the rest of Israel had fled. Like Eleazar, Shammah brought salvation, and salvation in his case literally meant food; victory produced an abundance of food, as Christ's victory allows us to eat at His table.

Verse 13 begins a new section about three men who aided David. These were different men from the official "Three." They were "three of the Thirty chief men," which means, whoever these three were, they were included in the Thirty. The list of "the Thirty" in verses 24–39, however, does not include the "Three" described in verses 8–12. A distinction is thus drawn between the "Three" cornerstones and "the Thirty" who (architecturally speaking) make up the rest of the foundation of David's military house.[18]

Prior to the list are three stories about particular members of "the Thirty." The first is the most elaborate and has been seen typologically. David was in the "cave of Adullam" and the "stronghold" (vv. 13–14), which indicates that this event took place while David was an outlaw, fleeing from Saul (see 1 Sam. 22:1, 4). The Philistines had taken possession of David's hometown and set up their garrison.[19] In the midst of the battle, David longed for the water of Bethlehem, and three of the thirty heard David's wish and fought through the Philistines to bring it to him. David refused to drink the water, and though his response seems cruel and ungrateful, he was actually paying homage to his men. He realized they had risked their lives to bring him this water, and that meant the water was as good as their blood. Eating blood was specifically forbidden by the law (Lev. 17:10–13), but to David this prohibition had wider applications than the literal meaning might suggest. The law that prohibited eating blood forbade men from being bloodthirsty and prohibited the king from sending men to risk their lives for the sake of pleasure or personal gain.

"Bethlehem" means "house of bread," and here we learn that it was a place of unequaled water as well. It was a small-scale "land

[18] A further argument for distinguishing the two sets of "three" has to do with the total number of the Thirty. According to 23:39, there are thirty-seven among "the Thirty." This may mean that "the Thirty" was a symbolic number and that there were actually more in the group at any one time (as "twelve tribes" was used though there were actually thirteen or fourteen separate tribal entities), or it could be that men would die and be replaced. This list includes the full number of members of "the Thirty" over David's entire reign; at any one time, there were only thirty, but over the whole course of his reign, thirty-seven different men were in this elite group. Another difficulty is to explain where the number thirty-seven comes from. If we assume that there were two "sons of Jashen," then there are thirty-five in the list. If we add Abishai and Benaiah, then we get thirty-seven, and we reach this total without including any of the "Three." This confirms that "the Thirty" does not include the "Three."

[19] The Philistines set up camp in the valley of Rephaim, a word derived from "Rapha," which means "giant." Again, we have a hint that David and his armies are giant-killers.

of milk and honey," a garden-like setting of rich food and drink. David wished for the goods of his garden-like home, and his men burst through the camp in the valley of the giants ("Rephaim," v. 13) to get it. Some older commentators suggest that David was expressing a deeper wish, not just for the water from the well in Bethlehem but for the water of life that would flow from the One born in Bethlehem as a son of David's house. David craved the ultimate deliverance of the garden from the possession of the ultimate enemy. If we take the story this way, David's decision to pour out the water may also have typological associations. Access to the garden does not come through the blood of David's mighty men, but only through the blood of David's Son, an even mightier Man. By pouring out the water, David acknowledged that the final redemption had not yet occurred. The water could not yet come from Bethlehem because Jesus was not yet glorified.

The next story involves Abishai, who was the chief of the Thirty but not among the Three. Abishai was the brother of Joab, whom David placed in charge of the whole army at one point. The story here is a general one, similar to the story of Adino the Eznite. Abishai killed three hundred with his spear (vv. 18–19), but, unlike Adino, it is not said that he killed them at one time. Thus, it may be a cumulative total over his whole career.

Benaiah's story is more detailed and intriguing. Benaiah was chief of David's bodyguard, known as the "Pelethites and the Cherethites" (2 Sam. 8:18; 20:23), and here we learn that he was from Kabzeel, a town in the tribal area of Judah (Josh. 15:21). In a number of ways, his exploits mimicked David's, showing again how a righteous king stamps his image on his men, how the glory of the sun king is reflected in his followers. Like David, Benaiah killed a lion; just as David killed Goliath, Benaiah killed an "impressive" Egyptian; like David, he fought the Egyptian with an unusual weapon, a club, rather than with a sword or spear; like David with Goliath, Benaiah killed the Egyptian with the Egyptian's own weapon.

The story about killing a lion in a pit on a snowy day is intriguing (2 Sam. 23:20). Benaiah also killed the "two sons of Ariel," and the Hebrew word "Ariel" means "lion." Benaiah not only literally defeated lions but also fought lion-like men. Benaiah's attack on a lion is comparable not only to David's combat with a lion, but more particularly to one of Samson's exploits, and the link with Samson is quite close (Judg. 14:5–14). After Samson killed the lion, he came back to find that the lion was filled with honey. In the context of Judges 14, killing the lion was parallel to Samson's defeat of the Philistines. The lion with sweetness in it contained a promise that Samson's victory over the lion-like Philistines would make the land flow with milk and honey: Sweetness would come from the corpses of the Philistines. Benaiah's victory over the lion had similar results. By killing the lion in the "cistern," Benaiah saved the water supply, just as Jesus descended to battle the roaring lion and to make living water available to us. David brought fertility to the land, like rain upon the earth, by inspiring men like Benaiah to secure the water supply against lions.

DELIVERANCE FROM PESTILENCE, 2 SAMUEL 24:1–25
Several structural considerations will help to illuminate the purpose and significance of this final episode in 1–2 Samuel. Most immediately, this is the last section of the chiasm that begins in chapter 21, matching the story of the famine that occurred because of Saul's attack on Gibeon. In both chapters, a curse fell on the land because of a king's sin; in both cases, the curse was removed by a sacrifice; and there is a clear parallel in the final clause of each story ("the Lord moved by entreaty for the land," 24:25; 21:14). The twin themes of deliverance and of the ideal king are highlighted once again. In chapter 21, David reversed the evil effects of Saul's sin, while here he first caused the plague, but then, unlike Saul, took immediate steps to rectify it. He was willing to take the punishment upon himself (v. 17), rather than allow the sheep to suffer. This shows the true king at work, not a sinless king but a king who,

once he sees the evil of his actions, turns and becomes like the morning sun rising and bringing health to the land.

As noted at the beginning of this chapter, this incident concludes the story of the house of Yahweh that began in the early chapters of 1 Samuel. At the battle of Aphek (1 Sam. 4–6), the house of the Lord at Shiloh was attacked, dismembered, and destroyed by the Philistines. For over a century, the worship system of Israel was in disrepair. David brought the ark to Jerusalem, but the whole system was not put back together. At the conclusion of the book, David made preparations for the permanent house when he purchased the threshing floor of Araunah and used it for sacrifice. According to 1 Chronicles 21:26, the Lord lit the altar that David built here with fire from heaven. Fire from the Lord was the sign that the tabernacle had been erected (Lev. 9:24), and again the Lord consumed the sacrifice as a sign that this was the place where sacrifice should be offered, the house of Master Yahweh; 1 Chronicles 22:1 and 2 Chronicles 3:1 record that Solomon's temple was later built on this threshing floor.

A new section begins at 24:1, but the last phrase in the previous section was the name "Uriah the Hittite." Uriah's name, and indeed the whole list of "mighty men," sets up a military context and emphasizes that the story in chapter 24 is about David's relation to the "hosts" of Israel. David's census was a mustering of military personnel, as verse 9 makes clear. As he did with Uriah, David sinned in relation to the military. Another general connection is that chapter 24 records the second great sin of David, immediately following a reminder of the first. More specifically, as in the Uriah story, a prophet came to David to tell him about a curse coming on the land because of his sin, just as Nathan confronted David after the sin with Bathsheba and Uriah. In both cases, the sin of the shepherd causes the sheep to suffer (v. 17).

The other, and more important, key to understanding this passage is to see the connections with the exodus. The most obvious parallel is that Israel suffered from a plague. In verses 13 and 15 the word for "plague" is *deber*, which is not used for the exodus plague, but the exodus word for "plague" is used in verses 21 and 25 (*magge-fah*). Further, the pestilence was spread by the "angel of the Lord" (v. 16) who struck down the people (v. 17), another exodus motif. 1 Chronicles 21:30 says that the angel had his sword stretched out against Israel, and particularly against Jerusalem, as the Lord had gone out against Egypt on the night of Passover.[20] Also like Passover, the angel was turned away by a sacrifice.[21]

This exodus theme helps us to understand the whole story, and the reason why David's census is a sin in the first place. The problem cannot be the census itself. Yahweh Himself ordered a census (Num. 1:1–3), and Exodus 30:11–16 made it clear that Israel's hosts might be mustered again. Exodus 30 indicates that there was a proper procedure for mustering the army, with each man paying a half-shekel of "atonement money." Since the war camp of Israel was a holy space, paying the money covered the men as they made the transition from the common state to the holy state of the war camp. Some commentators suggest that David was punished because he failed to follow this procedure, but this explanation is insufficient. There is no allusion to this law in the text, and Joab opposed the census as such, not merely the way it was conducted (v. 3). When Ahab later took a census during a war with the Arameans, he did not collect atonement money, and yet there was no plague (1 Kgs. 20:15). Others argue that David wanted to find out how big his army was so he could boast about it, or he was putting his trust in numbers of men rather than in the Lord's strength. This is possible, but there is nothing about motivation in the text, and Joab's objections, again, were to the census itself. More generally, the Bible rarely focuses attention on motives exclusively.

---

[20] Interestingly, as Bergen points out, this is the only place in the Old Testament where the angel of the Lord is turned against Israel. Normally, he stretches out his sword against Israel's enemies (Balaam; Assyrians in 2 Kgs.). See Bergen, *1, 2 Samuel*, 478, fn. 63.

[21] Verse 16 says that the Lord stopped the pestilence before the sacrifice was offered, but in 1 Chronicles 21, the Lord relents in response to a sacrifice.

The exodus background provides a more plausible perspective. David suffered plagues as Pharaoh did, and this suggests that he committed a sin analogous to Pharaoh's. Pharaoh killed the boy children of Egypt, but before that he sinned by putting them to work on his building projects (Exod. 1:8–15). When Israel first settled in Egypt, they were placed in Goshen, a separate territory, where they were to live as a semi-autonomous people. They were not part of Pharaoh's army nor were they his subjects (Gen. 47:1–6). Pharaoh began to arouse the angel of death when he seized the holy people for his own projects. And David did something similar. Israel was God's holy people, and that meant they belonged to Yahweh, who, as the High Commander, had the exclusive right to muster His hosts. When David mustered the men, he was seizing a holy people, claiming them as his own, committing sacrilege. The connection with the Bathsheba-Uriah incident supports this view, since in that case, too, David's sin was not just adultery, but seizing a woman that was another man's wife from the "sacred" protection of her husband's house. He made his sin worse by using his military to cover up his sin and having them arrange for the death of Uriah. In each of these sins, David was acting like a Pharaoh, like a king of the nations.

Despite Joab's objections, the census went forward. Joab's fact finding tour went in an elliptical loop around the land. First, he crossed the Jordan to Aroer (fifteen miles east of the Dead Sea), up to the northern portion of the Transjordan, and then back west to Gilead (above the Sea of Galilee), and to Dan (northernmost border of tribal areas), as far west as "Tyre" and then back south to Beersheba. This route shows that David controlled a significant portion of Transjordanian territory and, if the "fortress of Tyre" (v. 7) is "Old Tyre," the mainland portion of the city, his dominions stretched into Phoenician territory. Hiram of Tyre helped David build his palace and would later help Solomon, but 2 Samuel 24 raises the possibility that Tyre was a tributary state or ally during David's time. Yahweh's promises to Abraham were coming to pass, as the boundaries of the land extended to Abrahamic proportions.

The numbers made the same point. If there were 1.3 million fighting men, the total population must be close to five or six million.[22] Israel was becoming as numerous as the sand by the sea.

David's heart troubled him as soon as the census was over, and he responded with prayer (v. 10). As in the Uriah story, he confessed his sin outright, admitting that he had done a "very foolish" thing. The phrase "arose in the morning" (v. 11) may indicate that he kept an all-night vigil, as he had done in the earlier event with Bathsheba and Uriah. Later, he prayed a second prayer interceding for the people (v. 17). David's response of penitence was crucial. As Eugene Peterson observed, "David does not always obey God, but he always *deals* with God."[23]

In response to David's prayers, Yahweh sent Gad to offer three choices, of which David chose a three-day plague (vv. 10–14). Though shorter, this was the most severe of the others (70,000 died in three days, v. 15) and more certain to cause death, since ancient peoples had virtually no weapons to fight disease. David chose pestilence because he wanted to fall into the hands of God and not man; if he had to be vulnerable, he would rather be vulnerable with God.[24]

The passage emphasizes the number three (some manuscripts even have Gad offering "three years" of famine, as in 1 Chr. 21:12). A three-day judgment was an act of mercy, because it meant that God was not carrying out His judgment to a full week. On the third day of this pestilence,[25] David offered a sacrifice (on Mount

---

[22] The numbers were divided among "Israel" and "Judah." As noted above, there are hints throughout David's reign of a division among the tribes, and David treats them as separate administrative districts. Dividing them for census purposes may have exacerbated divisions even further.

[23] Peterson, *First and Second Samuel*, 264.

[24] How could famine force him to rely on other men? Buying food from other countries, as Jacob was forced to do in Genesis, would put David and Israel at the mercy of men who would drive hard bargains and make it difficult for him to supply his people.

[25] The plague lasts until the "appointed time" (v. 15), and this probably refers to the third day as mentioned in Gad's prophecy. The word choice is odd, since it usually refers to the holidays of Israel's religious calendar (*mo'ed*). This hints at the festival aspects of what happens here, which is a new Passover.

Moriah) that stopped the plague . The location links this event with the sacrifice of Isaac, which also took place on the "third day" on "Moriah" (Gen. 22:2, 4). Like the "third day" of Isaac's "sacrifice," the third day of the pestilence was a day of resurrection. The Lord was moved by entreaty for the land, and the plague was held back. The land was revived on the third day.

The emphasis in the rest of the chapter is on David's purchase of the site,[26] which included negotiations between David and Araunah (24:21–24), which remind us of the negotiations between Abraham and the sons of Heth about the purchase of a burial site (Gen. 23:1–16). In that passage, Abraham gained legal right to a portion of the land as a pledge of his future inheritance of the whole land. Abraham did not seize the land, but bought it. We can push the analogy between these two incidents in a couple of ways. The Hebrew name "Araunah" seems to come from a Hurrian word that means "lord," and this suggests the possibility that it was not a name but a title. This interpretation is supported by the fact that he is called "*the* Araunah" in the Hebrew text of verse 16. Verse 23 may also indicate that Araunah was a Jebusite official. Though translated as "Everything, O king, Araunah gives to the king," it could be understood as "Everything king Araunah gives to the king." Thus, Araunah may have been the former king of Jebus, the defeated lord of the city. Almost certainly, he was not merely a private person, and what happened here was not only some real estate deal, but the transfer of the rights to the capital city. By bowing before David, the Araunah recognized himself as a vassal of David. In this way, this event marked the completion of the conquest, and, along with the building of the temple, completed the exodus (1 Kgs. 6:1). And, interestingly, this completion of the conquest hearkened back to the beginning of the conquest. In Genesis 23, Abraham purchased the first plot of land that Israel owned in the

---

[26] Notice also that the place for the temple is a threshing floor, where wheat and chaff were separated. This is part of the symbolism of the temple: Israel appears in the presence of the Lord for review and judgment.

land. The beginning of the conquest and its end were marked by negotiations with the people of the land; Abraham's negotiations and David's frame the whole history of conquest and settlement. Surrounding the story of war was the story of a centuries-long real estate transaction.

No doubt, the event in chapter 24 is out of chronological order, but in narrative terms, it forms the conclusion to the story of David in Samuel. And, like the story of Israel, David's story ended at the threshing floor on Moriah:

Israel	David (2 Samuel)
Babylonian exile, 2 Kgs. 25	exile in Mahanaim, 17:27–29
return from exile, Ezra 1	return from exile, 19:11–43
numbering of the people, Ezra 2	census, 24:1–9
altar built, Ezra 3:1–3	altar built, 24:25
temple completed, Ezra 6:15	temple site purchased, 24:18–24; cf. 2 Chr. 3:1

Viewed from this perspective, it is clear that, far from being a clumsy or anticlimactic ending to the book, chapter 24 brilliantly draws together narrative and thematic threads. It reaches not only across the book of Samuel but back to Genesis, and then forward to "the distance," providing a preview of the future history of old covenant Israel. And more: In this incident, we see in a shadowy form a Son of Abraham and of David who would offer sacrifice to turn away Yahweh's wrath and to secure a place for the Lord's house.

David was Israel embodied in one man. David was the anointed of Yahweh. David was a type of the last Adam. Given these facts, how else could the story of David end?

SCRIPTUREINDEX

2 SAMUEL (CONT.)

I learned the characters and events of the Old Testament in Lutheran Sunday School, and though profoundly grateful for this training, I realize now that there were some significant weaknesses. The least important of these was that the teaching was very selective. . . . A more serious problem was that the story was never quite finished.

Children learn a story here, a story there, but they do not get the sense that the Bible is telling one story and that each of the little stories is an episode of something bigger. And this weakness is rooted in an even more fundamental hermeneutical flaw. Christians teaching the Old Testament are constantly tempted to treat it as a collection of moral fables. Abram "lies" to Pharaoh in Genesis 12, and we draw the conclusion that Abram's faith was not sufficiently strong, and that lying is a bad thing. But the story ends with Abram being treated well by Pharaoh and receiving all manner of livestock (Gen. 12:16). How such an ending discourages lying is not exactly clear: Abram does not just get away scot free— he is richly rewarded for his "lack of faith." To make this work, the moralizer has to say that the riches Abram receives are "deceptive riches," rather than the true riches received by faith. Moral piles on moral, all of them obscuring the passage they are supposed to illuminate. If we cut through the layers of moralizing, we realize that the story is not well-designed as a warning against lying. Why does Abram have to go to Egypt to lie? Why *this* lie? Why is he rewarded? One must simply say that something else is going on in Genesis 12, something that a moralistic reading of the Bible does not even hint at.

A HOUSE FOR MY NAME
A SURVEY OF THE OLD TESTAMENT
PETER J. LEITHART

Made in the USA
Monee, IL
09 October 2024

66964767R00204